Religious Talk Online

In the online world, people argue about anything and everything – religion is no exception. Stephen Pihlaja investigates how several prominent social media figures present views about religion in an environment where their positions are challenged. The analysis shows how conflict creates a space for users to share, explain, and develop their opinions and beliefs, by making appeals to both a core audience of like-minded viewers and a broader audience of viewers who are potentially interested in the claims, whether ambivalent, or openly hostile. The book argues that in the back-and-forth of these arguments, the positions that users take in response to the arguments of others have consequences for how religious talk develops, and potentially for how people understand and practice their beliefs in the twenty-first century. Based on original empirical research, it addresses long-debated questions in sociolinguistics and discourse analysis regarding the role of language in building solidarity, defining identity, and establishing genres and registers of interaction.

STEPHEN PIHLAJA is Reader in Stylistics at Newman University, Birmingham, UK, where he teaches and researches language use around religious interaction. Originally from Chicago, he has previously lived and taught in Japan and Malaysia.

Religious Talk Online

The Evangelical Discourse of Muslims, Christians, and Atheists

Stephen Pihlaja
Newman University, Birmingham

CAMBRIDGE
UNIVERSITY PRESS

CAMBRIDGE
UNIVERSITY PRESS

University Printing House, Cambridge CB2 8BS, United Kingdom

One Liberty Plaza, 20th Floor, New York, NY 10006, USA

477 Williamstown Road, Port Melbourne, VIC 3207, Australia

314–321, 3rd Floor, Plot 3, Splendor Forum, Jasola District Centre, New Delhi – 110025, India

79 Anson Road, #06–04/06, Singapore 079906

Cambridge University Press is part of the University of Cambridge.

It furthers the University's mission by disseminating knowledge in the pursuit of education, learning, and research at the highest international levels of excellence.

www.cambridge.org
Information on this title: www.cambridge.org/9781107157415
DOI: 10.1017/9781316661963

First published 2018

Printed in the United Kingdom by Clays, St Ives plc

A catalogue record for this publication is available from the British Library.

Library of Congress Cataloging-in-Publication Data
Names: Pihlaja, Stephen, author.
Title: Religious talk online : the evangelical discourse of Muslims, Christians and atheists / Stephen Pihlaja, Newman University, Birmingham.
Description: 1 [edition]. | New York : Cambridge University Press, 2017. | Includes bibliographical references.
Identifiers: LCCN 2017042369 | ISBN 9781107157415 (hardback : alk. paper) | ISBN 9781316610183 (pbk. : alk. paper)
Subjects: LCSH: Christianity and other religions–Computer network resources. | Social media–Religious aspects.
Classification: LCC BR127 .P534 2017 | DDC 261.20285/4678–dc23
LC record available at https://lccn.loc.gov/2017042369

ISBN 978-1-107-15741-5 Hardback

Contents

Preface

A book on religious talk online is likely to attract interest from three broad groups: people interested in religion, people interested in language, and people interested in the Internet. However, given the nature of academic research, it is unlikely that one person will be doing work in all three areas. The studies of "religion" and "talk" in particular are likely to draw audiences from decidedly different theoretical and methodological backgrounds.

As the author of the book, and a scholar interested in both these topics, a mixture of methods and theories is what makes academic work interesting to me – the ability to learn from and speak across disciplinary boundaries to describe and analyze the social world. For me, the joy of writing a book like this one is how to bring different scholars together at the same table with a shared focus on understanding religious life and experience through analysis of language use.

At the same time, you may find this book frustrating, depending on your discipline. If you're a linguist, you may likely find the work to be less empirical than you'd like, with less data than you'd expect in a monograph focusing on language. If you're a religious studies scholar, you might find yourself looking for a more nuanced discussion of things like religious identity and the sociohistorical context of the interactions I'm writing about.

Knowing this tension exists, I have attempted to write *Religious Talk Online* in a way that appeals to both audiences, but more importantly, provides a rigorous, empirical analysis of the language data. For me, as a scholar – a stylistician and discourse analyst – analysis is useful when it is valid and reliable and tells us something about the nature of reality and how language and society are mutually shaping forces.

Importantly, religious discourse remains relatively unrepresented in the field of communication and language study, with the best research being done by scholars in religious studies. This book is an attempt to address that gap in a small way and to bring discussion about religious discourse back into focus, particularly in a moment when technology is again playing an important role in the emergence of atheism.

Finally, discussions of faith and religion are often extremely personal. Interaction around faith online, moreover, can be laced with negativity and insults. Throughout this book, I've attempted to include examples of text and talk that are typical of the contexts I'm investigating but do not reflect my own opinions or beliefs about the users. *Religious Talk Online* is a snapshot of a moment in history, when social media played a key role in how some people expressed their own faith and used new technology to reach out to others. By focusing on this moment, we will see how historical ways of doing interreligious dialogue present themselves in new contexts and the effects technology can have on how differences in belief are managed and negotiated, and how its lasting effects might be seen on the role of religion in social life.

Acknowledgments

Yoko, Naomi, Mei, Mia, Beau, Mandy, Mom, Dad, Lynne, Daniel, Billy, Sylvia, Andreas, Peter, Lachlan, Kerry, Helen, Elizabeth-Jane, Chris, Tom, Newman University, Jeannette, Alice, Graham, Lettie, Peter, Caroline, Philip, Ann, Ruth, Susan, Michael, Quarter Horse Coffee, Woodbrooke Quaker Centre, Greg, Theron, Chris, Naomi, Jannis, and Heythrop College.

1 Introduction
Religious Interaction Online

A brisk spring night in 2014, I attended a debate between a Christian and a Muslim, held at a local Islamic center in the UK, in Perry Barr in Birmingham. The event featured Shabir Ally, a Canadian Islamic Studies lecturer and host of the Canadian public access TV show *Let the Quran Speak.* On the show, Ally is interviewed by a young woman in a *hijab* – headscarf – and answers questions about Islam and Muslim practice in Canada. The videos are posted regularly, with a range of topics and guest hosts through the year.

Ally looks the part of a Muslim scholar, dressed in a *thobe* and *taqiyah* – the traditional Muslim male robe and hat – with an impressive white beard. His accent is distinctly Canadian, and Ally in many ways embodies the image of the so-called moderate Muslim. He is pious and learned, while also being practical. He is pragmatic without appearing liberal, and he takes positions in a reasoned, understanding way, always displaying a careful consideration of context and how Islam should be practiced in Canada.

While *Let the Quran Speak* is shown on terrestrial television in Canada, the packed room in Birmingham knew Ally from YouTube, where his show and videos of his lectures and debates regularly appear. He is a kind of micro-celebrity, "Internet famous" among a very specific group of people. In YouTube videos, Ally can be viewed debating Christian fundamentalists in a variety of different settings before friendly and hostile audiences. In Birmingham, the audience was decidedly friendly. Ally debated a Seventh-Day Adventist representing Christianity, but the actual opponent seemed to be irrelevant: the group of people who had gathered were there to see Ally. The night was structured to allow Ally to speak about the supremacy of Islam over Christianity, and the Qur'an over the Bible, while listening politely to the Seventh-Day Adventist.

The debate was held in a small studio, set up to film the debate, with lights on the two lecterns. The room filled up with young men, mostly Southeast Asian and Muslim, with only a few women and one family with small children. I found a seat near the edge and waited for the event to begin, wondering how badly I stood out as the one white American academic in jeans and a sport coat. A young man wearing a *thobe* and a parka came and sat next to me, introducing himself. He settled into his seat and after checking his phone, asked whom I had come to support. I awkwardly tried to explain my position, that I wasn't supporting anyone – I had just come to listen. He nodded understandingly and turned to his phone, which he was using to read YouTube comments.

When Ally arrived, he was whisked to the front of the room as everyone looked on expectantly. His opposition was a middle-aged black man who was clearly not a religious scholar – he lectured at a local university, but in information science and was missing the prominent "PhD" after his name that Ally had. The man seemed understandably uncomfortable in a room that, though respectful, was unsympathetic to him. The debate went on cordially, with the Seventh-Day Adventist making classic apologetic arguments about the nature of Jesus – *was he a liar, lunatic, or might he have actually been God*? – while Ally held up different books, dismantling arguments about the reliability of the Bible and the deity of Christ.

The formal debate ended and there was time for an open discussion. A long queue quickly formed at a microphone with men who asked pointed and leading questions of the Seventh-Day Adventist, trying to trip him up on contradictions in the Bible. After the questions, and once the organizers thanked everyone for coming, a crowd formed around Ally. People took photos with him, giving congratulatory pats on the back, while largely ignoring the Seventh-Day Adventist. When the debate attendees finally filed out of the studio, happily chatting and checking their smartphones, it was clear that the debate had served its purpose, but it was not clear if there had actually been a meaningful discussion between both sides.

Ally's popularity among a Muslim community in Birmingham was in part the result of social media, of YouTube, and the spread of his videos by fans. In a small way, the debate shows how technological advances have given people of faith unprecedented access to new voices across the globe. In a utopian model of the Internet, this access also affords the presences of dissenting opinions, challenging users to reconsider their positions in light of new evidence. The debate in Birmingham, however, showed that access does not always translate into significant engagement. The arguments both men made about the existence of God or gods, and whose God was the real God, stubbornly followed the same pattern as they have for more than a thousand years. The Internet may have had an effect on the medium of transmitting these arguments, but the extent to which the arguments themselves have been transformed is still an open question. For scholars attempting to understand and place this interaction in a historical context, the complex interaction between the online and offline worlds presents new challenges for describing how social interaction develops. The global arguments about faith become local and situated, and when filmed and posted on YouTube they contribute to larger global trends. Social media and mobile technology increasingly marry the offline and online contexts, creating new ways of interacting.

1.1 The Internet

In the early twenty-first century, the Internet has become a key site for social interaction. Mediated communication now occurs regularly on social media sites like Facebook, Twitter, and YouTube. While early research on Internet interaction focused on anonymity and its negative effects (Kiesler, Siegel, and McGuire, 1984; Siegel, Dubrovsky, Kiesler, and McGuire, 1986) has remained influential in computer-mediated computer (CMC) research, social media sites have facilitated meaningful connections between named users, often showing their faces and using their real names. Social media connections can grow into a real sense of intimacy even while users are separated by time and space (Wesch, 2009). The Internet, however, has changed substantially since the 1990s when people first started becoming aware of it. To understand and analyze interaction online at a particular point in time – in this book, interaction on social media as it existed in 2014 – we must first take a historical perspective on the development of the Internet.

In a material sense, the Internet is a network of computers and servers sharing information in geographically remote places (Herring, 2003) and the use of the Internet can be seen in tandem with the development of technology in three phases. In the first phase, the Internet was used primarily as a way to access information and communicate using messaging tools like email or Internet Communication Relay (ICR) (Herring, 2003). In the second phase of development, often called "Web 2.0," users took a much more active role in the production of content (Herring, 2004b). Web 2.0 included the rise of social network sites (SNS), which allow individuals to:

(1) construct a public or semi-public profile within a bounded system,
(2) articulate a list of other users with whom they share a connection, and
(3) view and traverse their list of connections and those made by others within the system. (boyd and Ellison, 2007, p. 211)

These include sites starting with MySpace and eventually overtaken in popularity by Facebook. Twitter and YouTube can also be included here, as users were both producers and consumers of content, and "friends," "followers," and "subscribers" are used to describe connections among users in these different sites. These "connections" are not the same as online "communities," but rather a technical description of who users can access and what they are able to see or not see on other users' profile pages.

In the third phase, mobile technology has brought the Internet into the day-to-day lived experience of users, particularly young people, and the idea of "going online," where a user would sit at a computer and interact with others apart from their physical environment, evidenced in Facebook's shift to a mobile app from a previous focus as a desktop based website (Baron, 2008; Goggin, 2014). Mobile technology means content sharing can happen in real time, with apps on smartphones allowing users to "check-in" to physical locations and increase interaction between users' physical and online presences (Gordon and e Silva, 2011; Wilken, 2014). Although SNS were developed prior to the launch of the first iPhone in 2007, their development as key sites for social interaction has increased dramatically. They bred numerous other sites and applications that build on the notions of social connection in online space.

As social network sites, YouTube and Facebook have persisted as central places of interaction, with Facebook having over a billion users by its tenth anniversary in 2014 and more than 500 million users accessing the site via mobile phones at the same time (Sedghi, 2014). Similarly, YouTube also retained an important staying power through the transition from Web 2.0 to the era of mobile Internet. Users may not necessarily be active in YouTube communities (either by making their own videos or commenting on others), but with over a billion users and more than half of the views coming from mobile technologies (YouTube, 2016), YouTube is a central site of media consumption. Furthermore, both YouTube (owned by Google) and Facebook cannot now be seen only as online platforms, but important global economic forces with far-reaching consequences. Mark Zuckerberg, the founder of Facebook, has often attracted criticism for his views of privacy online and how Facebook encourages the presentation of personal information in public spaces, with Zuckerburg famously pronouncing the end of the age of privacy as a social norm in 2010 (Barnett, 2010). As a dominant force both socially and economically, Facebook's decisions have effects well beyond their own platforms. Their corporate decisions made about privacy, copyright, and security affect the way the Internet continues to develop, not only as a site for social interaction, but also with political influence on how people come to think about privacy and surveillance (Fuchs, 2012).

The openness of social media has created a new kind of "networked publics" (boyd, 2011) in which users can publicly view others' interaction and online presence across a variety of new media platforms. This presents unique opportunities for a broad range of users – from television evangelists to users with no viewers – to post their videos and present their worldviews in a variety of different places, with the nominal notion that anyone can view their content and potentially be influenced it. However, the ability to access material is not a promise that it will be accessed, and although users can have access to a variety of voices and perspectives, there is evidence that users do not necessarily seek out alternative perspectives for the purposes of widening their own horizons. Instead, evidence suggests that social media can result in an opposite effect, causing users to become more entrenched in their beliefs and avoid dissenting voices (Heatherly, Lu, and Lee, 2016). Users can curate their own pages and friend groups on Facebook, sorting out disagreeable information and opinions in a so-called filter bubble (Pariser, 2011), and becoming more inclined toward ideological messages to which they are already predisposed.

The public nature of some social media interaction also creates another complication, as the multiple identities that users have are often awkwardly forced into the same online space, like Facebook, where a user might be "friends" with a range of users including their family, co-workers, and "off-line" friends. Marwick and boyd (2011) have described this as "context collapse," where users must maintain authenticity to a variety of different audiences at the same time, often being unsure of who their audience actually is. This creates difficulties especially for users who are specifically interested in highlighting a religious identity online, and are attempting to spread their faith to others. Users might portray authentic religious identities which are recognizable to the faithful within their own community, but also appeal to and are oriented toward the beliefs and identities of the people they are attempting to reach. Moreover, they must also protect against users who are openly antagonistic to them and their beliefs and who might actively attempt to derail them and their message.

Social media provides the medium for interaction analyzed in this book, but the Internet is only the latest iteration in a long line of technologies that have affected how human-to-human interaction is mediated generally, and how religious faith is practiced more specifically. While the Internet is often viewed as revolutionary, its effect on social interaction and development must be considered as one of many technologies that have had a remarkable effect on society and religious practice, such as the printing press and the radio. Moreover, the interaction between people of different faiths does not appear for the first time with the invention of the Internet: they often have long histories that embed in them long-standing disagreements. The histories of contact among Christians, Muslims, and atheists are the foundation for religious talk online.

1.2 Outreach and Dialogue in a Historical Context

Interaction among people of different faiths is often entangled in larger political, ethnic, and cultural themes (Goddard, 2000; Watt, 2013), with categories like "Christianity," "Islam," and "atheism" all having their own complex histories, doctrinal differences, and strands. Evangelical movements within the religious traditions of Christianity and Islam are as old as the traditions themselves and necessarily a part of these complex histories of interaction. Understanding evangelism and interaction among people of different faiths on social media then requires understanding of how interaction fits broadly into a larger history of "evangelical" movements. The interactions among these traditions in some cases have been long-standing, particularly Christians and Muslims (Goddard, 2000; Lewis, 1993). While users on social media might not be aware of the how Muslims and Christians have interacted over the years, the history is profoundly important in how users talk about and conceptualize others when presenting their own beliefs. To understand what motivates people to take particular positions, we first need to go back to the origins of evangelism in each tradition and the historic interaction between groups.

Evangelism in Christianity has its roots in the biblical teaching of Jesus himself, who is reported to have said to his disciples, "Go into all the world and preach the gospel to all creation" (Mark 16:15, New International Version). This injunction is then followed up in the Acts of the Apostles with a description of his disciples being "filled with the Holy Spirit" (Acts 2:4) and preaching the message of Jesus to the Jewish community in Jerusalem. The New Testament also deals with some difficult issues of inter-religious dialogue, as the Apostle Paul's writing in particular worked to explain the emerging theology of Christianity in light of the Jewish context (Renard, 2011). The context of early faith, as it is today, was one of mixed religious communities and voices.

The injunction from Jesus himself to spread the message of the gospel to "all the world" led quickly to missionary activity to non-Jewish communities with the preaching and ministry of the Apostle Paul. Paul's message, while initially oriented to Jewish audiences, grew broadly throughout his ministry. Both his own letters to Christian believers and narratives about his ministry in the Acts of the Apostles focus on an explicit interaction with both the theologies and believers of other faiths beyond Judaism. Most strikingly, this included a direct attempt to explain Christian belief using the faith of the Greeks, for example, in his preaching at the meeting of the Areopagus in Athens. The story, related in the Acts of the Apostles, describes Paul preaching the message of Jesus specifically to believers in a foreign religion by addressing an altar for an "unknown god" he sees in Athens (Acts 17).

With the conversion of Constantine, Christianity became inextricably linked to secular rule (Renard, 2011) and discussion of Christian missionary endeavors have been deeply embedded in political movements. Still, the notion of Christian missionary work as "spreading the gospel" without an explicit commitment to political goals also has a long and extensive history, developing from the practice of the disciples through to the present day. Christian missions by the Catholic Church have often included other endeavors beyond simple religious teaching like education and charity work, creating a spread not only of Christian theology, but a framework of socio-political ideologies with it (see Neill, 1964). Under the British Empire, the spread of Christianity was tied to colonialism, which used religion explicitly for political aims (Renard, 2011) and had important consequences particularly when considering interaction between Christians and Muslims. Most recently, Christian missions have been centered in the United States and made a more active and public attempt at self-reflection, but missionary endeavors remain embedded in the theological and political ideologies of the cultures sending missionaries (Yates, 1996). Because of the prominence of American Christianity in the development of missions, American Evangelical ideology, rooted in notions of the Protestant work ethic (Weber, 2002 [1905]) and individual responsibility, is also tacitly spread in missionary endeavors.

The history of Islam charts a different path from Christianity, given the difference in constitution between the two religions. Christianity was co-opted by the Roman Empire following its theological development, while Islam developed simultaneously as a political and theological system (Hick, 1991). Islam, like Christianity, appeared in a context of other religious belief systems but unlike Jesus Christ or the Apostle Paul in Christianity, the Prophet Muhammad served as both a political and religious leader. Moreover, the development of Islamic theology saw continuity through the prophets, rather than a reinterpretation of a sacred text (Renard, 2011). These differences mean a comparison between Christianity and Islam is not straightforward, particularly when it comes to considering how both traditions have approached the spread of their messages. Although there is a belief in the West that Islam was spread initially "by the sword," Renard (2011) points out the fallacy in thinking that Muslim forces acted primarily on religious motivations. Islam does indeed have a distinct notion of the teaching and sharing of the faith, known as *dawah*. Dawah (or da'wa or da'wah) literally means "call" and like Christianity was historically tied to commercial endeavors or military conquests. It was "the function of the caliph [political-military ruler of Muslim community], extending authority over Muslims outside Islamic lands and promoting Islamic unity" (Esposito, 2003). However, as Bijlefeld (1995) points out, although dawah in Islam and mission in Christianity are significantly different, they can come to refer to the same realities – the notion that it is the responsibility of individual Muslims to share their faith through deeds and words, with the goal of propagating the religion (Poston, 1992). This is particularly true of the use of "dawah" among the people in this book, who treat dawah in similar ways to Christian evangelical outreach.

The historical relationship between evangelism and conquest means the interaction between Christians and Muslims has long been tied to political endeavors and has had a long and often violent history (Goddard, 2000). It is impossible to fully understand dialogue among Christians and Muslims without first understanding the influence of the Crusades in the Middle Ages and later of colonialism on how both groups have viewed one another (Ernst, 2004). Distinguishing violent interaction driven by primarily political interests from missionary activity with explicit theological goals is a difficult task. Ernst (2004) argues interaction between Western Christianity and Islam was, until the very recent past, marked by a gross misunderstanding of Islam by Western Christians (who often knew little Arabic) and deeply embedded in racist narratives. With first British and then American colonizers at the front line of interaction between Western Christianity and Islam, interaction between the religions became entangled with political positions and suspicion of Islam in the West.

This animosity and misunderstanding is, however, only part of the history of interaction among Christians and Muslims. There is also a long tradition of dialogue and argument among scholars in the faith traditions (Watt, 2013), and currents trends in debates like the one between Shabir Ally and the Seventh-Day Adventist do have clear historical precedence. Moreover, the themes and topics of these discussions often highlight differences in the views of each other's faith as well as differences in the theology of each belief system. From an Islamic perspective, Christianity, Judaism, and Islam all share a common Abrahamic ancestry, with roots in monotheism. Shafaat (1991) describes this "Abrahamic ummah," a multi-faith community that existed in Medina with a shared history and belief. From the Muslim perspective, the mistake in Christianity is not the presence of the figure of Jesus, who is also revered and respected in Islam, but rather the belief that Jesus is also God, which Islam views as idolatry (Solomon, 1991). The fault is not with the basic belief in God and his revelation to humankind, but rather the corruption of the original message of Jesus through retelling and translation. In a similar way that Christians view Jesus as the culmination of Jewish scriptures, Muslims view Muhammad and the revelation of the Qur'an as a fulfillment of the revelation of God to Christians and Jews by the Prophets (Kerr, 1991).

Historically, the Christian perspective on Islam has been decidedly more negative, with criticism focusing on Muhammad's military exploits and his marriages (Ernst, 2004). Ernst highlights the roots of these criticisms in traditional Christian views on celibacy and nonviolence, which have been seen as hallmarks of Jesus's own exalted nature, which set him apart from other prophets and humans. For Christian apologists, Muhammad is not a Prophet, but a kind of political leader driven by personal ambition and his own physical desire, while disregarding the political and cultural conditions of Muhammad's life, and playing into ongoing racist stereotypes of Muslims which marked early Christian interactions with Islam. Christian Evangelicals interested in "reaching" the Muslim world with the gospel and who see Muslims as potential target for missionary endeavors have increasingly recognized the colonial and historical negativity of previous attempts at converting the Muslim world, arguing that it is a potential obstacle for outreach (Parshall, 2003).

These criticisms also highlight theological differences in how Christians and Muslims view Jesus Christ and Muhammad. Christian arguments against Islam can focus on how Muhammad is not like Jesus, but this criticism misses the key difference between Islam and Christianity. Whereas Christians view Jesus as the revelation of God to humans, and indeed, as God himself, Muslims view Jesus as a "son of God," to be revered and respected as a pious human, but not as God himself (Ayoub, 1995). In Islam, Muhammad is not seen as God, but as a messenger of God, a prophet to whom God revealed himself. This has, of course, important theological implications for Muslims, particularly in comparison to Christian belief about Jesus. While Muhammad is deeply respected and revered as a prophet, he is not to be worshipped. His humanity and distinction from God is reinforced in the *shahada*, or the Muslim profession of faith, translated in English as: "There is no god but God. Muhammad is the messenger of God." This contrasts considerably with the common belief espoused by Christians in the Nicene Creed, a common profession of faith among Christians, which claims Jesus to be "very God of very God, begotten, not made, being of one substance with the Father." For a Christian focused primarily on the divine nature of Jesus Christ, Muhammad's humanity necessarily results in a lower status.

This background on Christian-Muslim interaction and beliefs is certainly not intended to be comprehensive, but rather to lay a historical groundwork for the interaction between Christians and Muslims online. As with many phenomena on the Internet, very little is actually new, particularly in terms of theological arguments. The histories of these interactions are indeed important for understanding how people of faith and no faith understand their own positions and responsibilities in "sharing" what they believe with others and attempting to convert others. The arguments, however, go back for many centuries, with users often drawing implicitly on the storylines that are available to them about the other. At the same time, social media and the Internet force a need to rethink how the collapse of space affects the ways in which discourses can be challenged directly by those about whom one is speaking.

Despite the key differences between Islam and Christianity, the two share more in common with each other than they do with atheism, defined here as a disbelief in the existence of a God or gods. In the first instance, "atheism" is not a belief, but a lack of belief. Although there is a long history of movements which include atheism, like secular humanism, in the West, progressive secularist movements have been notably focused on positive claims that favor "naturalistic and scientific thought over supernatural explanations of reality" (Cimino and Smith, 2007, p. 408). While secularism took hold in Europe in the twentieth century, Cimino and Smith (2011) note the resistance to secularism in the American context. Despite a significant growth in the number of people identifying as "atheist" or "agnostic" in the early 2000s, the number of atheists in America in 2014 was still well under five percent (Lipka, 2015).

In unpacking what it means to be an "atheist," LeDrew (2012) sees a distinction between "scientific atheism" and "humanistic atheism." The trajectories of these two forms of atheism are, LeDrew (2012) argues, independent with different focuses. Scientific atheism includes "non-believers [who have] focused their engagement with religion on science, explanation and knowledge vs. ignorance" while humanist atheism focuses on "religion as a social phenomenon and a symptom of alienation and oppression" (p. 71). LeDrew (2012) goes on to say,

> The distinction between scientific atheism and humanistic atheism is thus necessary because the term "atheism" does not precisely identify the nature of the epistemological and political orientations that characterize various formations of non-belief, as "atheism" is ordinarily defined in terms of a position on nature . . . rather than in terms of humanist philosophy or a sociological position. (p. 71)

This description of atheism sees it in two ways: first, as an approach to how knowledge should be gained and tested; and second, as a way to respond to injustice and oppression.

Though it may be possible and useful to distinguish between these categories, the lived experience of atheists in narrative research (see for example, Cimino and Smith, 2011; LeDrew, 2013; Smith, 2011, 2013; Smith and Cimino, 2012) suggests that atheists do not necessarily experience this distinction in a meaningful way and there is evidence that features of both can be prominent in the videos of atheists on social media. Indeed, LeDrew (2012) points out that though the scientific approach may be dominant among scholars like Richard Dawkins and Daniel Dennett, there is still tension with a humanist approach and the relationship between the two should be further investigated as they develop. Richard Dawkins, for example, is both a scientist and prominent antagonist of religion.

Attempting to track a history of dialogue between faith communities and atheism is a difficult task for several reasons. First, although there has been a presence of atheism in America (where YouTube and Facebook have developed) in the context of secular humanism, atheist and secular institutions like the American Atheists have had only modest membership and influence (Cimino and Smith, 2007). Until recently, atheism has simply not had a serious presence in the culture. Second, the very concept of so-called New Atheism suggests a contemporary social movement tied to atheistic belief and having roots in the world of social media (Cimino and Smith, 2011; Taylor, 2006, December/January). It may be possible to trace the ideology informing the development of atheism, but its presence in the context of the videos investigated in this book is in many ways a product of the Internet, and social media in particular. This development of atheism online in the early twenty-first century is understandable. Considering the marginalization of atheism in the broader culture, minority groups like atheists or free thinkers may feel alienation in their local context. Internet activity allows for contact with like-minded individuals who may not live in close physical proximity. Indeed, evidence suggests that the media environment in the early 2000s created a context in which atheist voices could gain traction in a way that had not been possible until then (Cimino and Smith, 2014).

The history of YouTube atheists is therefore much more contemporary when compared to users of faiths with centuries of existence. Christians might draw on the example of Paul at Athens or Muslims on the experiences of Muhammad in Medina, but atheists on social media look to contemporary examples of evangelical messages like Richard Dawkins and Sam Harris who form a kind of canon of atheist literature (Cimino and Smith, 2011). While the historical roots of atheism do, of course, go back further, with atheists claiming affiliation with figures like Charles Darwin and Thomas Huxley, these figures are connected not necessarily to a disbelief in God or gods, but rather their advocacy for the scientific method generally and evolution specifically: the roots of scientific atheism (LeDrew, 2012). The lack of institutional hierarchy and sacred texts within atheism limits the potential for figures to emerge in the same way as Christianity and Islam, which focus on the revelation of God to particular people at particular moments in history.

The relatively recent emergence of atheism in the context of social media makes the development of Web 2.0 an important cultural moment, particularly as it relates to the development of faith and how it is presented in public contexts. In many ways, the history of inter-religious dialogue which now includes atheism in an explicit way is being written on social media. The long history of interaction among Christians and Muslims may include the repetition of old argument in novel contexts, but the emergence of atheism offers a new perspective on both faiths, with a new challenge from a growing minority questioning what has long been taken for granted: what if there's no God at all? For all users and groups, how they respond to this new challenge affects not only how they respond to questions, but how they present their own faith and, potentially, how they personally (re)evaluate their own faith.

1.3 Conversion, Reversion, and Coming Out

Although social media sites exist in online space, the owners and producers of the sites exist in specific geographic locations, with their own cultural backgrounds and ideologies. YouTube (owned by Google) and Facebook are multinational companies, and their development and design have been embedded in American capitalist notions of self and community. Social media, for Mark Zuckerberg and Facebook, can be a way to build one's own personal "brand" and connect with "audiences" to curate an image and identity for oneself (Vogelstein, 2009). Interaction on social media becomes not just a way of engaging in ideas with others, but also a means for websites to "harness" relationships for financial gain (Barker, Dozier, Weiss, and Borden, 2015). In this model, the user is profiled and monitored, often without their awareness, and then sold as a commodity to advertisers (Turow, 2012).

This commodification of gaining followers, subscribers, and friends has important implications for the study of inter-religious dialogue on social media sites. Both YouTube and Facebook are driven by advertising revenue which benefits from extended use of sites. YouTubers also benefit financially from engagement on their videos when revenue from ads is shared with users. In the same way that interaction among Christians and Muslims in the last 600 years cannot be understood without understanding the context of the Crusades and colonialism, commodification and the pressures users might explicitly or implicitly feel to produce content, are important in considering what content is produced. In a social media economy where users can generate social and financial capital by performing in ways that consolidate interest and support from a core community of viewers, while expanding their audience, the economic factors affecting behavior can play into the choices that users make, particularly if they are in some way supporting themselves financially through their presence online.

Religious identity is an additional complicating factor in managing a personal brand, particularly when a user's faith includes a mandate to testify to it. Evangelism, conceived as the spreading or sharing of a specific religious belief, has been of particular importance in the American religious landscape for the whole of its history, but with the rise of popular evangelists like Billy Graham who placed evangelical outreach as the most important mission of the Christian church (Sider, 1975). On YouTube, Evangelical Christianity is often present in religious talk, both with Christians spreading its message, and atheists opposing it. Evangelical outreach is fundamental part of the faith – people must be led to a moment of conversion in which they explicitly and consciously choose to affirm their belief in Jesus (Bebbington, 1989). The emphasis on the individual conversion places particular importance on narratives about faith experiences, and privileges individual spiritual experiences, provided Christians are able to articulate their experiences in ways that are recognized by others who share their faith (Smith and Emerson, 1998). While notions of conversion are certainly present in Islam and atheism, the focus on articulating the experience as a single narrative testimony and "witnessing" for the purpose of conversion is a key part of Evangelical Christian belief and mission.

Equipping Christians to share their individual testimony and lead others to conversion can be seen in the focus of Christian mission on apologetics in second half of twentieth century, led by prominent theologians like Cornelius van Til (1955) and more recently Ravi Zacharias (2008) and William Lane Craig (1993). This outreach places importance on logical arguments that can be made for the existence of God, rather than on mission as taking the gospel to "unreached people" , which had been the emphasis of missionary work up to and through the twentieth century (Neill, 1964; Yates, 1996). Christian apologetics can be less about "going" to preach the gospel, but rather providing an account for faith in day-to-day life, particularly in postmodern, pluralistic environments (Feinberg, 2013). There are numerous resources both on and offline, focusing on how to argue for and support one's faith with evidence.

Similar patterns for sharing faith can be observed between Christianity and Islam, particularly in Western contexts and in people like Shabir Ally who engage in arguments with Christians, effectively attempting to accomplish the same goals but from the opposing perspective. Still, "conversion" as it is conceived in Christianity is not directly analogous to the process of becoming a Muslim – indeed, even the description of someone "becoming a Muslim" is not necessarily accurate. Poston (1992) remarks that accounts of conversion, which play an important role in the discourse of Christianity, are noticeably absent in Muslim literature. Christian Evangelical culture may focus on the articulation of a personal testimony, but dawah has traditionally focused on the printed word and the distribution of literature through study rather than proselytization (Poston, 1992). While the notion of "conversion" is particularly important in Evangelical Christianity, being "saved" from one's sinful nature and coming into harmony with God, Islam sees human beings as naturally and innately in submission to God, with the need to "revert" to a submissive state.

Islamic proselytization has historically been treated differently than Christian outreach in research, and particularly following the terrorist attacks on the World Trade Center in 2001. There has been a growing focus on Islam, reflected in the dominance of research of Muslims which often views them as the "other" and investigates how religion feeds into larger issues that affect the assimilation of Muslim immigrants in Western countries. Interest can be seen in how Muslims engage in politics (Leonard, 2003), the relationship between growing piety and radicalization (Heffelfinger, 2011; Karagiannis, 2012), and the role of dawah in identity and teaching of young Muslims, particularly immigrant children, about the faith (Janson, 2003; Kelly, 1999; Peek, 2005). This research presents dawah as inwardly oriented, focusing on the Muslim community and using dawah as a tool of attracting individuals who are either already predisposed to the religion in some way, or members of the community who are being taught about the religion of their family.

However, dawah organizations and Muslims do make open and outward calls to Islam, much in the same way as Christian missions. Sites like "Mission Dawah" (Mission Dawah, n.d.) and "Just Dawah" (Justdawah.org, n.d.) serve a dual purpose, both drawing non-practicing Muslims back into a more pious lifestyle and expanding the Muslim community with reverts from Christianity and other religions. Like Evangelical Christian calls to outreach, these organizations and preachers highlight individual responsibility rather than community identity and promote dawah as an obligation for all Muslims (Justdawah.org, n.d.). The sites provide information about teaching tactics and methods for street dawah, provide manuals for doing dawah, and produce videos about the best ways to talk with potential reverts. The sites and resources are oriented toward Western audiences and assume a pluralistic rather than exclusively Muslim society. They focus on helping users of the materials explain the uniqueness of Islam in comparison to other religions and the logic of its beliefs. In contrast to the research done on the political nature of dawah, the dawah preachers this book focuses on often avoid discussion of political contexts and discussion of terrorism and radicalization, instead speaking exclusively about Islam as a faith.

Bunt (2009) suggests that the Internet has provided an affordance for Muslims to challenge old models in which scholars and authority figures held Islamic knowledge and were not challenged. The Internet now facilitates discussions which can result in a range of dissenting views on a range of topics, including religion (Etling, Kelly, Faris, and Palfrey, 2014). Like other users, Muslims interacting online must also manage their own self-presentation taking into account a "context collapse" that might include members of their own family and members of the Muslim community, but also non-Muslim friends and colleagues. In this context, the tactics of the Evangelical Christian approach to apologetics can prove useful. Where Muslims might be challenged about the nature of Islam, particularly given media exploitation of terrorism leading to Islamophobia (Gottschalk and Greenberg, 2008), they are placed in a defensive position to explain their faith in opposition to these competing storylines. Whether or not testimony is historically important to Islam may be less important than the immediate need of responding to pressure to explain Islam to a hostile audience.

Like Christianity and Islam, evangelistic language and endeavors can also be observed from within atheism, which like Islam often focuses on logic. However, given the nature of atheism as a lack of belief, the notion that an individual can "convert" to atheism as one would to a belief system is problematic and one that atheists reportedly resist (Simon, 2008). Thoburn (2003) notes that the American context has long lacked a structure for atheism and social context in which it is appropriate. Instead, as Cimino and Smith (2011) write,

> The practice of "coming out" as an atheist has not been simply a matter of publicly claiming atheism along a well-worn, legitimate route. It has involved emerging from invisibility to claim a personal and social identity that has carried a fair degree of stigma. (p. 25)

Rather than co-opting the language of religious conversion, Cimino and Smith use the language of pronouncing one's homosexuality in a hetero-normative culture. In this construction, identifying as an atheist is identifying with a distrusted and suspect minority group, a process that Smith (2011) shows includes questioning theism, rejecting theism, and "coming out" atheist. Because the atheist identity includes rejecting a dominant worldview, the construction of atheist identity is often around what it is *not* rather than what it is (Smith, 2011).

Unlike conversion to Christianity or reversion to Islam, there is no institutional structure around "becoming" an atheist and people describe the experience in different ways. LeDrew (2013), for example, shows that atheists can also construct their atheist identity not only as a "coming out," but as a progression, seeing "atheism is the end point of a gradual progression from religiously fuelled ignorance to scientific enlightenment" (p. 437). LeDrew (2013) argues that this diversity in atheistic identity can lead to different outcomes, including those who privately identify as atheists, those who publicly do so, and "atheist activists," working in some way to promote atheism. LeDrew warns against seeing "coming out" as a necessary precondition of being an atheist. Indeed, people can take different approaches to their interaction with atheism, with varying degrees of activism. With no belief to profess and no customary practices or institutional membership, when and how one "becomes" an atheist is process each individual must negotiate themselves.

At the same time, customs and practices for "coming out" as an atheist have emerged. The "blasphemy challenge" is one such example, in which YouTube users recorded themselves denying the existence of the Holy Spirit, a practice that has been seen as making a singular and irrevocable rejection of Christian faith. The practice emerged as meaningful for a brief time, but did not have staying power. Users participated for a time, but it was not ultimately adopted as an important marker of becoming an atheist in a Christian context. Instead, practices of "coming out" or "converting" to atheism have taken different forms and atheists have adopted different practices for the spreading of their faith. Cimino and Smith (2014) argue that these tactics are embedded in atheists accepting their minority status in the USA and following three broad thematic tactics:

> First, they are competing and positioning themselves to attract "secular seekers," who are similar to spiritual speakers or "questers in their persistent search for authentic communities of meaning while remaining highly individualistic (Roof, 1999). Second, they have borrowed elements from their main antagonists – evangelical Protestants – in

> defining themselves and rallying others to their cause. Third, they have taken up the minority discourse and identity politics in pressing for group rights and equal treatment in society. (p. 22)

Each of these methods highlights different ways of conceiving of atheism and the connection of the individual to an atheistic identity. The outreach to others suggests a view that atheism, while in practice simply a lack of belief in God or gods, actually does have the potential to attract particular people together in a community. Importantly, however, atheism, in contrast to Christianity and Islam, does not have a "ready-made" identity (Smith, 2011, p. 232). Instead, individuals who come to atheism must in some way make a new identity for themselves, one that is not fixed in institutional practices and is often in opposition to their local community.

The extent to which the "tactics" of atheist movements affect the individual experiences of atheists also needs to be interrogated, given the lack of institutional authority in atheist organizations and lack of real "membership" in atheist communities that is mediated by specific rituals and practices. LeDrew's (2013) research shows the heterogeneity in terms of atheist experience results in different narratives that depended heavily on an individual's own history and whether or not they had held a strong religious faith at any point in their lives. Moreover, he notes that atheism is not a permanent condition and individual atheist identity can be a complex interaction of different factors and like other kinds of religious identity (Peek, 2005), is an "achieved identity."

Despite these different approaches to understanding a shift in belief system – be it conversion, reversion, or coming out – the influence of the language of Christianity on outreach in both Islam and atheism in the context of a dominant American cultural influence is important to recognize. Indeed, the contemporary notion of "sharing your faith" can be traced to Evangelical Christian culture in the USA. Its influence can then be seen on how other people of other faiths or no faith frame their own discourse about religion. Muslims in the West and the social media data analyzed in this book engaged in dawah co-opt the language of evangelical outreach, using the word *dawah* in a way more synonymous with Christian mission. Organizations like "Mission Dawah" use the terms together and co-opt the notion of "mission" to "create a buzz for dawah within a community" (Mission Dawah, n.d.). Similarly, atheists still speak of "converting" to atheism and share stories of their "coming out," similar to Christian conversion testimonials, which begin with a person feeling in some way incomplete or uncomfortable, coming to a realization, and feeling liberated and "free" in their new identity (Smith, 2011). While becoming an atheist or reverting to Islam are clearly different from the process of converting to Christianity, with important theological and cultural implications, within a dominant culture of Protestant Christianity, people of other faith or no faith must co-opt the language of the dominant culture to explain and express their own positions.

1.4 Belief and Community in Online Spaces

Campbell and Lövheim (2011), in their introduction to a special issue of *Information, Communication, and Society* on religious expression and practice online, quote Ess in reference to the potential impact of computer-mediated communication on religion:

> If CMC only partially effects the revolutionary transformations of values and social structures envisioned by its enthusiasts, then religion – as humanity's oldest expression of values and community – is likely both to impact and to be impacted by these transformations. (Ess, 1996, p. 9)

Ess's comment on the potential of CMC is prescient in many ways and reflects the overarching interest of researchers in CMC: to what extent does the technology we use change the way that we interact? (Herring, 2004b) As Campbell and Lövheim (2011) point out, the questions of how religious practice and religion itself has been "transformed" by technology are now genuinely empirical questions, and while the Internet remains young in historical terms (and social media, in particular), trends in use and changes can be observed in the way individuals both practice their own faith online and how their beliefs and practices change as they interact with others.

For Christians, Muslims, and atheists, notions of community around faith or lack of faith are important for how each conceives of their own identity in affiliation with and opposition to others with whom they interact, both on and offline. As we have seen so far, the socio-political context for faith in American society is still predominately Evangelical Protestantism. While local contexts different, the influence of the dominant cultural practices of Christianity on how faith and religiosity are understood and practiced, evidenced above as examples in the appropriation of "church" by atheists and "mission" by the Muslim communities. How religious communities emerge online and the extent to which they are, as Ess suggests, "transformed" by technological affordances is a key question.

The notion of "Internet community" has been historically a problematic topic (Rheingold, 2000) with researchers quickly realizing that "community" might too broad to be useful (Fernback and Thompson, 1995; Jones, 1995). Herring's early work (2004a) defined "community" for computer-mediated discourse analysis as similarities in structure (such as jargon, in-group/out-group language), meaning (exchange of knowledge, negotiation of meaning), interaction (reciprocity, extended [in-depth] threads, core participants), social behavior (solidarity, conflict management, norms of appropriateness), and participation (frequent, regular, self-sustaining activity over time). Although online communities may differ in the configuration of these features, they are all necessary for the development of an online community.

Studies of online discourse have continued to engage the concept of "community" to better describe interaction, focusing on how norms and practices develop in the engagement of online communities (Angouri and Tseliga, 2010; Graham, 2007; Luchjenbroers and Aldridge-Waddon, 2011; Stommel, 2008). This research focused on using language analysis to identify how membership in communities is negotiated. Stommel (2008) for example used conversation analysis to investigate a German forum on eating disorders. Stommel analyzed the interaction in terms of Herring's description of community to show how solidarity, a shared purpose, norms and values, conflict, roles, and hierarchies are attended to. In other studies, a community of practice framework (Lave and Wenger, 1991) has proven particularly useful in describing the social context of social media sites. Rather than view community as "structural units of cultural and social transmission" (Arensberg, 1954, p. 109), the community of practice framework sees community as emerging around a shared repertoire of negotiable resources, mutual engagement, and a joint negotiated enterprise. Communities of practice differ from other popular notions of community which view identity as key factor, particularly social identity theory (Tajfel, 1981; Tajfel, 1983; Tajfel and Turner, 1979) and speech community theory (Labov, 1972a) which focus on individual identity in relation to others and a cognitive conceptualization of groups as a product of people's self-perception (Hogg, 2004). In a community of practice, the focus in not on who one is, but what one does.

A notion of community which foregrounds identity can be problematic when observing and analyzing discourse. Lundby (2011) points out that "religion is understood through processes of mediation and patterns of belonging rather than as defined "communities" (p. 1219) and usefully draws apart the experience of the individual in the community. Religious community involves individuals understanding themselves in relationship with others and institutions that often act as gate-keepers for religious ritual and practice, as in the case of the Catholic Church. While religious communities can be embedded in physical spaces and institutional hierarchies, the individual sense of "belonging" is a much more useful analytic frame for research into religious communities online (Campbell, 2005). For Lundby, "belonging" is the link between a network of users and a community. While an individual community is difficult to identify and analyze as an entity, user experience and in particular the practices and patterns that lead to the sense of belonging can be investigated.

Ess's (1996) expectation that technology had the potential to impact and transform religious practice (and specifically religious interaction online) has largely been accurate. In some ways, the development has been predicable as in Hutchings's work (2007, 2011) on online churches. These communities emerge in online spaces, but in ways that are largely analogous to and influenced by offline realities, becoming places of genuine religious experience for many users and allowing for a new presence of a religious community within one's life (Estes, 2009; Hutchings, 2007). At the same time, the affordances of the Internet have also affected religious practice in ways which would have been unpredictable in the early days of the Internet, including how authority has been sustained and upended, the presence of mobile technology in day-to-day life, and the "context collapse" of the social media.

As a starting point, the democratizing force of the Internet has provided a means to challenge and question, in particular fundamentalist, religious authority (Barzilai-Nahon and Barzilai, 2005). The increased activity of people in online discussions has required religious leaders to adapt practices to take into account threats to authority posed by opposing viewpoints represented in online spaces, as Cheong, Huang, and Poon (2011) have shown in research on Buddhist leaders in Singapore. Participants in this study focused on the need for embodied, special experiences in the practice of Buddhism and thus the need to be physically present with students, while still making concessions for the necessity of the Internet for communication. My own work has shown the difficulty of assuring particular interpretations of religious texts in online environments, where users can challenge one another and the only agreed upon authority is the Bible (Pihlaja, 2013a). In this case, institutional religious authority was entirely absent from the discussion. Instead, lay practitioners took on authoritative voices, appropriating second-order discourses about the text (Foucault, 1981), and attracting users as supporters.

While religious authority can be upended in new technologies, with increased access to diverse information outlets, new authorities can also emerge. As Anderson (2003) shows in the use of new media by Muslim innovators, modern technologies can be used to challenge the goals of Modernism even while existing within the technological affordances they provide. Moreover, technology allows for voices entirely outside a religious tradition to be present in the life of a believer, challenging their own personal beliefs as shown in LeDrew's (2013, 2012) and Smith's (2011) research into atheist activists. The upending of religious authority has consequences for not only controlling the interpretation of sacred texts by the faithful, but access to other voices can also entirely upend a system of belief for an individual. If the Internet allows users to become aware of different belief systems and potential issues of continuity within their own system, it poses a risk to religious authority structures and institutions.

Research into religious practice online has also looked at other ways in which the Internet can change or challenge practice, for example in how offline communities have appropriated online spaces for religious ritual and practice. Becker (2011) looks at how rituals such as making *dua* (or praying) are appropriated in online chat forums consisting of Muslims following the Salafiyya Movement within Islam. While these appropriations of online space for ritual, as in the case of taking a virtual *hadj* (Bunt, 2009), Becker (2011) notes the limitations of online appropriate of offline ritual and argues that for ritual to be effective, three dimensions must be present:

(1) they must keep the sacred protected from the profane;
(2) they need to be a communal endeavor wherein a significant part of the community of believers participates and/or accepts them as legitimate; and finally,
(3) they must maintain and reproduce the core values and fundamental beliefs of a religion. (p. 1186)

Here, the limitations on offline experiences of religious practice being appropriated in online spaces are clear, as found in Cheong, Huang, and Poon's (2011) study of Buddhist leaders cited above. Meditation, for example, as a physical ritual cannot be accomplished in online spaces, and religious experience associated with it cannot be fully enacted online. Where a rich history of offline ritual exists, as in the case of Islam, Buddhism, and Christianity, and physical experience is essential to the ritual (as in the taking of the Eucharist or a physical journal to Mecca), online spaces cannot replace the experience.

Although there remains a useful distinction between the offline and online religious communities and practices, Campbell (2012) argues that in the development of Internet interaction and the ubiquitous presence of mobile phones in day-to-day life, offline/online distinctions have grown more problematic. Wagner (2012), for example, investigates the proliferation of different apps, which facilitate prayer, ritual practice, sacred text reading, and social networks of connected believers. For example, Trammell (2015) discusses a popular app called "Jesus Calling" which encourages users to interact with daily devotional content and focuses "almost exclusively on users' anxieties, burdens, and hardships" (p. 223). Trammell further highlights concern that the use of the app focuses on individual, rather than communal practice. While the mediatization of religious practice is not necessarily new, as Trammell points out by drawing an analogy to televangelism in the 1970s, the individualization of experience certainly is. Whereas the commercialization of evangelical televangelism focused on the creation of shared desires among viewers, the mobile app focuses on customization for the "felt needs" of the user (Trammell, 2015, p. 229). In this case, technology is not facilitating religious community, but rather individual religious experience, how and when a user chooses to engage it.

Trammell's comparison and contrast to the medium of television is also an important reminder that while the technological affordances of the Internet might be new, technological mediation in religious practice is not. Further, innovation through technical advancement is not unique to Christianity. Anderson (2003), for example, argues that new interpretations of Islam have historically been connected to media innovations, from the printed word to cassette sermons to satellite television. The technological affordance creates a new medium of sharing a religious message, but the medium itself changes how users interact with the message. Satellite and terrestrial television provide a useful example as the technology created a new context for broadcasting theological messages beyond local contexts, and spreading messages nationally and internationally. The technology facilitated a change in how the message was then shared, as preachers needed to communicate beyond a physically present, local audience, to a largely unknown, physically absent audience. While the Internet has also offered an affordance of "broadcasting," in the sense that it allows users to reach broad audiences in global settings, it has also increasingly led to "narrowcasting" with the development of mobile apps which are oriented toward individual users. Trammell (2015) draws a comparison between the "Jesus Calling" app and "Our Daily Bread," a devotional series sent through the post. Because of the customization abilities of the app, the message an individual believer receives is now different, something that was not possible with the postal devotion series.

Considering the effects of apps like "Jesus Calling," the commodification of social interaction that underpins the economic model of social media companies like Facebook and app developers remains a key issue. The technological affordance of the smartphone is a predecessor to the apps which are developed for it. These technologies, while appropriating the language of socialization and "friendship," are designed for individual user technologies. While "digital religion" (Campbell, 2012) can and is effectively facilitated on these devices, their design is not oriented toward collective religious experience. If using Facebook is, as Mark Zuckerberg quoted above argues, about developing a personal "brand," "digital religion" on Facebook sits *within* this context. Although designers and users can act to appropriate or even subvert technology for different purposes, the economic interest of social media providers (like Facebook, Twitter, and YouTube) and their parent companies (like Google), and the companies that produce the technologies to access them (like Apple), must always be on the analyst's mind when investigating how they are used.

The relationship between the online and offline religious practices can often be more implicit, and online interaction is informed by offline experience. Stewart (2011) shows this influence in the development of online practices and text production by looking at charismatic Christian women and how restrictions to their participation in offline practice have clear continuity within online spaces. Interpretive practices in online spaces are also often based in offline practices, with users co-opting new social media spaces like YouTube to engage in practices that mimic offline practices, such as using Biblical evidence in argumentation (Pihlaja, 2014a). These practices can be upended by the presence of users who do not share the same faith background, or are members of different denominations, resulting in complex interactions between both scriptural interpretation and social disagreements (Pihlaja, 2011, 2013a). Because social media and SNS are not designed exclusively for religious communities, when they are appropriated by religious users, particularly for evangelical purposes, the presence of these dissenting voices can be unexpected and powerful.

Online affordances also facilitate the emergence of specific religious movements around specific topics, which would not have necessarily been possible in offline contexts. Howard (2011) shows how early technologies like Usenet newsgroups could be used to propagate and develop fundamentalist messages and create topical communities oriented toward specific issues, like the so-called "End Times." While these topical communities can have positive effects, topical community formation can focus exclusively on negative issues, as in the rise of *jihadi* propaganda communities (Bunt, 2009). These topical communities can create dissonance with offline communities, but also within themselves, as topical communities around religious interaction can attract users from many different sides of an issue (Pihlaja, 2014a).

The notion of an online community is also particularly important for groups that have been marginalized in local contexts. While atheists in America may have historically felt isolated within local community contexts where Christian faith was the norm, online spaces allow for connection and discussion (Cimino and Smith, 2011). If "coming out" as an atheist is similar in some ways to identifying as a member of a marginalized sexual community (Smith, 2011), the "community" of atheists may be less about the adherence to a particular belief system (or lack of belief), but as a means of supporting others who have also taken on the marginalized identity of "atheist." "Coming out" as atheist often requires, as Smith (2011) shows, taking on an identity that is in opposition to one's community and family. This community might be more analogous then to forum of transvestites negotiating politeness and the representation of gender norms (Planchenault, 2010) than Muslims using online virtual words like Second Life to perform a virtual *hadj* (Bunt, 2009).

Atheism provides an interesting case study in the discussion of digital religion because the Internet served in many ways to facilitate its growth (Smith, 2013; Smith and Cimino, 2012). At the same time, while the offline religious practices of Christianity and Islam have in some way provided a framework for how believers might practice their faith online, there is no obvious starting point or analogous set of rituals for atheistic expression in online spaces. Indeed the different trajectories of "scientific atheism" and "humanistic atheism" (LeDrew, 2012) and their different focuses also complicate describing "communities" of atheists, both on and offline. Cimino and Smith (2007) prefer to consider atheists as a kind of "sub-culture" rather than a community in the American context, arguing that atheists are "assuming a subcultural identity and engaging in defensive competition in order to create a secularist market niche in American society and the American religious economy" (p. 413). Particularly for "humanistic atheism," atheism is a response to religious practice rather than an identity in and of itself, and does not exist in a meaningful way as an identity except in contrast to a dominant culture in which religious belief is seen as the norm.

Although the description of atheistic communities is problematic, there is also clearly a push for a collective atheist identity for example in the so-called "atheist church," Sunday Assembly in London (Wheeler, 2013) or the Reason Rally on the National Mall in Washington, DC (Cimino and Smith, 2014). Atheist, secular, and humanist organizations maintain collective identities to accomplish particular social and political goals, despite disparate membership and a lack of a clear or specific creed. This is particularly an issue among "active" atheists, as LeDrew (2013) shows in interviews with attendees at a national atheist conference and in Smith's (2013) work showing a perception among atheists that many atheists are still not "out" in their communities. The goal of rallies and assemblies is to overcome the lack of organizational structure and providing "closeted" atheists a context in which to "come out" (Smith, 2013, p. 84). The assumption among atheists in this research is that the lack of structure and organization is a barrier to a collective identity and group consciousness, but also assumes that a collective of identity of atheism is something worth pursuing.

Religious ritual, practice, and community online can be inwardly focused. However, social media, SNS, and the implicit pressure to share and broadcast your own content has created a new affordance for religious interaction and community. Gillespie, Herbert, and Greenhill (2013) argue that social media has impact in changing religious practice, first, in conjunction with mass media to propagate discourses of religion and spirituality; and second, challenging existing religious communities to negotiate new spaces where users from a broad spectrum of religious positions. Atheism has flourished in this context, giving "out" atheists a platform for presenting their lack of belief in a way that allows them access to audiences without the filters of broadcast or traditional media. The shift in atheist views of themselves in the world can even be felt in the progression of research cited so far, where atheist have grown more bullish in carving out a place for themselves, and a collective atheist identity in the culture. Smith (2013) remarks, "Organized atheists perceive both the possibility, and necessity, of not just defending their views, but growing, increasing their influence, and becoming an accepted part of the mainstream" (Smith, 2013, p. 96).

Interaction around religious issues is not always best described in terms of "community," and collective action can occur even when "community" is not present, for example when SNS movements lead to collective action to support or oppose a specific side in one specific issue. Al-Rawi (2016) shows this in researching messages on a Facebook page set up to protest a short anti-Islam film called *Innocence of Muslims*. In this case, discourse about religion and primarily pro-Islamic messages were produced on the Facebook page, but they did not necessarily emerge from or result in a specific community of users. Instead, the issue and the specific Facebook page allowed for a kind of "one-off" expression of shared identity.

For Christian and Muslim users of social media, the issues could be different, given the established communities already present in offline contexts. A Christian user may, for example, find themselves friending church members on Facebook and joining a church Facebook group, creating a situation where members of their faith community are present in their day-to-day online life, and perhaps requiring some modification to how they interact on the site. Research I've cited so far has suggested that online spaces can and do affect the way that faith is practiced. However, the question of how people of different faiths interact with one another on SNS remains unresolved. SNS create a context somewhere between community and network, between public and private, where users are oriented toward people and spaces where they feel a sense of "belonging," but are, at the same time, aware of their own self-presentation, their "brand." Different SNS offer different ways in which these issues are negotiated, be they making videos public or private on YouTube, or controlling settings on Facebook posts to limit who may or may not see certain content. When users choose to make their content publicly available, as in YouTube videos, there is the possibility that users who both support and oppose them will view the video and respond.

However, attention, both negative and positive, is not something users necessarily avoid and since the nature of SNS is, in some way, self-promotion, the promotion of one's religious identity can be a part of that promotion. This can result in positive experiences of felt sense of belonging, or negatively when users respond in negative ways. These responses can, at times, be difficult to manage and users might not necessarily be able to predict who will support or oppose them. My own work looking at the interaction of Christians and atheists on YouTube showed that shared ideological positions or identity was not necessarily a guarantee of support, with users often arguing with others who shared similar ideological positions and affiliating with users whom they opposed (Pihlaja, 2014a). Because SNS are dynamic, social spaces, users must take into account a range of factors in deciding whom they will engage and how they will engage them. Users in my research actively sought out engagement with people they opposed. Rather than being a reason to avoid SNS, antagonistic interaction was one of the reasons to use YouTube, a finding that other researchers studying YouTube have also found (Lange, 2007a; Moor, Heuvelman, and Verleur, 2010).

Significant debate remains about the extent to which the Internet and social media either facilitates discussion among users of different beliefs, or rather operates as an echo chamber or "filter bubble" (Pariser, 2011), where users only interact with and reinforce the beliefs of users with whom they already agree (Prior, 2007). Interaction on SNS can, of course, be limited to relatively homogeneous groups, but SNS encourage interaction beyond one's immediate circle of "friends" to one's friends connections (McLeod and Lee, 2012). Heatherly et al. (2016) investigating the extent to which SNS users interacted with users of differing political positions, showed some optimistic findings, suggesting that SNS did lead to "deliberative democracy," as it related to American political discussions. While Heatherly et al. (2016) cite research showing the polarity of positions in blogging (Hargittai, Gallo, and Kane, 2008; Adamic and Glance, 2005), their findings show that SNS provide a different context for interaction, one where users are exposed to "cross-cutting discussions." This seems to suggest that both kinds of interaction are possible and are not necessarily exclusive: users can seek out and consume media that specifically supports their own ideological preferences while, at the same time, engaging with users who differ from them.

1.5 Key Questions

"Digital religion," Campbell's (2012) term for religious practice and expression online, has changed substantially from the early days of social media. It is now an increasingly more integrated space in which offline and online realities are difficult to separate. Users engage in religious communities which have both online and offline components. The bulk of this research, however, has focused on how users talk about their experiences of digital religion and their own reporting on experiences in online spaces. Moreover, the research into interaction among Muslims, Christians, and atheists has largely been historical, and not entirely analogous to the interaction that can be observed now. On YouTube and Facebook, Christians, Muslims, and atheists interact together in the same online space, speaking directly to one another and drawing others into the conversations. A gap remains, therefore, in analysis of this interaction on SNS, looking past the reported experiences of users, or quantitative data about their use of the site, but close discourse analysis of the actual interaction among users.

Religious Talk Online aims to fill this gap, by focusing on the videos users make, their interaction with commenters and others within their videos, and the interaction among users in comments. Rather than asking users what they think they are doing, I use a case study of interaction among Christians, Muslims, and atheists to answer the following questions:

- How do users on social media present themselves and their beliefs to others? What is the effect of the medium on the presentation of belief?
- How do users employ language to align with and oppose other users? How do disagreements arise (and potentially resolve) in interaction? What is the role of conflict and antagonism, when it is present?
- What themes can be observed across the different channels? What correlation can be found between particular beliefs and kinds of interaction that takes place?
- In what ways do communities of users emerge in the interaction and how do they differ depending on the ideological or theological positions that users take up?

To provide empirical answers to these questions, this book looks at a specific series of videos, embedded in the social media profiles of three public religious figures: an Evangelical Christian, a Muslim, and an atheist. Using their own words and the comments on their videos and pages, how users position themselves and others using language can be observed, as well as the consequences positioning has for the development of users that employ SNS and the development of religious communities they are members of more broadly.

In the following chapter, I discuss the methods, making a case for an empirical study of language use in interaction among users of different religious affiliations or no affiliation. I present a narrative description of the users and dataset that I will analyze and set out my methods.

To present my analysis, I will organize the findings around three main themes that emerge from the data: *Conflicts*, *Stories*, and *Themes*. The *Conflicts* chapter looks at how users deal with those who may disagree with them, both users who share their ideological position and those opposed to them. The *Stories* chapter will focus on how user narratives – about their own lives or taken from sacred texts or those of others – are used, either in the purpose of proselytization of others or in encouragement of their own community. The *Themes* chapter will focus on how users employ social media for particular ends, investigating if different uses of the SNS correlate with belief.

The final chapter draws together the main findings and discusses them in relation to the research that I have so far discussed in this chapter, answering a larger question about the ways in SNS have transformed interaction around religion online and what the future may hold.

2 Finding and Analyzing Religious Interaction

Religious interaction occurs all over the Internet. From online churches hosted on independent websites to Facebook groups for physical churches to Twitter evangelists, any discussion of "religious talk online" requires difficult decisions about what counts as "religious talk" and what platform to focus on. Importantly, when users talk about what they believe or don't believe, they often have some history on the platform they are using – religious talk online doesn't just appear out of thin air. To offer a robust description and analysis of how the sites and modes of communication affect the ways users represent themselves, interaction needs to be observed over time and particular attention must be given to *what* discourse is analyzed. My analysis will focus on users who have been successful in attracting an audience and who are engaged in the life of social media, including 1) users who interact with people with whom they agree and disagree; 2) users who are stable, with the content posted in the past still available to access at the time of analysis; and 3) users who generate content which is popular and is part of a developing online presence that can be observed over time. This chapter will present my methods for gathering and analyzing my data.

2.1 YouTube and Facebook Videos in Context

YouTube, founded in 2005, began as a largely unregulated video-hosting site, with users posting clips of popular television shows, contributing to both the success of YouTube and the shows whose copyright had been infringed (Burgess and Green, 2009). Coupled with the development of cheaper means of capturing video, with webcams and digital cameras, the site provided the means for a logical next step to blogging. Initially, however, YouTube grew in prominence through the posting of copyrighted material on the site, and much like the struggle in the early 2000s between Napster (the music sharing service) and the music industry, became the site for an important debate around copyright and the "sharing" of digital content. In 2007, the American mass media company Viacom sued YouTube over the posting of television content owned by Viacom on the site (Stempel, 2014). YouTube also introduced a means for users to share ad revenue through a "partner" program (Biggs, 2007), leading to users starting to make money from producing videos for the site.

While the Viacom lawsuit became a flashpoint for arguments about copyright online, from the beginning, YouTubers were also producing their own original content. "Vlogging," the video version of the "blog," for example, emerged as a model for interaction. Users like Renetto, the original "King of YouTube," began moving from producing viral video content to focusing on YouTube community engagement (Lange, 2007c). Users made videos that addressed the broad audience that YouTube afforded, but they also responded to specific users. The "video response" feature of the site allowed users to respond back and forth to one another in video, and conversations could expand and develop as YouTube videos could be posted as responses to other videos (Pihlaja, 2011). The "video response" remains an important part of the YouTube community and can develop into a thread of videos, as users build on what others have said and add to the discussion, pushing it forward until a particular topic is no longer of interest. YouTube, however, has removed the function to attach response videos to the original, so tracing a video thread requires careful observation of how users interact with one another around specific topics and knowing who is speaking with whom.

As a social media site, YouTube has been unique in that users produce videos for an audience and grow a "subscriber" base, rather than building a network with users based on "friend" connections. The communities that initially emerged were oriented toward the creative work of users in their videos. Early research into YouTube by Lange showed that the site was serving as more than a video depository and that users interacted on the site often in antagonistic ways (Lange, 2007a, 2007b). There was also often a clear tension users felt in balancing "freedom of speech" with being intolerant of abuse. Moor et al. (2010) did important early work on the notion of "flaming" (which they defined as insulting, swearing, or using otherwise offensive language) in the YouTube community, showing that although many people experienced "flaming" as a negative feature of the site, it wasn't always the case. They found instead that flaming was a part of the entertaining features of the site, something that made YouTube interesting, rather than something to be avoided.

The relationship between individual personalities and their viewers was an important mechanism for some minority groups to gain ground in presenting themselves to a larger audience. Particularly, the platform was important for an emerging presence of atheists who shared videos from prominent atheists such as Richard Dawkins and Sam Harris. Dawkins's and Harris's popularity grew in part thanks to the sharing of videos of their lectures, TV appearances, and discussions of their books. The atheist presence on YouTube came into the public eye at the end of 2006 when an atheist activist group called the "Rational Response Squad" issued "The Blasphemy Challenge" where users were encouraged to post videos of themselves denying the existence of the Holy Spirit, an act of "blasphemy" that was argued to be an unforgivable sin. In return, the group offered the first 1,001 users to post videos, a copy of the DVD *The God Who Wasn't There* (Rational Response Squad, 2007). Christian organizations responded with warnings that users were risking damnation, and creating their own challenges, including the "Praise the Lord Challenge" (Bansal, 2007). Arguments among and between Christians and atheists often mirrored larger theological disagreements, but worked out in the context of YouTube. Interpersonal and social disagreements could devolve into name-calling with users arguing endlessly, not only among categorical labels (i.e., Christians and atheists), but within their own communities (Pihlaja, 2014a).

YouTube has changed significantly as technology has developed. Between the founding of YouTube and 2014, there was a shift from desktop to mobile computing, and other social media sites like Twitter and Facebook had grown in prominence. YouTube was acquired by Google, becoming an important source of advertising revenue, thus moving from a "virtual village" to a more professionally oriented site (Kim, 2012). The introduction of advertising revenue created financial incentives for all users and the development of new business models to capitalize on the changes. For example, the development of multichannel networks, which allow individual users to pay part of their advertising revenue to join larger networks of users (Vonderau, 2016) and increased use of the site for "talent" to become paid entertainers (Cunningham, Craig, and Silver, 2016). While there had been great interest in "vlogging" as a way of keeping a personal "video diary" that could be shared with others (Burgess and Green, 2009), YouTube shifted toward a site of consumption and has grown more powerful as a media outlet wherein a smaller number of people make videos, and a majority of users simply watch the videos rather than making their own.

The commercial development of YouTube has indeed changed how YouTubers interact with the site and view the production of their own content, but YouTube continues to play a role in publicizing and magnifying events without an explicit goal of revenue production. Videos can still go "viral" after being posted and being shared by users (Broxton, Interian, Vaver, and Wattenhofer, 2011), although an element of unpredictability remains over which videos become popular and which don't. Going viral reflects the interaction of a complex set of online and offline factors. Viral videos also have the effect of taking local issues and recontextualizing them, for example in the case of police violence (Reilly, 2015) where a single instance of police violence can become a much larger, international issue as users view, comment on, and share the content.

The monetization of YouTube, its history as a social network site, its interaction with other social network sites (SNS) such as Twitter and Facebook, and the unpredictability around which videos will gain a large viewership has created a complex environment to research. How users produce content for public consumption – while interacting with the content of others – became an important part of the "participatory web," where new content is not just created, but content is remixed and retold in different contexts (Androutsopoulos, 2010). Manipulation of content can happen in different ways, be it simply by sharing content (and changing its meaning in recontextualization), or by remixing or spoofing or "mashing up" content (Georgakopoulou, 2015). This can be seen in the development of video "memes," derivative content centered on a particular theme which users reinterpret in local contexts (Gal, Shifman, and Kampf, 2015; Shifman, 2012). They can also be effective ways of arguing, by parodying the positions of others through spoofing.

Interaction around religion on YouTube, and in particular the three users that are the focus of this book, exhibits both traits of YouTube as a social network site and YouTube as a media outlet. In the videos analyzed here, all three present themselves as public figures who are authoritative figures and who are trying to grow their audiences. All three engage with the content of other users in a "participatory" way – they mash up and remix others' videos in their responses. They spoof the content of other users to support their own views and criticize and ridicule others. They encourage viewers to share of their content, and all three have had "viral" videos which were shared well beyond their normal subscriber base and picked up and discussed outside of their normal circle of influence.

Many early YouTubers were drawn into antagonistic interaction around political and religious issues. Although sometimes these arguments fell predictably along ideological lines, early YouTubers often argued with users that ostensibly held the same political and ideological commitments, a topic I have written about since 2011 (Pihlaja, 2011, 2014a, 2015, 2016b). The antagonism was similar to other arenas of online interaction, where asynchronicity and displacement led to users being less accommodating and more confrontational than they might otherwise be in face-to-face interactions but was also new in its scale (see Kiesler et al., 1984 for an early description of the social psychological effects of computer-mediated communication [CMC]). With the introduction of video, users could attack others with confrontational "in-your-face" videos. Responding to and mocking others became a way for users to increase their own popularity, gaining "subscribers" or users who opted into receiving notifications when new videos were posted.

A user's subscription number was and remains a significant sign of popularity on the site, with YouTube presenting gold framed "play" buttons to users who attain one million subscribers or more (Cohen, 2012). Those who generated controversy could increase their subscriber count by "p'wning" others – a neologism meaning to dominate another user completely, as in an online game (Pfannenstiel, 2010). Atheist users p'wning Evangelical Christians was a common practice, and theamazingatheist was a part of arguments with other users around issues of religion and politics. The drama featured varying levels of severity, from petty arguments about who had insulted whom, to the posting of sex videos of other users' partners. One notable instance ended with the Christian user VenomfangX being threatened with legal action by the atheist user Thunderf00t ostensibly over filing false claims about owning the copyright of Thunderf00t's videos (see Thunderf00t, 2008).

The extent to which any threat materialized with offline consequences is difficult to say, particularly from the perspective of a viewer, but a lack of clarity around what threats had real, offline consequences and which were just the noise of Internet boredom was part of the compelling nature of this drama. It was always hard to tell what was real and what wasn't. Indeed, one of the first YouTube phenomena was lonelygirl15. The vlog featured a young girl, Bree, talking to a camera in her bedroom, but questions about the authenticity of the vlog – whether it was a genuine vlog or an actress playing the role of lonelygirl15 – led to its increased popularity (Rushfield and Hoffman, 2006). The controversy around the series highlighted the extent to which video, even with its visual element, could not ensure authenticity online. It also opened up the possibility that videos could be produced specifically for the YouTube platform and develop into successful creative content beyond the site, with the questions of authenticity driving interest in the creator and the series. In one sense, whether it was real or not was less important than the unresolved question about its authenticity, which allowed for arguments to develop around it and increased its exposure.

Much of the in-fighting between users – particularly the focus on p'wning others – shifted significantly as YouTube introduced monetization of videos in 2009. Different moderation rules made it harder to attack others without facing some consequence, notably the removal of one's channel for not following community guidelines. Most seriously, rules related to infringing on the copyright were established to provide assurances that users would not violate YouTube's terms of service and users would provide content that did not infringe on the copyright of others and appealed to advertisers. "P'wning" and antagonism of other users became riskier in a new business model where growing one's audience into the hundreds of thousands required in some way rising above the "drama" of the YouTube community and creating content that appealed more broadly.

The changes in YouTube, while making it harder for users to interact in antagonistic ways, has created a market for the growth of daily vloggers and other so-called micro-celebrities (Page, 2012), who are able to grow specific audiences around personality. Although there has been research interest into antagonism on the Internet and YouTube specifically, discourse analysis of micro-celebrity vlogs has been of significantly less interest. That is not to say it has been entirely absent – some work has been done to look at how the discourse of comments develops. Eronen (2014), for example, has looked at rhetorical practices in YouTube comments, showing how hierarchies of moral norms are absent. Research has also looked at impoliteness from a pragmatics perspective in the comments sections, showing a perhaps unsurprising preference for so-called on the record impoliteness in comments, where users attack others and don't mitigate the attack (Bou-Franch and Garcés-Conejos Blitvich, 2014; Lorenzo-Dus, Garcés-Conejos Blitvich, and Bou-Franch, 2011). However, this research has a static notion of the YouTube page, taking comments at a certain point and analyzing them in relation to one another, rather than doing close analysis of video discourse. This research is certainly useful in describing how commenters use the site at particular times, but it does not necessarily give a clear picture of how users interact over time.

The Facebook videos investigated in this book function in many ways like YouTube – the video plays prominently in a browser window, there is a "like" function, and users can comment. However, Facebook as a social media site has followed a much different trajectory from YouTube. While pragmatically, the videos on both sites are content for public audiences how each site developed is important to understand for successful analysis. Founded in 2004, Facebook developed at the same time as YouTube, but with different priorities for user experience and interaction. YouTube's primary feature was to store and publish videos (with social networking as a by-product) while Facebook functioned as a way of connecting with friends, family, and colleagues (Kwon and Wen, 2010). Unlike YouTube, the focus is not on the content that is being produced, but on building a social network.

While illegal "sharing" of copyrighted content fueled YouTube's rise as a social media platform, Facebook grew in a very different way. Previous network sites like MySpace and Friendster focused on developing relationships in online spaces, but Facebook successfully created an online social network site with a focus on users connecting with people they already knew in their offline lives. Mark Zuckerberg's early description of "The Facebook," launched initially at Harvard University, compared it to an online directory of people, allowing users to network with other students (Tabak, 2004). Unlike YouTube, the importance of "critical mass" (Sledgianowski and Kulviwat, 2009) – or having enough members that finding friends on the site would be possible – was key to Facebook's success. Facebook, as a social media site, attained success by becoming the place that users went to connect with others that they already knew in their local life, highlighted by the development of Facebook first on individual university campuses for classmates to connect.

YouTube and Facebook therefore differed initially in the reasons a user would access each site. When accessing YouTube, users mostly land on specific video pages, to watch specific video content, often produced by someone they don't personally know. Facebook, by contrast, has historically been less about the specific content of a page, but rather an individual user's reporting of their lived experience as the content. Page (2010, 2013) has focused on this presentation of self in terms of personal narrative – social media is about telling stories of one's lived experience and sharing them with others. These stories are not necessarily interesting in and of themselves, but they are meaningful when shared with others who, in one way or another, have an interest in the life of their Facebook "friend," be they a colleague, a family member, or an offline friend. Unlike YouTube, where users develop content to attract viewers, on Facebook, the person creates content through status updates, posting information on their own "wall" or timeline, and commenting on others' content (Caers et al., 2013). Although there is still the chance for and the presence of antagonism, the actions on the site are much less "deindividuated"; that is, users interact with people they know in other contexts, be they old high school friends (Ellison, Steinfield, and Lampe, 2007) or someone else they know well in the offline world (Subrahmanyam, Reich, Waechter, and Espinoza, 2008).

Facebook as a social network site was prescient in one sense, seeing online and offline life as converging. With the development in mobile technology and smart phones, computing has moved away from the desktop experience with online groups, to a much more integrated world in which users are regularly using their mobile devices to connect with friends geographically displaced and those with whom they are physically present. At the same time, Facebook has also developed features which have moved it away from being a site where users engage only with their own "friends," but also with brands and celebrities (Vorvoreanu, 2009). Vorvoreanu (2009) shows in a small study how the "liking" of a brand or celebrity on the site becomes a part of one's identity, shared with other information about who one is and how they want to be perceived. The integration of the social network site with one's consumer preferences further extends the use of the site beyond simply connecting with friends and colleagues to interacting with corporations and celebrities.

Although Facebook initially was conceived as a "closed-garden" social network site where users needed to be members of the site and friends with someone to see the content that they shared, Facebook has increasingly developed functions which are public facing, encouraging users to keep profiles and share information publicly. What is or is not considered "public" on the site has, however, long been considered problematic, with an experience of "fuzzy" or non-binary public/private boundaries for users (West, Lewis, and Currie, 2009) and some users being unaware that their profiles are completely public (Brandtzæg, Lüders, and Skjetne, 2010). Where interaction can be viewed beyond a core group of "friends," many of the same trappings and problems of sites like YouTube, which are historically used to publicly publish videos, appear. This is evident in the increased presence of commercial pages on the site, where profiles are no longer just representative of individual people, but can represent companies or products or events.

As Facebook became an increasingly important site of social interaction, it also became a site of media sharing, and a new way for content creators, either individuals or corporations, to push content to consumers. Pages on Facebook now resemble other sites of media distribution, like YouTube, that feature content rather than "status updates" which was the core function of the site initially. Although the actual appearance and user experience of viewing a video posted on Facebook and YouTube might be quite similar, the functions of the sites are different, with different histories and apparatuses for engaging in content, with different concerns and cultures attached to what users might expect to experience. Although these differences have been described in terms of community expectations (Angouri and Tseliga, 2010), users' experiences of the sites might be more implicit, with the histories of experiences on the sites having a tacit effect on how one might come to and interact with a YouTube video compared to a video on Facebook.

The differences in how Facebook and YouTube are used have consequences then for the sort of interaction which develops on each site. While YouTube's comments sections, and their anonymous nature, have often been of interest, research into Facebook has been more focused on how individual users represent themselves and maintain relationships using their own pages and the difficulties this poses (see Caers et al., 2013 for a full reveiw of this research). YouTube users all have the ability to make and upload videos, but many users employ the site just to watch content. Facebook, however, is different in the sense that developing and maintaining a network of friends on the site includes having and maintaining your own page. This leads to a focus on how individuals present themselves and manage things like their privacy and public identity (Georgalou, 2016). These issues become recurring themes in articles about Facebook, where unlike YouTube, users are much more conscious of being monitored and of the consequences of doing something which might bring them negative attention offline.

At the same time, there are significant similarities between Facebook and YouTube. Researchers have looked at how social movements can emerge around particular events on the Facebook, like the response to the *Innocence of Muslims* film on Facebook (Al-Rawi, 2016). The analysis in Al-Rawi's article mirrors other work done on YouTube videos, taking a large corpus of data and looking at how patterns of responses developed in comments on the video. Other researchers have looked at how Facebook can affect political engagement, in terms of how political organizations use the site (Nitschke, Donges, and Schade, 2016) and whether Facebook does or does not encourage civic and political engagement for young people (Theocharis and Quintelier, 2016). Research has also been done on how "fan pages" on Facebook create involvement with brands and celebrities. Yung-Tzu and colleagues (Yung-Tzu Joyce, Meng-Yen Tom, and Kuo-Chen, 2015), for example, have shown how post reach correlates with positive engagement, meaning the more people that see a post, the more likely it is that people will be positive toward it.

While it may be possible to draw distinctions between Facebook and YouTube as a researcher and while it is important to take into account the differences in the development of sites, there is something to be said about the "complicated" nature of social media and the relationships among different sites for users, as boyd (2014) has found in their study of teenagers' engagement with social media. The social media world and how users engage different platforms is not a simple formula. Overlap across social media sites and managing different content in different forums is a necessary skill in a culture of being "always on" (Baron, 2008). How platforms influence the development of discourse, particularly around sensitive or important issues like religion, is a key question, having looked at the development of digital religion up to this point. Attempting to understand any particular interaction online requires taking a scaled, longitudinal approach and taking into account the different affordances, histories, and communities of users is essential.

2.2 "Dear Mr. Muslim; Dear Mr. Atheist": Description of Data

A unique perspective can be gained about users and communities looking at how positions, affiliations, and arguments shift as users respond to one another, but gathering this data can be difficult. To investigate how language use develops in dynamic interaction around religion on social media, it is necessary to identify a series of interactions between users from different faiths. By its nature, interreligious dialogue occurs across different communities online, and is then likely to occur on the public pages of users representing different positions.

Considering the research questions in this book – what popular "evangelical" outreach looks like on social media for users from different perspectives, particularly in a context of confrontation with users with which one didn't normally agree – theamazingatheist, a prominent and longstanding presence in religious discourse on YouTube, provides a good starting point. theamazingatheist has an online persona that his username embodies. One of the original YouTube atheists, theamazingatheist made a name for himself by attacking and mocking religion and religious users on the site. He's built a successful business around theamazingatheist, supporting himself through ad revenue and donations from subscribers for both his YouTube channel and his podcast, through the crowd-funding platform, Patreon. He's sold shirts and books and has a clear sense of how YouTube micro-celebrity can be used to motivate a fan base around a particular topic, in this case, mocking and attacking religious fundamentalists. By 2014, theamazingatheist's channel remained one of the most viewed atheist channels on the site, but he had shifted his channel to a model which represented the current trends on the site, producing videos for a niche audience while also trying to grow his channel. theamazingatheist still confronted other users and public figures, but these users were often public figures – politicians, sports stars, and popular online preachers, including Joshua Feuerstein.

Joshua Feuerstein is known for his in-your-face approach to Facebook, mixing tough pronouncements of judgment that are always couched in the language of love. He describes himself as a "husband and father to four beautiful kids. A former television and radio evangelist, he has turned to social media with his personal story of redemption and the hope of how Jesus Christ can heal a hurting heart!" (Feuerstein, 2016b). He cultivates a presence that is imposing and aggressive but also kind and loving. Feuerstein's page has featured videos of him holding firearms while commenting on his "love of Jesus" (Feuerstein, 2016a), a juxtaposition that can be jarring for those not familiar with Conservative American Christian culture. He continuously reminds the viewer of the love of Christ and how the path of Christian faith provides "love, joy, and peace." With almost two million likes on his page by the end of 2015, Feuerstein's appeal as a preacher is clear. Feuerstein's popularity has grown thanks to the juxtaposition he cultivates – taking a hard-line doctrinal or political stance, attracting hate and anger from users who do not share his theological and political positions, and then using the hate to increase his own credibility within his own community. Feuerstein takes positions that are viewed as unpopular to a broader Internet culture but often attract support from users who "like" his page on Facebook. His positions are attacked not only by individual Internet users in comments and videos about him, but increasingly in larger, more visible arenas, such as being denounced on Huffington Post (Hanson, 2015) and *The Washington Times* (Moyer, 2015). While much criticism of Feuerstein addresses his style and the lack of rigor in his arguments, Feuerstein claims the criticism as a kind of persecution for his faith, one which he says is unpopular because of his willingness to speak truth that others find offensive.

A series of interactions between Feuerstein and theamazingatheist began when Feuerstein made two videos in May and June 2014, titled *Dear Mr. Muslim* and *Dear Mr. Atheist.*[1] In both videos, Feuerstein did not appear to target anyone in particular, but rather spoke about issues related to atheism and Islam in a general way. In both cases, Feuerstein claimed to have contact with people whom he categorized as "Muslim friends" or "an atheist" who had insulted him, but who the particular "Mr. Muslim" and "Mr. Atheist" were was never explicitly stated. In both videos, Feuerstein represented himself as opposing what he perceived as positions held by both categories, arguing for the divinity of Christ in his video to "Mr. Muslim" and arguing against the validity of evolution to "Mr. Atheist." In both cases, the videos did not seem to be generated by specific comments or emails and in neither case did Feuerstein read from another text or refer directly to another source.

The response by theamazingatheist was in some ways unsurprising. theamazingatheist had made his career in calling out "Creationist bullshit" and for years had addressed different Evangelical Christians who had challenged him with similar arguments. The response by another user, however, John Fontain, to the video *Dear Mr. Muslim* was more unexpected. Fontain, a white British Muslim "revert," had built a small channel around recording and posting videos of his dawah outreach in the UK and beyond. A red-headed, white British man dressed in a *thobe* and speaking Arabic, Fontain is not the stereotypical face of Islam online – commenters remind him regularly that he's a "ginger." Born and raised in a Christian home, Fontain reverted to Islam as a young man, the result of Muslim outreach to him. With few exceptions, Fontain's message comes back again and again to the transformative power of following Islam and the benefits of sharing it with others. Fontain had published an evangelical pamphlet called "Jesus and the Injeel" arguing for a new reading of Jesus's ministry in the gospels, that Jesus was spreading the "Injeel" or the message of Allah. Fontain's message focuses on responding to Christian values and doctrine and arguing that the Bible not only supports Islam, but that Islam provides a more "pure" form of Christian religion.

Before responding to Joshua Feuerstein, Fontain's videos did not regularly engage other online users. Instead, his channel served as a site for storing his more traditional content, which included television shows, interviews of other Muslim scholars and reverts, and videos of Fontain doing street dawah – or evangelical outreach – in a variety of contexts. Fontain used the channel to show how his method for dawah was effective and to promote his pamphlet. Throughout Fontain's videos, there is a focus on how Muslim viewers can

[1] All videos referenced in this section can be found in the Appendix.

share their faith, and Fontain regularly recorded himself talking with people on the street and spreading the message of Islam. Unlike theamazingatheist, Fontain doesn't suggest that he is performing, or that his online presence is a performance, with the exception of one "parody" video in which he pretends to be a British nationalist, making a video about how Muslims are corrupting Britain, only to be welcomed into a mosque in the end of the video. The videos are carefully produced and edited, often including interviews with Muslims who are in some way engaged in dawah.

When Feuerstein published his video *Dear Mr. Muslim*, Fontain responded in a typical YouTube style, similar to the video produced by theamazingatheist, called *Dear Joshua Feuerstein Muslim Response John Fontain*. The response took clips of Feuerstein's video edited together with Fontain responding to Feuerstein point-by-point. Although markedly less antagonistic than theamazingatheist, Fontain also subtly mocked Feuerstein, turning his hat backward in one clip and mimicking Feuerstein's style, before becoming more serious and making an argument typical of his channel: Feuerstein was a good, moral man who needed to take his faith one step further and accept Islam as the final revelation of Allah. Fontain's video used Feuerstein's presentation of Christian belief, as it related to Islam, to show how Christians misunderstood Islamic belief. However, Fontain was not hostile in the video, instead offering an invitation to Feuerstein and all the viewers of the video to learn more about the Islam and the teachings of the Prophet Muhammad.

The interaction among these users provides a useful starting point for data collection because it includes videos made around religious topics, which are also explicitly oriented toward the three audiences which each user seemed to be addressing: an oppositional audience (of users who did not share the same belief and were openly hostile to it), their own viewers (including fans and users who shared the same belief), and a general audience of users who might not be affiliated one way or another but might be persuaded to join their community. Feuerstein's videos and the responses represent an exemplar case of interreligious dialogue on social media at a particular point in the development of the platforms, showing how dialogue often represents patterns of interaction. Also, given the visibility and popularity of the three users, the comments sections in the videos also provide evidence of how each community responded to the positions presented.

2.3 Approaching Public Social Media Exchanges

In the previous chapter, much of the evidence cited to describe the experience of individual users on SNS and discuss how they have developed as sites for religious practice and interaction was taken from a sociological perspective. Indeed, the study of "digital religion" as presented by Campbell (2012) and others has focused on methods and descriptions of communities that aren't exclusively concerned with how language is used. The research in this book takes a markedly different approach to religious practice online. Rather than asking users about their experiences of social media, it focuses on the language surrounding experiences, analyzing interaction as a starting point for describing how patterns of religious dialogue develop.

2.3.1 Discourse Dynamics

Choosing to look at interaction requires taking a perspective on how to understand language in social life. My research starts with two key assumptions about the nature of interaction – that language is a social practice and that interaction is a complex, dynamic system. In terms of the social nature of language, linguistic ethnography, an approach to language as social practice and building on work in linguistic anthropology and interactional sociolinguistics (Creese, 2008) provides several important key points, namely that "language and social life are mutually shaping, and that close analysis of situated language use can provide both fundamental and distinctive insights into the mechanisms and dynamics of social and cultural production in everyday activity" (Rampton et al., 2004, p. 2). Analysis of language then must "combine close detail of local action and interaction as embedded in a wider social world" (Creese, 2008, p. 233). These assumptions offer a useful frame for starting research into religious discourse on social media, drawing attention away from only reports of experiences by users to the analysis of "local action" – the minutia of interaction that might be lost when people think back on and report their own lived experience.

Language in use – discourse – can be viewed as a complex dynamic system (Cameron, 2015; Larsen-Freeman and Cameron, 2008), and Cameron (2015) has developed a discourse dynamics framework for investigating how the system develops over time. While complex dynamic systems are difficult to conceive of in the abstract, we regularly experience them in our lives. For example, traffic patterns are the result of a variety of different factors that contribute to whether a given street is congested on a particular day or not. Some of these patterns are predictable and long term, such as the number of people living in a particular place and daily contributing to the traffic congestion. Some patterns are predictable, but less regular, such as different national holidays affecting the traffic. Some other patterns are not predictable, such as whether or not a traffic accident occurs at a given time or in a given place. With so many factors at play, some predictions about the dynamics of traffic flow on a particular street can be made, but things can also change suddenly and unexpectedly.

As a complex dynamic system, discourse has features of predictability in some ways, and dynamism in others. Complex dynamic systems are, importantly, non-linear, meaning that there is not always a clear cause-effect relationship and no clear beginnings and endings (Cameron, 2015). Complex dynamic systems theory holds the following positions:

- Central to complex dynamic systems are notions of connectedness and change;
- every aspect of a situation that we investigate and theorize is connected to other aspects of the situation;
- many, if not all, aspects of the situation are in flux, always changing, i.e., dynamic;
- the connections between aspects of the situation are themselves dynamic. (Cameron, 2015, p. 31)

Thinking again of the traffic example, there are different ways in which any individual event can affect future events. If there are road works, for example, on a given day the traffic flow will change. Less obvious events, however, might also affect the system. A baby may have kept someone up all night, leading them to be more tired than normal when they head out for their morning commute and causing them to be less aware of a cyclist they accidently hit. This could lead to a traffic jam that causes someone to be late for work and miss an important meeting. Where these networks of causation begin and end is indeterminable given the interconnected nature of the world. What is clear, however, is that nothing occurs in isolation.

A discourse dynamics approach attempts to apply the notions of complex dynamic systems to language and bring together theoretical positions about the role of personal, cognitive, and physical contexts (Simpson, 2004). It describes discourse and the development of discourse in real time as the result of the interaction of a variety of components without focusing on or favoring one as a starting point for analysis. In this approach, patterns are understood from a bottom-up description of the particular conditions of a given interaction. Cameron (2011, 2015) has used this approach to describe complex interactions particularly as they relate to metaphor use in conciliation discourse and in talks aimed at developing empathy in dialogue and interaction between tribes in Kenya in conflict with one another. Cameron shows in both cases the need to analyze discourse, working to understand how different components affect the outcome of interaction.

By accepting, as a starting point, the interconnectedness of social interaction, a complex dynamic systems approach to linguistic analysis demands a careful management of macro and micro perspectives on language data. It is important to have a broad scope for data collection, looking beyond narrow commitments to particular analytic frameworks that assume a focus on a limited set of linguistic features, but instead allows for the potential that interaction can and does develop in particular ways for a multitude of reasons. This does not mean that the analyst is always aware of the elements contributing to the development of a system, but it does mean that more and perhaps unsuspected elements can be identified and analyzed. The analyst works to understand the contours of the system, what can and can't be known, identifying not only at what is present in the interaction, but how it compares to other interactions, paying attention to what might be absent in addition to what is present.

A discourse dynamics approach focuses on identifying and analyzing how all the components come together to produce a unique interaction, which can be influenced by how different agents and/or elements may interact at a particular time. Like Bakhtin's (1981) notion of "heteroglossia," there is a tension between the momentum of a system and the disruptions which can bring change, given the right circumstances. Complex dynamic systems may tend toward stable states, creating patterns that can continue to reoccur. However, because the system is open, when new components enter, they have the possibility to change the interaction. A discourse dynamics approach to interaction on social media also helps to dissipate concerns about collecting the "right" data or "all" the data from the interaction. Instead, the researcher can look for data which represents the system at particular times, and which can provide some explanatory power why interaction occurs in the way that it does.

Cameron (2015) describes how there are five interaction levels in discourse dynamics:

- [Point Zero] is the initial conditions of an interaction, the state of the system immediately before the event being modeled or investigated.
- Level 1 represents activity on a timescale of milliseconds, such as automatic responses to another person or experience.
- Level 2 represents the level of minute-by-minute engagement and more controlled responses, e.g., in conversation or language learning activity.
- Level 3 is the level of a single discourse event.
- Level 4 encompasses accumulated level 3 patterns that stabilize as attractors in the system, for example as learned vocabulary items, empathic understandings, idioms, discourse genres, or ethical codes. These operate on a longer timescale beyond an immediate event, and may, as social change, spread across communities, groups or nations, as with the signing of a peace agreement. (Cameron, 2015, pp. 44–45)

Taking all of the levels of the system into account, a discourse dynamics approach seeks to understand interaction in terms of macro and micro trends. An analyst might focus on how specific interactions between Muslims and Christians online might be a part of a larger historical pattern of interaction, as well as the contour of every interaction across a particular timescale, which Cameron (2015, pp. 45) argues can be bound as "discourse events." These also lead to new initial conditions, the "Point Zero" of the next discourse event. Considering interaction in this way is particularly useful in thinking about social media because it gives a theoretical structure for talking about specific moments in the context of what comes before and after, and in relation to how they relate to larger trends on larger scales of magnitude. By separating out the different timescales and levels that the interaction occurs on, the analyst can then establish where their analysis is focused at any given time.

Dynamic systems can be difficult to conceive of in an abstract sense, but they become clearer as we think about the specific interactions analyzed in this book. If we can consider the development of interaction among Christians and Muslims, we can understand in some sense why it has developed in the way it has. When displaced geographically, dialogue between Christians and Muslims emerged in a particular way, with stable ways of describing one another. At different times in history, new technologies or political realities resulted in a disruption to a stable way of talking about the other. After a disturbance in the system, new ways of talking to and understanding the other emerged, and along with them, new stabilities. Because complex systems are open, predicting what might affect the system in the future is difficult. It isn't enough, for example, to understand the historical context of contact between Christians and Muslims to describe the interaction of particular users online. We must understand the individual agents, with their own motivations and histories. How this interacts with historic precedence, or how interaction normally occurs on the given social media sites, are all incredibly important for understanding a particular instance of religious talk on social media.

This description of language use focuses on how language and context are always mutually influencing one another. While regularities can be observed in interaction, important and meaningful parts of discourse are the result of interactants speaking together and constructing meaningful social realities. Cameron's work, for example, has focused especially on how metaphor use can show how speakers come to make sense of abstract concepts like conciliation (Cameron, 2011; Cameron and Maslen, 2010). In these cases, tracing interconnectedness and change in the interaction allows the researcher to see how users from very different personal, physical, and cognitive contexts attempt to communicate and build or block empathy, issues which are of importance when investigating language data taken from users on social media from vastly different backgrounds.

Methodologically, the discourse dynamics approach follows these steps:

- Start from interaction: e.g., face-to-face talk, use of text, situated discourse.
- Interpret an instance of the interaction – a literacy event, a conversation, a task – as a trajectory of a complex dynamic system.
- Unpack the elements, connections, and dynamics of the system.
- Investigate the detail with appropriate tools.
- Make every decision with moral/ethical responsibility. (Cameron, 2015, p. 43)

The analysis starts with interaction, moving from the situated discourse across different timescales and scales of magnitude. While a discourse dynamics approach to interaction serves as a useful theoretical starting point, it does not necessarily dictate how interaction should be analyzed. Instead, the focus is on using "appropriate tools," which suggests that tools may different depending on the context. While Cameron and my own work focuses on the use of metaphor (Cameron, 2011, 2007; Pihlaja, 2014a), a discourse dynamics approach does not prescribe a particular set of linguistic tools for collecting the data and analyzing it. Therefore, building on the theoretical notion of interaction as a complex, dynamic system, it's necessary to develop a toolkit of analytic resources which will help to collect data and to do linguistic analysis that takes into account both micro and macro perspectives, without ignoring potentially important components in the system which could be affecting the outcomes we observe.

2.3.2 *Discourse-Centered Online Ethnography*

To identify data for analysis, this study employs key elements of "discourse-centred online ethnography" (Androutsopoulos, 2008): longitudinal observation followed by close discourse analysis. From the perspective of discourse-centered online ethnography, simply analyzing web pages as fixed artifacts, be they webpages or YouTube video comments, doesn't allow for a description of their dynamic elements. Social media sites are not static environments, but develop over time, interacting with a variety of different factors that can't be observed by simply extracting and analyzing them. By observing sites and doing analysis within the perspective of the observation, the analyst can provide a much more comprehensive perspective on why certain trends or patterns might emerge.

In discourse-centred online ethnography, data collection itself is a recursive process that involves some amount of analysis to decide how a project should develop. While a researcher is "in the field" in online communities, key issues, characters, and conflicts begin to emerge and with them, specific questions about the users and the context. In previous research, I employed longitudinal analysis to identify instances of "drama" within a community of users and chose a specific instance of drama to analyze, based on the questions that emerged from the observation (Pihlaja, 2014a). The longitudinal observation not only allows the researcher to take into account changes in how users employ technology over time and to situate discourse analysis, but it gives a rich understanding of why certain arguments or topics of discussion arise. The framework also offers a useful theoretical starting point for taking into account how different elements on a YouTube video page and Facebook videos (i.e., spoken discourse in the video and comments) interact with one another. It sees the different elements of the pages as dynamic and networked to other videos and topics both on the site (in this case YouTube) and beyond the site, as in this book where arguments emerge on Facebook and are responded to on YouTube.

While in the field, my approach has taken several key departures from online ethnography. First, I have not, as a researcher, fully participated by making videos, joining conversations, commenting, and messaging or contacting other users. The idea of "participation" is, however, problematic, in that my use of YouTube is in many ways the same as other community members. I watch videos on YouTube, and follow certain users and discussions, and have uploaded a variety of family videos, research lectures, and conversations with my brother. I watch videos from a variety of topics and comment on some videos, although very rarely. This might not make me a full-participating member of the community, but I am clearly a "viewer," which is a valid and indeed most common position in the YouTube community. While I am an active user of Facebook as well, I also did not engage in any way with the pages I analyze in this book. Second, I have not attempted, for this research, to contact any of the users to be interviewed or to talk about their experience. In online ethnography, this emic perspective would be essential for describing the lived experience of users. For my research, however, I am less interested in what users privately say they are attempting to do. The social media content I am analyzing is public, and I am focused on the public interaction of the users.

In this initial observation period, my analysis focused on finding key themes, following Owen (1984) and looking for recurrence, repetition, and forcefulness in the discourse. This analysis is impressionistic and does not yield empirical findings: it is not systematic and it is not replicable. It does, however, help the researcher identify questions and potential data sets. Observing larger channels and users and the responses to them to find data allows the researcher to comment not only how people present their own beliefs, but how communities develop around them. In particular, given the focus on "religious talk" more generally, interaction among Christians and

Muslims and atheists was a good potential area of focus theamazingatheist led to Joshua Feuerstein and John Fontain, through the interaction I described above.

Online data collection poses several complicating issues. In the first instance, there is a question of when to collect the data. On some videos, particularly popular ones, users can post comments that are deleted either by the user themselves, by the video page owner, or removed by YouTube for breaching their terms of use. Because of this, the page that you see at one moment is not the same as the next. Content, particularly after a video has just been posted, is likely to be garnering more and more views and more and more comments. Data collection immediately when a video is posted could potentially track some of the most dynamic elements of the interaction, but is problematic because the researcher is often not aware of which videos will be useful for analysis until after the video has been posted for many days. Monitoring a large number of video pages becomes too difficult because the process of choosing videos cannot be automated unless the researcher simply wants to focus on particular users.

Waiting to collect data until after a video has reached a more stable place and new comments are not being added at a high rate allows for a more complete view of the interaction. These issues apply not only to YouTube videos, but also Facebook videos, where content can also be posted and removed. Although the page is not dynamic in the way it is when a video is first posted, the whole of the interaction is preserved in a way that allows tracing arguments through the comments section and comparing the information from the comments with the knowledge gained from the longitudinal observation. It also allows for the researcher to choose video pages to analyze which are particularly relevant to the research questions that have developed. This does mean, however, some loss in the ability to trace the moment-to-moment interaction occurs. If, however, the focus of the study is on overall patterns, the loss of this data is not consequential for the analysis, particularly as numerous examples of spirited arguments remain on the pages. Because the starting point of my data collection was longitudinal observation, I was looking for users to compare, not data sets to compare. Once the argument among the three users was identified, I began to think about how a data set could be collected from their interaction, which would give insights into their individual uses of social media, the communities around them, and their talk to and about a variety of other users.

The three users made very different kinds of videos, for different audiences. I decided to gather videos from both the main videos the three users made addressing each other, and a selection of videos around the event to see how the users employed social media not just in their interaction with one another, but more generally. As a rough starting point, I decided to collect twenty videos from each user, which allowed for a good sense of the user's overall engagement. I also decided to pick the videos manually, rather than choose videos from a particular strict time period or through random selection. This reflected an awareness of the different kinds of videos that users made and allowed me to avoid collecting more videos of one type which make have given a false sense of the video maker. For example, John Fontain made a series of videos of him doing dawah during the World Cup. Rather than select all of these videos for analysis, I only included two, to ensure that my collection of videos from Fontain represented his diverse use of YouTube. I also ultimately gathered seven additional videos from Feuerstein, as he consistently made very short videos and I wanted to ensure that there was enough spoken discourse to compare with the other users. These criteria were, however, rough and reflected the awareness I had from watching the users over time. The data set was, by its nature, subjectively constructed and the video choice reflected my interest in comparing the users and their use of the sites, not to produce the most balanced data set. Looking at the different ways that users employed the sites, this would have been impossible anyway, which I will discuss below.

In this study, I used only publicly accessible YouTube and Facebook data, consisting of three types: my transcripts of the videos, the written content produced by the user themselves when posting a video (including descriptions, tags, and titles), and the comments on the videos. The authorship of the video page content is the owner who produced the text and has, at least from the user agreement standpoint, responsibility for its content. The comments, however, are less straightforward in terms of ownership. Although the commenter produced the content and was able to remove the content, the comment exists on the video page of another user's video, who controls and curates the content, with the ability to remove comments. Authorship of comments is also not always straightforward. While on Facebook comments are linked to user pages and profiles (with users' "real" names), on YouTube, users don't necessarily need to provide their real names, or link the comments to a consistent online identity. In collecting the data, I chose to include all the content on the page, without deleting any automatically generated text or usernames, choosing after the analysis on which parts to include or not in the writing up of the research.

For the video discourse, I produced the transcripts of the spoken language in the videos. I transcribed using intonation units (Chafe, 1994), following a full description of this methodology in Stelma and Cameron (2007). I did not transcribe closely for intonation to ensure that words were searchable using corpus linguistics tools I employed. By using whole word transcription, I could search between the video discourse and the comments and compare occurrences of words easily. I also did not attempt to transcribe the visual representations on the video, choosing instead to keep the transcripts focused on the verbal communication while referring back to the video during the analysis. In several instances in Fontain's videos, there were also extended greetings or recitation of verses from the Qur'an in Arabic, which I did not transcribe. I did, however, transcribe the use of Arabic as single discourse markers, when the Arabic did not extend beyond two full intonation units. I have represented written comments as they appear online, without any editing. I will discuss patterns of visual representation in my analysis of positioning later in the chapter but only as a way of supplementing and corroborating evidence from the spoken discourse. While video data offers many different frames for analysis, with focus on different modes, the decision to focus on discourse represents a need to focus on a data set which would best and most efficiently address the research questions.

2.3.3 *Description of Data*

The whole of the data set consists of 67 videos comprising over six hours of video and 60,888 comments. A full list of the videos, titles, and URL addresses can be found in the Appendix. The data set started with roughly the same number of videos from each of the users, but because the different users varied in popularity, the number of comments on each video (and subsequently, the number of words) varied from each source.

Table 2.1 shows the basic information about the data set. In the first column, all three users are identified by how they are best known. While the number of video pages and the video length is determined by the site (either YouTube or Facebook), the word counts of the videos are taken from my transcriptions. The number of comments represents those I was able to cull from the pages but does not necessarily represent the number of comments that were posted on the page prior to data collection, as users can delete comments,

Table 2.1 *Data Set*

User	Video pages	Video length (hr:min:sec) and word count	Comments	Comment word count
theamazingatheist	19	2:49:18 / 30,638	48,414	2,355,873
John Fontain	21	2:58:39 / 29,490	4,196	227,797
Joshua Feuerstein	27	0:59:05 / 12,140	8,278	185,936
Totals	67	6:47:02 / 72,268	60,888	2,769,606

comments can be automatically deleted when an account is closed or removed, or the video page owner may delete them.

Differences in length and content of videos and the number of comments can occur when one chooses to use as the unit of analysis the video page, which consists of both video discourse and the comments. However, because a single video has only very basic restrictions in terms of its length and what an individual user can do while recording themselves, there is not consistency in terms of length of video, or indeed how much language occurs in an individual video. For example, while Feuerstein's total video length above is less than one-sixths of John Fontain and theamazingatheist videos, his are far denser in terms of words (only about one-third of both of the others). Also, while Feuerstein's videos are shorter, they have far more comments than Fontain, and far fewer than theamazingatheist. These don't necessarily reflect the popularity of each; indeed, Joshua Feuerstein had more than twice the number of likes on his page than theamazingatheist had subscribers. Instead, the differences reflected both differences in the platforms and how they users engaged with their audiences, which will be the object of the analysis going forward. For the purpose of this study, I've also focused my analysis on where users were most prominent (theamazingatheist on YouTube, Joshua Feuerstein on Facebook, and John Fontain on YouTube). All users maintained pages on all social media sites, often cross-posting the same content. Where it was useful, I searched and found pages where missing videos had been reuploaded. For example, although Feuerstein's *Dear Mr. Atheist* was deleted from Facebook, it was reuploaded several months later on YouTube. I have included the link to that page in the Appendix for reference, but the comments were not included in my analysis, as the original comments was not available on Feuerstein's Facebook page at the time of data collection.

These differences in length were expected and returning to the key premises of the discourse dynamics approach, the discourse event – whatever its contours – is the unit of analysis. Given the different ways that the users interact with social media sites and their respective audiences, video pages differ. Rather than getting the same amount of information in terms of words of talk or comments, understanding interaction between Feuerstein, Fontain, and theamazingatheist requires understanding the initial conditions of their relationships and what resulted from it as the users went forward in time. The goal of this data collection method was not to build a representative database of Christians', atheists', and Muslims' use of social media – a discourse dynamics approach is unlikely to offer comprehensive descriptions of whole categories of interaction or text types. The data set is not intended to be balanced in the way that allows comparing, quantitatively, the users. Instead, the data set is meant to represent how each of the users employed their particular platform during a particular time. Because the users employed their platforms in different ways and attracted different kinds and different numbers of users, the data collected from each was quite different.

Given my focus on discourse dynamics particularly as it related to users responding to one another, doing close analysis of a large range of users is not feasible. My method does necessarily limit the diversity of user voices represented, particularly in terms of gender (based on my observations, the users are overwhelmingly male) and in terms of location (primarily users from the USA and UK). Because the data collection method relies on longitudinal observation of popular users with the goal of identifying interaction among evangelical users from different perspectives, it is difficult to control for variables such as gender or geographical location. While limiting the generalisability of the study, there is an important place for close discourse analysis of particular interaction among particular users as it offers unique insight into how discourse unfolds, not simply its outcomes. As Cameron's (2011) work on conciliation discourse has shown, attending closely to the dynamic interaction of individuals can lead to fruitful insights about both the initial conditions and how patterns develop going forward.

2.4 Analyzing Public Social Media Data

To understand what was occurring in occurring in each individual interaction, and how those interactions might be unique to each user, I employed a two-tiered approach to data analysis: an analysis of "positioning" in video talk and comments, focusing on the discourse dynamics, and a keyword analysis of all the discourse of each user and the comments on their videos, to compare trends and patterns among the different users.

2.4.1 Positioning Analysis

After data collection and longitudinal observation, I undertook a focused analysis of how discourse develops both on individual pages and across the whole of the time period investigated in this book. To do this, I employed a method of discourse analysis that allows for a closer look at the minute-to-minute development of discourse activity, looking at how users position themselves and others interaction. Positioning analysis (see Bamberg, 1997; Harré and van Langenhove, 1998; Harré, Moghaddam, Cairnie, Rothbart, and Sabat, 2009) treats social positions as fluid and dynamic, in contrast to "roles" or "categories" which might be considered more fixed. Speakers and hearers position themselves and others in the course of discourse activity, both implicitly and explicitly, giving meaning to their actions and the actions of others. The naming and describing their own and others' positions can be identified in discourse often with the use of category markers, but implicit positioning is equally important, as people allocate incumbent responsibilities and expectations without explicitly describing what those expectations are. For example, a manager might allocate tasks to employees by forwarding an email to them. Without giving explicit instructions, the implicit expectation is that the employee will do the task in the forwarded email. This process positions both the manager and the employee, and reenforces an existing power structure and the actions that both people take are mutually defining.

A focus on positioning also potentially downplays other ways one might investigate interaction around religion on YouTube, be it in terms of membership categories (Sacks, 1992; Housley and Fitzgerald, 2002, 2009), social identity (Abrams and Hogg, 2010; Hogg, 2004; Tajfel, 1983), or group membership (Tajfel, Billig, Bundy, and Flament, 1971; Turner, 1981). Of course, all these approaches to social life and the role of the individual in larger social structures does have a place, but my analysis is focused on how these positions are accomplished, and what the differences in positionings reveal about social media as a place of interaction, about evangelism as a social practice, and about online community as it is realized by different groups of users. By looking at the positionings rather than more static conceptions of identity, community, and in-group/out-group interaction, this analysis places heavy emphasis on how positionings are realized in the moment and how these develop into patterns over time. Because the positioning is dynamic and situational, my focus is on how changes in conditions can create affiliations and communities that potentially go beyond "groups" and shared identity.

A key part of positioning is the concept of "storylines" (Harré and van Langenhove, 1998). Storylines are established ways of talking about and experiencing the world, and they provide interactants with moral directives and heuristics to navigate the world. They can be tied to common sense understandings of moral action. In the example of the manager and the employee, the storyline might be one of a good employee following a manager's instructions. These storylines are ones that people often know implicitly and might not actively think about them. They are, instead, simply the "way things are." Storylines might be culturally-situated and therefore differ depending on the culture context. They can also be tied to other moral authority structures, like sacred texts or institutions, which are particularly important when analyzing how religious beliefs interact.

Positioning, in Bamberg's (2004, 1997) framework, focuses on storytelling and describes a process that occurs on three levels, taking into account the different social spaces and positions that storytelling afford. In the first level, there are the positions allocated characters within a given story or narrative. The second level is the positioning of the speaker and the listener as a story is being told. Finally, the third level is the storyteller's own positioning of themselves beyond the context of the story being told and how they see themselves in the larger social world. These three levels of positioning can be explicitly separated to show how the elements of the story being told (the first level) relate to the social interaction in which the telling is occurring (the second level) as well as a storyteller's own values and beliefs about themselves (the third level). This taxonomy, much like the discourse dynamics approach, encourages the analyst to think about the connections between different scales of discourse and the role of the storyteller and listener in relation to larger structures and patterns.

In my analysis, I use positioning analysis on two levels. First, I take a global view and consider what positions are allocated and defined on the level of the video as a whole. Often times, while the narrative of a given video might be segmented into several sections, the overall positions that are allocated are stable. Moreover, these positions might also be stable across more than one video, with particular users positioning themselves in consistent ways over time. This analysis then allows for the description of storylines, showing how consistent positionings across different videos reveals accepted ways for talking about and conceiving of social interaction. Understanding these positions then allows for a comprehensive answer for the main questions of this study: how do users present themselves and their beliefs, how do they interact with others with whom they may disagree, and how do communities form in affiliations and shared storylines?

Second, I move downward to the "minute-by-minute" interaction to uncover the specifics of positioning as they develop. At this stage of analysis, I focus first on the video as the primary data on the video page because it is the content with which any viewer of the page will have interacted, be it by clicking a link on their own Facebook feed, looking at a subscription list on YouTube, or being sent a link from another place. The comments are secondary: not all comments are read and comments are produced over time, meaning that while the content of the video will not change, what comments are visible can be much more dynamic over time, depending on when a user visits the page. I therefore identify positions within the video on a line-by-line basis in the transcript, looking for places where shifts occur, using all three levels of Bamberg's (1997) framework. I then look to the comments, to analyze responses to the videos and to see where positions are accepted or contested. I also, in investigating interaction among users, consider how users position one another in the text comments and the relation this may or may not have to the content of the video.

This is particularly important in looking at how positioning is contested in discourse. Although I have so far presented examples of positionings which are accepted by both the person doing the positioning and the person being positioned, Harré and van Langenhove (1998) in their description of positioning point out that there are several orders of positioning. In "first-order" positioning a person locates themselves in a storyline, one that also includes moral obligations and responsibilities. The boss emailing the employee a task implies that the boss has the authority to make this request of the employee, one that the employee accepts and affirms by doing the task. "Second order" positioning, however, occurs when a position is contested and negotiation occurs, for example, if an employee rejects the boss's request saying that it's not their job to do the task they've been given. Positioning can also be malignant; that is, it can have a negative effect on the person being positioned, and resulting in the positioned individual subsequently being treated negatively by others (Sabat, 2003). In malignant positioning, certain rights of the positioned individual are taken away as in Sabat's work on patients suffering from Alzheimer's disease. The right to speak was taken away from the patient and others spoke about them without giving them agency (Sabat, 2001). Malignant positioning is of particular interest in this study when users position members of other religions in specific ways, which can lead to negativity toward the positioned user being compounded.

So far, I have focused on video discourse and how it was captured, transcribed, and presented for analysis. However, the visual element of the video is also a potentially rich source of data for analysis, one that has been increasingly the focus of developing frameworks over the last twenty years (see Kress and Van Leeuwen, 2006; Van Leeuwen and Jewitt, 2001 for comprehensive overviews) as video recording technology has become increasingly more accessible. Although the focus of this book is on discourse on social media, I also use principles of positioning analysis to consider how users represent themselves visually, and what effect this has on how they position themselves and others. Bamberg's (1997) levels of positioning can be used to discuss how user talk is reinforced or undermined by their appearance, their representation of the words and videos of others, and their own identity across videos. For example, in Feuerstein's choice to record himself with his phone, with his face dominating the frame, the positioning of himself as a close confidant is re-enforced.

Much of what is revealed in positioning analysis is the structure of interaction that the analyst might already know from a longitudinal observation. Unlike other forms of discourse analysis, such as critical discourse analysis which looks to uncover ideology hidden in the discourse (Fairclough, 2001, 1995), positioning analysis may seem rather straightforward. It is easy to see Joshua Feuerstein is positioning himself as a friend and confidant, using his language and the positioning of the camera to build an intimacy with the viewer. What positioning analysis offers, however, is an empirical description of this feeling, one that is built from a line-by-line analysis of discourse activity to not simply say what the overall effect of a Feuerstein video might be, but how intimacy is constructed and how the medium is effectively (or ineffectively) used. It also illuminates larger structures and common-sense understandings about the world, which can be then used to understand conflict between users. As my previous research has shown, it's not accurate to simply say disagreements between users emerge from differing beliefs (Pihlaja, 2014a). This is part of the interaction, but it is not necessarily the definitive element. What positioning analysis, in tandem with the corpus-assisted analysis, provides is a fuller picture of the system, one that considers interaction from a variety of perspectives and offers explanations that are not reductive.

For this research, I have chosen not to attempt to contact the users directly and ask them about their intentions and motivations for making videos. Considering the research questions, I have purposely downplayed what users might privately report as their intention for making videos. Moreover, I have not contacted members of the communities of any of the users to discuss how the videos are viewed in "real life." This choice in focus contrasts in many ways with much of the analysis I cited earlier in the book discussing the sociological aspects of Internet use for religious and non-religious users. While I don't discount the value of asking users about their intentions and experiences online, there has been considerably less focus on the discourse between and among users on social media as it develops in a public and public-facing way. Because the focus of my analysis is explicitly on the effects of context collapse on how people share their faiths, analysis of public interaction brings attention back to actual discourse activity and the language of social media. As an analyst, I am less interested in what a user might reveal to a researcher in a private conversation as I am in what they are actually doing online, day in and day out, in their interaction with others.

2.4.2 *Corpus-Assisted Discourse Studies*

Given the size of the data set (particularly the video comments), I supplemented the close discourse analysis of the videos with macro-analysis of the whole data set. Corpus linguistics, as a field of study within linguistics, has for many years now has been a powerful tool for describing patterns in language use by looking at very large collections of texts (a single corpus or several different corpora) and querying them using computer software. By doing so, corpus linguistics has provided important insights about the relationship (among other things) between lexis and grammar, particularly through the use of statistical measures to describe patterns in language and language use, often using statistics (Partington,

Duguid, and Taylor, 2013). Increasingly, however, there has been a move toward employing corpus linguistic tools as resource in discourse analysis. While historically corpus linguistics has been used to develop dictionaries and grammars, specialized corpora can be useful for describe specific forms of discourse and provides a useful tool for describing one variety of discourse in relation to another, using empirical measures.

While corpus linguistics provides useful tools for the descriptions of large bodies of texts, an approach to a corpus as a static body of texts is less useful when considering the dynamic notions of discourse that I have so far introduced in this chapter. Corpus tools traditionally treat all texts in a corpus as equal statistically, with the goal of providing unified descriptions of language use. However, rather than produce a description of language generally or even a particular text type, this study aims to describe a particular interaction from a longitudinal perspective, and the data set was produced in a way that favored capturing the content of a series of interactions. Still, the tools available from corpus linguistics are useful, particularly in parsing a large data set and offering insight about the contents of a corpus that simply can't be attained easily or reliably with one analyst attempting to notion patterns.

The term "corpus-assisted discourse studies," first coined by Partington (2004), describes uses of corpus linguistics methods beyond a statistical, quantitative analysis of texts. Partington and colleagues (2013) write,

> Unusually for corpus linguistics, [corpus-assisted discourse studies] researchers typically engage with their corpus in a variety of ways. As well as via wordlists and concordancing, intuitions for further research can also arise from reading or watching or listening to parts of the data-set, a process which can help provide a feel for how things are done linguistically in the discourse-type being studied. (p. 12)

From a corpus-assisted discourse studies perspective, the tools of corpus linguistics shouldn't be seen as an isolated tool, useful for quantitative descriptions of large bodies of texts that are treated like a "black box" with all the necessary information for analysis contained within the corpus (Partington et al., 2013, p. 12). Instead, analysts can and should look, to the discourse in context and longitudinal descriptions. From this perspective the corpus is treated as a useful resource in understanding the interaction, one that can help answer reliably and validly the questions of this research: what are different users discussing on their pages, and how do those themes differ both from other users in the study and from discourse more generally?

One way corpora can be employed to answer these questions is through identifying keywords (Baker, 2006; Baker, Gabrielatos, and McEnery, 2013). Keywords occur statistically more frequently in one form of discourse compared with another. For example, in a corpus of texts produced by Christians about their faith, one would expect the words "Jesus" or "faith" or "God" to occur more frequently than in a corpus of newspaper articles. This doesn't necessarily mean that any of these words would be the most frequently occurring within the Christian discourse; it simply means that they are comparatively high. The keywords are used to offer descriptions of talk more broadly, allowing for macro descriptions of different users' style and register. Styles and registers associated with particular groups can also be investigated by querying the corpus as a whole and breaking the corpus into sub-corpora to look for themes in discourse among particular pages or channels, providing descriptions of how themes differ.

In the first instance, one user's videos and comments are compared against other users within the data set, and then against a separate reference corpus. The aim of this research is to not only compare and contrast users within the interaction and to highlight themes in the discourse activity for further analysis, but to also show how the users compare to a larger set of speakers. As O'Halloran (2014) rightly points out, keywords should not be used to assume "a homogenous set of opinions on a topic" (p. 5). They do, however, allow the researcher to get a sense for the themes in discussion, to test whether or not the assumptions that may have developed from the longitudinal observations are correct, or more often, the specifics of those themes. For example, watching videos produced by theamazingatheist, I had the sense that science and argumentation were more important than on Feuerstein's Facebook page, but this was little more than a "hunch" for which keyword analysis provides a reliable, valid description. Partington, Duigid, and Taylor (2013) describe this well, saying "most corpus research, by steady and repeated observation of data, results in telling us more about what we know already" (p. 9). The value of this can't be understated, particularly when trying to unpack the differences among the users in the data set. Searches of a corpus allow the analyst to build on what they have may have already observed and focus and sharpen the analysis with increased precision.

Keywords can be used to identify themes, or *topoi*, (Wodak and Meyer, 2002) in the data, and with the aid of the semantic tagging software WMatrix (Rayson, 2008), key semantic domains can identified. These themes allow for a kind of "bird's eye view" of the kind of discourse being investigated, showing where in the text important issues might be coming up. By identifying main themes, instances where keywords within the themes are discussed can be identified, to see what role it is playing in the development of discourse. If a theme is indeed central, it can be used to describe the nature of the goals and aims of particular channels. In the case of discourse about science on theamazingatheist's channel, it shows how atheist users often choose this topic as the main argument against Christians, often drawing more fundamentalist Christians into arguments about science and religion. In a recursive process, the researcher investigates themes in the corpora from the keyword search, revaluates the uses in context, and adjusts thematic coding of both keywords data and comments.

While corpus analysis can be used in a much more in-depth and statistical way, the analysis this book generally does not rely on statistical measures to make claims about the validity of findings beyond the rather straightforward compiling of keyword lists. The data sets gathered do not lend themselves to direct comparison because of the different levels of popularity of the users, the different ways they use social media, and the kinds of discourse on each page. Although some basic descriptions like keywords and topic or content analysis can tell us something about basic differences in the users, without have comparable data sets in terms of size or constituency, it's difficult to make a valid argument about the differences using statistical measures. In the spirit of corpus-assisted discourse studies, I will make use of keywords and themes, as well as collocates and clusters, to describe the data set as a whole and to identify places where further investigation is needed.

2.5 Ethical Issues in Online Data

The use of social media data for research is also potentially a problematic ethical issue. Research ethics debate about research on SNS have developed with technology, and guidelines and advice from different contexts have been put forward about how researchers should use SNS data and whether or not informed consent should be sought from users (Bruckman, 2002; Fossheim and Ingierd, 2015; Markham and Buchanan, 2012; Walther, 2002). At the same time, debate has also grown over the role of copyright law (which forbids reproducing others' original creative work) and fair use or fair dealing exceptions (which allows for some use of others' copyrighted material in one's own original creative work) for the use of online data (Aufderheide, Milosevic, and Bello, 2015; Edwards, Klein, Lee, Moss, and Philip, 2013; Freund, 2014). Still, whether the average user understands or is concerned with copyright law, is debatable and indeed, the use of sites like Facebook in particular does not necessarily suggest that users are treating their own public content as creative content. While social media sites are very clear that any "public" postings are publicly available to any Internet user, the extent to which the ramifications of this are felt by most users is an important question for researchers. Citing the terms of service for sites like YouTube, Twitter, or Facebook as evidence that users have a particular intention when they click the "accept" box on signing up is problematic. Research shows that users do not regularly report reading the terms carefully, if at all (Smithers, 2011). The knowledge that user have of the terms of service can be incomplete at best, particularly as terms of service can change without users being aware (Vie, 2014) and terms of service are particularly onerous for users to read and understand, in terms of time commitment (McDonald and Cranor, 2009). In a separate article (Pihlaja, 2017), I discuss in-depth the issues of ethics in online research, particularly around copyright and social media, but in this section I will simply address issues related to this particular project and when data should be attributed to content creators as copyrighted material, and what should be anonymized, or not used at all, to protect users anonymity.

Ethical guidelines for using online data for research have thus far focused on what might be called "average" users of social media who do not use these sites for their livelihood and are often detached from arguments about copyright. The Association for Internet Researchers (Markham and Buchanan, 2012), for example, only has brief mention of copyright in their guidance, suggesting that only in some disciplines is copyright law more significant than human subject regulation. Although this may be true of some uses of SNS, there is a case to be made that some social media content should be treated as copyrighted material. While there may be questions about the extent to which users understand the consequences of posting material online, in the case of the users in the book, it would be difficult to argue that they are unaware that their content is being viewed by a multitude of known and unknown audiences. Users are explicitly employing the sites to promote or disseminate their content to a general audience. On sites where growing a social media following is the expressed goal, posting videos is intended to increase social media presence and stature. This is often tied to a desire to increase ad revenue as well, an influence that users can explicitly address in their videos.

In terms of their social media personas, the three main users in this book work to spread their particular messages in explicit ways. Joshua Feuerstein, for example, regularly encourages users to "Share if you care," repeatedly asking users to spread his content. While this doesn't necessarily mean that all users on Facebook or YouTube intend to have their content spread, when users like Feuerstein *do* encourage others to spread their message, this is compelling empirical evidence that attributing the videos and content as copyrighted material is both legally required and the most ethical treatment of the content. With both theamazingatheist and John Fontain, these same observations can apply. Therefore, in the cases where I use the spoken words or text produced by a content creator on their own page, I attribute their work with a citation to the appendix of videos.

Since the integration of YouTube and Google's social network site Google+ with the YouTube commenting function, comments can be linked to a Google+ profile. This was implemented to force everyone to use their "real-name" to reduce antagonism on the site but was eventually abandoned (Ruesch and Märker, 2012). Although users making videos should clearly be protected by fair use law, with citation of their work, the comments sections are slightly less clear. Given the history of YouTube as a public forum, and the orientation of the site's discussion toward public, rather than private, interaction, I chose to keep the user names, be they user's real names, pseudonyms, or screennames, as a part of analysis, rather than "clean" the data, as this allowed me to trace comment threads and identify particularly active users. However, when choosing which comments to publish and how to cite them, I kept users' names anonymous in the book to avoid drawing any unwanted attention to any specific users.

The Facebook data included in the analysis is slightly more problematic, given Facebook's history as site where users have traditionally commented with their "real names." This data can be accessed without creating a Facebook account and is publicly available in the same way any other public webpage might be. In this case, although users might not necessarily have the assumption that their comments are private, they are oriented toward the specific community around Feuerstein and the practice of tagging others suggests that care must be taken to involve users who might unwillingly be appearing on the page, simply because their privacy settings allow them to be tagged. Although some comments *may* also fall into the category of users attempting to publicize their own page, it is difficult to provide evidence that this is the case from what has been posted on the site. Indeed, there is also evidence that Facebook users aren't always aware of the consequences of disclosure on the site or that their information is publicly available (Brandtzæg et al., 2010).

While fair use allows copying data for my own research, whether or not to cite the user comments was more complicated. Like my initial impulse with YouTube comments, I felt compelled to cite users by their names and with their content, assuming that since they have posted on a public place, they are aware of the consequences of their posting. However, the value of this approach seemed limited, particularly when I was less interested in mapping the development of discourse over time on the page, but rather interested the overall content of the comments. Knowing, for example, the name of the user commenting "God bless you Bro. You are doing a great work for the Lord" was less important to me as a researcher than the content of the comment. I chose instead, where I quoted comments in my own writing as examples, to anonymize them, following the suggestion of Wilkinson and Thelwall (2011).

2.6 Conclusion

Approaching discourse as a complex system requires developing tools for analysis that work across the different levels. By using a mixed methods approach, descriptions of talk that are empirically grounded and reliable can be developed. Data sets then need to be focused on interaction between users.

Having the data from the interaction and a rich knowledge of the socio-historical context, explanations for the development of the system can be explored based on all the available information gathered from watching a group of users over time. While considering the state of the system, the following analysis will explore how presentations of belief and interaction between users can be understood both as unique to this particular set of users and part of larger patterns of social media use.

3 Conflicts

3.1 A Culture of Conflict

Antagonistic interaction between users goes back to the beginning of the Internet, and the negative effect of anonymity in the "global village" has been a prominent recurring theme in research about computer-mediated communication (CMC). Interaction on Facebook and YouTube is further complicated by social and economic pressures, which push users toward more engaging, controversial content to garner more views. Users like Joshua Feuerstein, theamazingatheist, and John Fontain are spokespeople for ideological positions and also entertainers, whose online personalities are developed to attract more viewers. For the theamazingatheist, this includes a performance of anger, creating conflict which may or may not be genuine, but which generates controversy and more engagement with his videos. Why users get drawn into ongoing "drama" and what effect it has on interreligious dialogue are also not simple questions to answer. In this chapter, I will look specifically at the conflict that is at the center of the interaction among Feuerstein, Fontain, and theamazingatheist and show how it provides users with the affordance to take positions in relation to others.

Antagonism in computer-mediated communication can be traced back to the 1980s (Kiesler et al., 1984; Siegel et al., 1986), with research focused on how communicating through computer technology led to deindividuation, or a sense of anonymity. As research into online interaction developed, a description of negative behavior online as "flaming" emerged. Flaming has been described as the sending of aggressive individual messages "related to a specific topic and directed at an individual user" (Crystal, 2001, p. 55) or "scathingly critical personal messages" (Cosentino, 1994) or "rude or insulting messages" (Schrage, 1997). Brown and Levinson's (1987) notion of a "face-threatening act" has influenced the development of descriptions of online impoliteness (and impoliteness more generally), with notions of categorizing different kinds of "flames" (O'Sullivan and Flanagin, 2003). With the rise of mobile technologies, and the embedded nature of the Internet in everyday life, the questions around how and why conflict arises online has become a much more diverse and complex question. While "flaming" was sufficient in some way to describe responses to emails or other text-based messaging services, it doesn't encompass the range of negative interactions that can be present in all the different contexts we might consider. The same could be said of "trolling," which Hardaker (2010) has attempted to classify, with some frustration for the imprecision with which these words are often used in online contexts. They are often neologisms or metaphors that are by their very nature vague. What one does when one "trolls" another user might have some consistency in patterns of usage, or it might differ greatly, depending on the context and the particular action being described.

Research into impoliteness online has, understandably, been interested in describing larger trends in interaction on the Internet and explaining what motivates negative behavior online. There has also been interesting research into how politeness norms are managed as in online fora (Angouri and Tseliga, 2010), online communities (Nishimura, 2010; Planchenault, 2010), and interaction such email discussion lists (Haugh, 2010; Luchjenbroers and Aldridge-Waddon, 2011). While this research has focused on the effects of technology on the negotiation and understanding of politeness norms in online settings, they have also been primarily studies in asynchronous, text-based interaction. This is reflective of the development of technology, in which text-based interaction has remained a dominant form of CMC (Tagg, 2012; Seargeant and Tagg, 2014).

As technology has developed, there was a sense that part of the reason antagonism existed online was that people were only interacting in a written mode rather than exposing themselves visually (Lange, 2007a). If, as Kiesler and colleagues (1984) initially suggested, part of the reason for antagonism and negativity stemmed from other users being displaced and distant, then technology which allowed for a more multimodal experience of others may reduce the amount of negativity that users experience. YouTube, with its multimodal video page and ability to respond to others "face-to-face" had the potential to reduce the amount of negativity. This has largely not been the case, although it is difficult to judge what aspects of the experience on YouTube lead to negativity. YouTube remains well known for its negativity, particularly the comments section which despite the integration with Google's social networking application Google+ are often anonymous. My own work (Philaja, 2014a) has looked at the ways in negativity is also present in the making of "drama videos," where users seem willing to often speak out loud and with their face on camera many of the negative things that they might otherwise type.

The nature of YouTube celebrity and the pressure to "get views" might be partially responsible for the popularity of drama videos, since users in my data sets have regularly referred to the interest they generate. The early research of

Lange (2006, 2007b, 2007a), and Moor and colleagues (2010) focused on the experience of YouTubers on the site and how users understood things like "flaming" in comments, finding that in some ways, the negativity and ongoing drama was part of the interest of the site, with users seeking out content that includes conflict for its entertainment value. Facebook does not suffer from the same reputation of negativity as YouTube, in part due to the lack of anonymity of users who often know their Facebook friends from "real-world" settings and a focus at least initially on status updates, which encourage narrativity and shared experience with friends (Page, 2010). The site, however, is not entirely free of negativity, and Phillips (2011), for example, has studied the emergence of trolling on Facebook memorial sites. Troubling as well is the use of Facebook for bullying, which Kwan and colleagues (2013) have also investigated, showing that Facebook bullying can become an extension of offline school bullying. This research shows how Facebook can represent a clearer link between online and offline realities, differing from YouTube comments on video pages, where users are often not likely to have any offline interaction.

Research has been focused on particular moments of negative reactions around specific topics or videos, like analyzing rape threats against feminist campaigner Caroline Criado-Perez (Hardaker and McGlashan, 2016) or responses to the anti-Islam film *Fitna* (van Zoonen, Vis, and Mihelj, 2010, 2011; Vis, van Zoonen, and Mihelj, 2011) or comments on a single particular video, like the "Obama Reggaeton" YouTube video (Lorenzo-Dus et al., 2011). Less work, however, has been done on tracing how impoliteness and antagonism occur over sustained periods of times in particular communities, with a qualitative focus on the back-and-forth nature of Internet "drama," the "ongoing antagonistic debates" (Burgess and Green, 2008) that crop up regularly on social media. My own research (Pihlaja, 2011, 2014a) has focused on how understanding the nuance of particular arguments shows that there is often an important social history behind each interaction. Although different patterns and strategies for impoliteness might be observed, why they happen in each individual case is often quite complicated.

Apart from the negative role that conflict plays in the interaction among users, it can also be seen as a means of producing content. Conflict provides users with positions of opposition to "enemies," a view researchers have long held about YouTube antagonism and a historical role of argumentation (Billig, 1996) – by allowing users to take positions opposing others and present their case for their own positions and beliefs, in contrast to other users holding different positions. Argumentation is fundamentally a part of religious tradition as well, something Billig (1996) shows in his discussion of Talmudic arguments in Jewish traditions and I have shown in my own research on arguments on YouTube (Pihlaja, 2013a, 2016b). In addition to these larger issues, conflict can also be rooted in more mundane social interaction frustrations, like being insulted by someone, which are not rooted in deep theological or philosophical differences, but are simply the result of humans interacting with one another in a social space.

For religious talk online, what conflict *does* in the interaction and how it affects the relationships between people of different faiths or no faith is particularly important. When arguments do occur, they must be placed in a long history of contact between Christians and Muslims and a contemporary context of the emergence of atheism. The users exist within histories and Christian polemics about Islam (Goddard, 2000; Lewis, 1993) and atheism (Wilson, 2007; Zacharias, 2008), and the responses to these polemics are key parts of the ways people come to interact in new settings. The following analysis shows how these theological arguments are remade in online contexts and what the medium's effect is on the presentation of belief.

3.2 Positioning and Attacking

theamazingatheist has made videos calling out Christians for many years, but his first engagement with Joshua Feuerstein appeared in a video entitled, "Christian 'Disproves' Evolution?" posted on June 2, 2014. In the video, theamazingatheist responds to Feuerstein's video *Dear Mr. Atheist* by offering an explanation of evolution and arguing against and mocking Feuerstein. *Dear Mr. Atheist* was originally posted on Feuerstein's Facebook page and theamazingatheist used clips from the video in his response to Feuerstein. The clips show Feuerstein making an argument against evolution by claiming evolution is "not science." He says,

> hey guys
> Josh Feuerstein here
> you know the other day I had an atheist tell me
> that I was
> an idiot moronic and stupid
> for believing in God
> that He created this world because it took
> way too much
> faith to believe in a process like that while
> he believed in what he called the
> science
> of evolution
> well let's go ahead and
> let's do this
> dear mister atheist
> first of all

let me correct you
because
evolution is not a science
never has
and never will be
why?
because it cannot fit
within the parameters and parentheses of science
for one simple reason
it was never observed

(2014.06.02 AA Video)[1]

In this extract, Feuerstein presents his video as a response to an attack and positions himself as challenging an atheist user who has called him "an idiot, moronic and stupid" for his beliefs. This response is necessary, Feuerstein claims, to correct the misconceptions about himself and his faith and reassert what he sees at the truth. Feuerstein says, "Well, okay, let's do this," suggesting that he has some hesitation in making the video, but that the attack has left him with no choice. In Feuerstein's argument against evolution, there is little in-depth understanding of evolutionary biology represented. Instead, "science" as a concept is used to stage an argument for Christian belief. Feuerstein says to the generic atheist, "Let me correct you." However, the "correction" is based on a very basic understanding of evolution, reasserting claims that theamazingatheist has already challenged, particularly Feuerstein's focus on "chance" in his description of evolution.

The extent to which Feuerstein is aware that his own position is built on a disputable generalization is difficult to tell. Feuerstein does not engage in a back-and-forth dialogue with anyone on the specifics of what he says and does not respond to detractors in his comments or the comments of theamazingatheist's video. The main focus instead is a storyline about the world wherein God plans, designs, and exerts control over nature, something that becomes increasingly important considering Feuerstein's focus on presenting his own belief as true and accurate. What any user says in response is ultimately irrelevant because it can't challenge the fundamental truth of the Bible, a point Feuerstein regularly makes. He states at one point in reference to the Bible and how different people might have different interpretations: "It doesn't matter what you think" (2014.8.28 JF Video).

The positioning of himself as being attacked by atheists also provides justification for taking a stance against atheism, because he is defending himself and the truth, rather than aggressively pushing his own beliefs on

[1] Citations for videos are as follows: Year-Month-Day User. AA=theamazingatheist, JF=Joshua Feuerstein, JFo=John Fontain. The full list of videos can be found in the Appendix. All transcripts are represented using intonation units.

others. Instead, he is "correcting" what he states is a false claim. For Feuerstein, the unnamed atheist who called him an idiot is responsible for the response. By speaking in categorical terms, referring to "an atheist" rather than a specific person, the encounter can be presented as exemplar of a larger storyline that is scalable on several levels. Feuerstein is not simply positioning himself as being attacked at one point by a single atheist. He is positioning himself as someone who is regularly attacked for what he believes. This is a particular interaction with a particular atheist, but the conversation is one that he presents himself as regularly having and one that is indicative of a larger argument between Christians and atheists about evolution.

For theamazingatheist, Feuerstein and Christians like him provide a platform for attacking Christian belief as illogical and incoherent. theamazingatheist, like Feuerstein, positions himself as playing defense, responding to the *Dear Mr. Atheist* video with a video titled *Christian "Disproves" Evolution?* (2014.06.02 AA Video). theamazingatheist plays Feuerstein's argument back and responds to it, playfully quoting Feuerstein and parodying his voice:

> evolution's not a science
> who you gonna believe
> the scientists who say it is
> or the fat bearded guy wearing a stupid hat
> who says it isn"t
> I mean
> who the fuck appointed this guy
> the arbiter of what is and isn't science
> [...]
> the sad thing is that you're such a moron that
> even if some piece of evidence was produced
> that shows the evolution is true
> I mean there's plenty of pieces of evidence like that already
> like
> the entire fossil record
> retroviral DNA
> all of modern fucking genetics
> blah blah blah
> you know
> if you're not convinced by now
> nothing's gonna convince you
>
> (2014.06.02 AA Video)

theamazingatheist emphasizes Feuerstein's ignorance about science, positioning Feuerstein as being completely untrustworthy as a source. Importantly, theamazingatheist does this without addressing the claim "evolution's not a science," which is what Feuerstein originally stated. The argument is positioned as completely unworthy of a response. Instead, theamazingatheist attacks Feuerstein with personal insults, calling him a "moron" and reducing him to a "fat bearded guy wearing a stupid hat." theamazingatheist's response to Feuerstein also positions Feuerstein as disingenuous and not arguing in good faith, especially in his treatment of "evidence." This is, based on what I have shown so far, true in some sense. Feuerstein is not interested in engaging in a meaningful dialogue about evolution. The premise of dialogue, of addressing "Mr. Atheist" or theamazingatheist specifically, is simply a rhetorical device to present himself as engaged with the opposing point of view.

The notion that Feuerstein is arguing in bad faith is key to theamazingatheist's negative portrayal of Feuerstein and provides some protection from criticism that theamazingatheist is treating Feuerstein unfairly. theamazingatheist positions Feuerstein as uninterested in dialogue and acting as a demagogue which, in turn, allows theamazingatheist to treat him without respect. Despite this explicit dismissal of the Feuerstein as a reliable source, theamazingatheist does engage Feuerstein's argument, addressing it in point-by-point commentary. He continually returns to the idea that Feuerstein is completely unreliable as a source and everyone who accepts the video is equally foolish. theamazingatheist says:

> I don't know what sort of brainless morons out there watch this
> and found anything cogent
> or worth hanging their hat on
> but all I would say is that
> you're either
> so blithely incurious about the world that you live in
> that it's almost criminal
> and you're wasting your fucking life
> or you're so ignorant
> that you just are not even smart enough yet
> to know how stupid you are
>
> (2014.06.02 AA Video)

In this section of the video, theamazingatheist moves beyond attacking Feuerstein for his claims and ignorance about science and positions everyone who agrees with Feuerstein as "brainless," "ignorant," and "wasting your fucking life." This move to group Feuerstein and his viewers together serves an important function for theamazingatheist by allowing him to position Feuerstein as a kind of prototypical Christian, one who represents the beliefs of a large group of people. While theamazingatheist doesn't explicitly refer to this group of people as "Christians," there is an implicit linking between Feuerstein's rhetoric and Christianity, starting with theamazingatheist's joke that he is happy arguing with Feuerstein because he hates "arguing with Christians who are more attractive than me" (2014.06.02 AA Video).

theamazingatheist continues this mocking of Feuerstein and positioning him and his audience as ignorant throughout the whole of the data set, including making parodies as "Josh Moronstein" in a video entitled, *Gravity Disproved In 2 Minutes*. The video is shot in portrait mode like Feuerstein's Facebook videos and theamazingatheist wears a red baseball cap, both references to Feuerstein's video style. In the video, Moronstein goes outside with a helium filled balloon to prove that gravity doesn't exist. The video ends with Moronstein letting the balloon float away, declaring that he disproved gravity and that he is "the smartest person on the planet." This negative positioning of Feuerstein and his audience as "morons" and "blithely incurious" and "ignorant" suggests that theamazingatheist is not attempting to convince Feuerstein that his positions are wrong. The video is not an overt outreach to Christians in Feuerstein's audience or attempt to convert them. Instead, theamazingatheist is positioning Feuerstein as an "idiot" to support his own storyline. theamazingatheist and those who agree with him are positioned as intelligent and reasonable, while Feuerstein and other Christians like him are unreasonable and illiterate about key points in science.

While theamazingatheist doesn't explicitly encourage attacks on Feuerstein, users do follow his lead. The responses to the videos in the comments revoice the same arguments against Feuerstein in a show support for theamazingatheist. I will go into more depth looking at the theme of "logic" and "stupidity" in the subsequent chapters, but for now it's useful to see the effect of theamazingatheist's attack on the subsequent responses to Feuerstein in the comments. The words "idiot," "moron," and "ignorant" appear 189, 59, and 145 times respectively in an extended discussion about the merits of intelligent design in the comments of *Christian 'Disproves' Evolution?*:

> Joshua Loserstein makes the human race fail. His ignorant banter is stunting intellectual growth in our nation. What a shame. (2014.06.02 AA Video Comments)
>
> this guy is a fucking idiot. i hate that ppl believe in his bs (2014.06.02 AA Video Comments)
>
> Looked up Law of thermodynamics (cuz I don't claim to know everything) and the Christian dude is an idiot. Then.......the sun goes up!!!!!!!!hahahahahahah I'm dying right now LOL (2014.06.02 AA Video Comments)[2]

The comments follow the same thematic elements as the video, that Feuerstein is an "idiot" and "ignorant," and extend theamazingatheist's play on Feuerstein's name, calling him "Loserstein." More important, users follow theamazingatheist's lead in extending this positioning to other groups in each of the comments, although who is grouped together with Feuerstein is different

[2] All comments are presented as they appeared on the video page.

depending on the commenter, with the extension applied to the "nation" (because Feuerstein's "banter is stunting intellectual growth"), "ppl (who) believe in his bs," and "Christians" (as Feuerstein is a "Christian dude"). While the linking of Feuerstein to Christian belief might be expected, Christian belief which Feuerstein represents is also tied to a larger "American Christian" identity, which is also linked to anti-intellectualism seen in the comment: "great video mate gotta love the American Christians, that special blend of dumb and dumber is just perfect" (2014.06.02 AA Video Comments). This comment suggests a larger storyline in which "American Christians" are known for lacking intelligence.

Sabat's (2003) notion of "malignant positioning" (see pg. 74) describes the process in which the person positioned in discourse has certain rights deleted as a result of the positioning. The positioning of Feuerstein as an idiot does, it appears, have the effect for some viewers at least of removing Feuerstein's right to be heard. Some users do challenge theamazingatheist's positioning of Feuerstein, but for the users that accept it, there is no consideration of the points that Feuerstein has made. Instead, a revoicing of the arguments made by theamazingatheist in the video can be seen both in the comments of theamazingatheist's videos and on Feuerstein's page. theamazingatheist seems to suggest that Feuerstein is simply an idiot and incapable of presenting any logical argument for intelligent design. Moreover, the spread of the positioning to both a religious and national category creates a more complex conflict, one that is both theological and political, and highlights the intersectionality of identity in the YouTube context, where Feuerstein's ignorance is attributed not only to his theological positions, but also his nationality.

In *Dear Mr. Atheist*, however, Feuerstein doesn't attempt to challenge atheist positionings of him as "idiot" by showing how his position is the result of study and research. Instead, he argues that the atheist position is even more unreasonable, repeatedly referring to evolution as requiring faith to accept. Feuerstein's positioning of himself and of the generic atheists that he is addressing accepts the notion that believing something without evidence is illogical, and at least rhetorically, downplaying the importance of faith in accepting or not accepting something at true. Instead, Feuerstein attempts to position the assumed atheist "belief" in evolution as requiring more faith than Creationism.

> you see
> you think it takes a lot of
> of faith for me to believe in a god that created this world
> a god that created order and yet
> what if I were to tell you
> that
> somewhere in Oklahoma a tornado

rolls through a junk yard full of old cars and
and somewhere on the other side of that tornado
out of that junk pile
it magically produces a perfectly red shiny working Lamborghini
you would tell me I was nuts
you would tell me that I had lost it
you would probably try to admit me into the psychiatric ward
why
because that is absolutely stupid I mean
how much faith would it really take to believe
something as idiotic as that
and yet
that's exactly what science believes

(2014.06.02 AA Video)

The story that Feuerstein tells counters a positioning of Christianity as "idiotic" – "science" instead is positioned as something "idiotic." Feuerstein represents evolution as the belief that something ordered emerged out of something disordered, using the analogy of a tornado coming through a junkyard and producing a fully formed car. This story which Feuerstein tells is also not an original story, but rather a retelling of a common story in which manufactured items like cars or watches are used to illustrate the so-called theory of Intelligent Design, which claims that an intelligent agent must be behind the creation of the universe (Dembski, 2002) and is regularly refuted by biologists (Dawkins, 1986). The use of the story represents revoicing of an argument that is not Feuerstein's own, but one that he revoices for his own purposes, including elements like "Oklahoma" and "a shiny red working Lamborghini" that are unique to this particular telling. Their purpose, as they are in other tellings of the story, is to position the person who accepts a world without a designer as, Feuerstein states, "nuts."

This positioning of "atheists" as "nuts" and people who have "lost it" in the context of religious talk online is in an implicit response to the criticism of atheists of religious individuals as "moronic and stupid." Feuerstein's response doesn't detail how faith is intelligent, but to instead challenges the intelligence of the atheists, arguing a binary position: that atheists are in fact unintelligent. This positioning of "science" as being "idiotic" or "stupid" challenges the storyline that Feuerstein initially presents of being called an "idiot" for his belief. Implicit in this claim is an acceptance that belief must be supported by evidence, but what he agrees should or should not count at evidence is an important distinction with the "atheists" he claims to be addressing.

Claims and counterclaims – *logoi* and *anti-logoi* in Billig's (1996) terminology – are important parts of argumentation, and they are embedded in the positionings and responses to being positioned. Feuerstein's response to being called ignorant is to respond by positioning theamazingatheist as ignorant; his response to being told he is too dependent on his faith is to position atheists as having even more faith than he does. The arguments are not necessarily nuanced or critical but points and counterpoints that do little to move the argument forward. They establish and reestablish existing storylines always needing to be retold and recast when they are challenged. If Feuerstein has been challenged as having an unfounded faith, the response is to then argue that theamazingatheist has an even more unfounded faith.

Feuerstein's approach to the generic atheist and the lack of nuance in his discussion of evolution can be explained in part by the relationship between Feuerstein and his audience. While the video is addressed to "Mr. Atheist," Feuerstein's fans on his Facebook page are primarily Christian and supportive of his message. Comments show the extent to which Feuerstein's message is approved of, with the word "Amen" appearing 1,368 times. If the primary audience of the video is then not atheists, the specifics of the argument about evolution are less important than responding to the argument that belief is stupid. In Feuerstein's storyline, everyone believes something, and Christian belief is more rational than belief in evolution. At the same time, Feuerstein doesn't, explicitly apply to scripture for his argument, but instead to a notion of common sense and his own personal experience:

> it had to be by intelligent
> design
> so dear mister atheist
> who really has to have a lot of faith today
> to believe in their theory
> I believe in God because I've experienced him
> I've felt him
>
> (2014.06.02 AA Video)

Here, belief is the result of personal experience and Feuerstein positions himself as not simply relying on faith, but on the evidence of his own experience and his "feeling" of God. This "feeling" and "experience" of God plays an important rhetorical role in Evangelical discourse about a "personal relationship" with God (Packer, 1973), one that is foundational to descriptions of salvation. Feuerstein speaks in a way that appeals specifically to Christians who believe God can be "experienced" and "felt," but the argument is one unlikely to sway an atheist audience. Because Feuerstein doesn't make any explicit effort to offer a more careful rebuttal of the arguments against his understanding of evolution, his positioning of himself in relation to atheists appears focused on a Christian audience. The argument does not appear to be about creating a genuine dialogue or debate about science but reasserting his position.

Ultimately, being attacked by theamazingatheist is beneficial for Feuerstein, particularly given the vicious way theamazingatheist refers to Feuerstein's beliefs and his audience. By attacking Feuerstein and everyone around him, theamazingatheist can be positioned as an enemy of God and the truth, a positioning that users who already have a belief about the Bible and are predisposed to Feuerstein's argument will accept. Although Feuerstein doesn't explicitly say he is being persecuted for his belief, by saying he is being "attacked" for "his belief in God," any negativity that comes his way, particularly from atheists, can be explained as persecution. A commenter on his page explicitly states this, writing in response to a post Feuerstein makes calling out "haters,"

> Jesus said if they hated Me, they will hate you, don't be surprised when you face opposition and persecution. I believe that when you begin to stir up trouble for the devil he will react and respond with much rage, and just like God uses people, so does the devil. Keep the faith!!

Throughout the Facebook comments on Feuerstein's videos this theme of persecution emerges, with users referring to others who attack them as persecuting them. At least one user makes explicit reference to Bible passages that refer to persecution, particularly Matthew 5:11 (NIV) in which Jesus explicitly promises persecution to his followers, and says, "Blessed are you when people insult you, persecute you and falsely say all kinds of evil against you because of me." For Christian users, being insulted and ridiculed by others provides a kind of social capital in the Christian community because it is evidence that they are, in some way, doing what God has called them to do. theamazingatheist makes clear that he is not attacking Feuerstein for his belief in God, but rather his ignorance about science, but the explicit reason for the "persecution" seems to be less relevant than whether or not it can be positioned as the result of a belief in God.

While the atheists attacking Feuerstein is useful for the storyline of persecution, for theamazingatheist, Feuerstein is also a useful character, an issue that he explicitly addresses in his July 28, 2014 video, "The Amazing Atheist vs. Josh Feuerstein," responding to Feuerstein's sign off that includes the phrase "I love you."

> I love you because thus far
> I have made a lot of fuckin' money
> off of responding to your videos
> and off of pretending to be
> Josh Moronstein
> the character based on you
> so I have to thank you for just supplying me
> with tons of material
> it's been very
> very beneficial to me
> and I very much appreciate it
> and actually

the great thing about this is
after I make this reaction video
I can go ahead and make
an amazing atheist
uh
I can make a-a Josh Moronstein
parody of this video
so I get a double-dip

(2014.07.28 AA Video)

theamazingatheist makes the point that people like Feuerstein provide him with content, allowing him to make more money from responses. Implicitly, however, Feuerstein is also useful to theamazingatheist because Feuerstein fits into a larger storyline about Christians – they are ignorant and ill-informed and flagrant in this ignorance. Having this kind of Christian in the public eye serves the purposes of theamazingatheist by giving him an easy target to criticize. Feuerstein can be roundly rejected and ridiculed by the community, much to everyone's amusement, without having to argue against more challenging users who might be both more talented in debating and who might have a better understanding of evolutionary science. These opponents would likely be less interesting and result in far less entertaining content.

Insults also focused on the physical appearance of the users; for Feuerstein and theamazingatheist, their weight is constantly an issue. Commenters write, "We gonna believe the fat guy with a neckbeard . . . or the scientist?" in relation to Feuerstein and "It's hilarious to see a fat neckbearded atheistic fedorafaggot thinking he's intellectually superior" in relation to theamazingatheist. The proliferation of negative comments – the word "fat" occurs 572 times in the comments on theamazingatheist videos – suggests that this sort of attack is normalized on the site, something to be expected and a part of the culture of the site (Moor et al., 2010; Lange, 2007a; Pihlaja, 2014a). When it becomes a part of talk about religion and religious belief, they too become a resource in mocking and insulting others.

Insults related to appearance are less frequent on the Facebook pages, with only 26 uses of the word "fat" in the Feuerstein comment corpus, and nine uses concentrated in the following exchange:

User 1: Shut the fuck up with your fat ass. Stop putting the camera so close onto your fat ass face.
User 2: I always find it funny when people call him fat. Do you really think it phases him? Well it doesn't. To even post something of this nature screams self image issue
User 1: Firstly I'm pretty sure I'm not a fat bitch, secondly I'm pretty sure it does phase him that people call him fat. (2014.08.29 JF Video Comments)

This exchange provides a clear example of how insults can be perceived as unsuccessful, with the second user making the point that Feuerstein is likely "unphased" by the criticism and suggesting that the comment reflects poorly on the first user rather than on Feuerstein. This sense of expectation of insults without users responding explicitly to the "haters" is an important part of the ethos of the community. The negative comments serve as evidence of Feuerstein's effectiveness, with one user commenting, "The fact that you have so many haters Josh just proved you are doing something right! If you were on here spewing liberal propaganda then no one would have a problem with what you were saying." These comments seem distinctly different than more serious "trolling" involving rape or other threats of violence (Hardaker and McGlashan, 2016).

Feuerstein's own physical representation of himself is also used to attack him. Throughout the responses to Feuerstein, there are also a number of different photo comments, often taking the form of a "meme" image, with a recognizable image and text overlaid on the image. Some images employ screenshots from Feuerstein's videos to mock him. One comment with the text "More stupidity from this doofus" includes an unflattering image of Feuerstein with his mouth open and the caption "Believes in talking snakes; Thinks evolution is just silly." Another image shows Feuerstein's head photoshopped onto the naked torso of a morbidly obese man, with the caption, "Dear Mr. Atheist ... Allow me to destroy this cake in 3 seconds." Although the comments are not explicitly from users who affiliate with theamazingatheist, the tone and content which are similar to theamazingatheist's attacks suggest the success of a malignant positioning of Feuerstein, one that persists beyond theamazingatheist's video page and follows him onto his own page.

While both theamazingatheist and Feuerstein appear to be speaking to users with whom they share beliefs, the effect of their videos is worth considering particularly in terms of "converting" Christians away from their faith. For example, the research suggests that the presence of atheistic voices online are influential in encouraging people to come out as an atheist (Cimino and Smith, 2011; Smith and Cimino, 2012). Although theamazingatheist doesn't seem to be making a genuine appeal to Feuerstein and his viewers, the positioning of Feuerstein and his beliefs as illogical and doing so in a mocking way may have some positive effect on users who might be considering the weakness of the Christian faith in light of science. While there is clearly evidence of a core audience of like-minded individuals and an audience of users opposed to theamazingatheist's message, there is also potentially an audience of users who may be persuaded and for whom presenting a negative prototypical Christian might help convince.

Feuerstein is not the only object of derision, with commenters also taking aim at theamazingatheist on his own videos. Users write, for example:

> science isn't on your side fat fuck, any scientist that has watched your video says "wow this guys a fucking retard i hope people aren't associating his fat ugly ass with science because that would make us look bad" look, if you wanna be butthurt about people

believing in god, then leave it at that but don't ever talk about science because you don't know what the fuck you are talking about. you're not a scientist you're a fucking idiot. (2014.06.02 AA Video Comments)

The commenter takes issue with theamazingatheist's attempt to respond to the scientific inaccuracies in Feuerstein's video and challenges him aggressively for presenting himself as a kind of scientific expert. The commenter doesn't, however, appear to be affiliated with Feuerstein. Although Feuerstein's and theamazingatheist's arguments may suggest an "us" versus "them" mindset, the commenters do not always take such a simple approach. Here then, conflict is not limited to a simple storyline of Christians fighting with atheists. theamazingatheist's viewers and other atheists on YouTube do not simply take his side regardless of his position, an issue that is highlighted when he criticizes Feminism and receives criticism for his position from other atheists. While there may be a core of viewers that support him regardless of his position, atheists who oppose and ridicule him are also always present, something that isn't true of Feuerstein or John Fontain, the Muslim user.

The comment represents a larger difficulty with atheism as a category, where there is a tension between creating a community of atheism and atheists desiring independence in their individual disbelief (Cimino and Smith, 2011, 2014). While Feuerstein is, in many ways, an advocate for Christian belief, and his videos show his commitment to "spreading the gospel," theamazingatheist is not clearly advocating for atheism. When theamazingatheist does mention the atheist community, it is only to argue against people attempting to exclude him from it, something that he addresses in other videos. Rather than positioning himself as an advocate for or a leader of a community, he instead positions himself as a kind of antagonist, attacking people he finds to be ignorant or illogical, be they Christians, "social justice warriors," or feminists.

3.3 Appealing and Consensus Building

In contrast to his response to the atheist in *Dear Mr. Atheist*, the video *Dear Mr. Muslim* Feuerstein positions himself in a completely different way. Here he is not focusing on logic, but rather on the theological argument that Jesus was God. Like the video "Dear Mr. Atheist," the original posting of the video isn't available online but instead was re-uploaded by another user. John Fontain's response, *Dear Joshua Feuerstein Muslim Response John Fontain* was posted on June 1, 2014, suggesting that Feuerstein posted the original video around the same time as he posted his *Dear Mr. Atheist* video. From the beginning of the video, there is a clear departure from *Dear Mr. Atheist* in that Feuerstein does not engage "Mr. Muslim" from a point of defensiveness and does not present the video as a response to any attack. Instead, Feuerstein starts by praising his "Muslim friends," saying:

> Mr. Muslim
> now I must preface what I'm going to say by simply saying
> that my Muslim friends are some of the most kind caring
> compassionate
> incredible individuals I have ever met
> and to be quite honest with you
> and sadly so
> well your propensity towards prayer and
> dedication to your religion
> puts most Christians to shame
>
> (*Dear Mr. Muslim*, JF Video)[3]

Feuerstein does not initially position himself as opposing Muslims. Instead, by praising the piety of his "Muslim Friends," the initial positioning suggests shared experience, particularly around the prayer and dedication to religion, something that Feuerstein says "puts most Christians to shame." The kindness to a potential Muslim audience suggests that Feuerstein might be making a genuine attempt to reach out to Muslims, although there is little evidence that he has a significant Muslim presence on his Facebook page. Moreover, Feuerstein does not continue in other videos to make an outreach to Muslims a significant part of his preaching. The video could then be seen as Feuerstein attempting to bat down attempts by Muslims to build shared alliances against atheism online, which is one of the reasons Feuerstein gives for Muslims reaching out to him.

Feuerstein goes on to describe why he is making this particular video addressing Muslims, saying,

> and over the last week
> I have gotten a couple hundred e-mails at least
> from Muslims around the world that
> have congratulated me
> on the video I have recently made
> and yet at the same time
> they have questioned
> well they have questioned my claim that Jesus Christ
> is in fact the messiah
> however it is in those questions that I find a couple of contradictions
> how is it that Islam
> says that Jesus Christ
> is a prophet

[3] The transcript is taken from the re-uploaded version of the video. The original date of the video is not known.

a mouthpiece of God
that he is a good man
and yet when I look at the words of Jesus Christ
well they seem to contra-
well they seem to contradict exactly what Islam says
you see Islam says that Jesus Christ was not the Son of God
that he was not
the savior of the world
that he was not the messiah
and yet when I look at what Christ claims
it's exactly that
for he says I am the way the truth and the life
and no man comes to the father
except
by
me

(*Dear Mr. Muslim*, JF Video)

The "video that I recently made" appears to be Feuerstein's *Dear Mr. Atheist* video in which he made an explicit argument for creationism, a belief shared with Muslims, and a video that Feuerstein claims has resulted in receiving "a couple hundred" emails. By mentioning the praise of Muslims, Feuerstein also suggests that others have positioned him as sharing a common belief about evolution. The positioning of Muslims and Christians as sharing belief is, however, quickly challenged around the issue of how Jesus should be treated. From an Evangelical Christian perspective, the claim that Jesus is a "prophet" or a "good man" rather than God is an important distinction between the faiths, one that separates Christianity and Islam from one another into non-compatible categories.

This way of talking about the relationship of Jesus to God and about the deity of Christ is not specific to Feuerstein's video to Muslims. It is part of a longer ongoing argument among Christians and Muslims since the beginning of engagement between the two faith traditions (Watt, 2013) and one that is highlighted in Christian missions to Islam in the contemporary world (Parshall, 2003). Feuerstein's argument, like his talk about evolution, suggests a misunderstanding of the theological position of Islam, particularly as it relates to belief about Jesus being the "Son of God." Indeed, as we will see in Fontain's response, what Feuerstein presents as problematic is not necessarily problematic for Muslims. Instead, it is the belief embedded in the statement "Jesus is the Son of God" which, for Feuerstein, means that Jesus is also God. While the text doesn't explicitly make this point, for Feuerstein, it appears obvious, something that anyone looking at the text should see.

This belief in the deity of Jesus Christ results from an interpretation that over time becomes embedded in the verse. The text then carries with it assumptions and beliefs, referred to as a "shared repertoire" in a community of practice (Lave and Wenger, 1991), in which texts can have a "richness" that denotes deeper beliefs. These beliefs are not necessarily explicit in talk among people holding the same deeper beliefs because they do not challenge one another. When making the same statement to a Muslim, however, where the belief is not shared, the video lays bare the implicit belief about the text. How the "shared repertoire" of language and belief affects interaction is highlighted in Feuerstein's emphasis on Jesus being "the only way" to the "Father," which revoices John 14:6, where Jesus is speaking to the disciple Thomas:

> Thomas said to him, "Lord, we don't know where you are going, so how can we know the way?" Jesus answered, "I am the way and the truth and the life. No one comes to the Father except through me. If you really know me, you will know my Father as well. From now on, you do know him and have seen him." (John 14:5–7, New International Version)

In context, the passage is not clearly a statement about the exclusivity of Christian belief or faith in Jesus but is instead a metaphorical statement about how Jesus is the embodiment of the abstract concepts of the "way," "life," and "truth." However, in Christian apologetics, the passage takes on an important role in supporting the supremacy of Christ and Christian belief. That belief, however, is one that is built up from a specific set of interpretations of the Bible within a specific tradition. This context of belief is necessary for interpreting the scripture and providing a storyline with which Feuerstein can subsequently position others: that those who believe in Jesus can come to the Father and those who don't believe in Jesus cannot. For Feuerstein, however, if it is only necessary to assert the verse with the expectation that others will understand why he is quoting the verse. It is not a meaningful argument for Muslims because it doesn't seem to take into account any Muslim belief about the nature of Allah or Jesus in relation to God.

The use of scripture in this way also highlights a belief in the "common meaning" (Malley, 2004) of the Bible, that the message contained in the Bible is consistent and coherent across all the parts of the collected writings that make up the text and a belief that the Bible is the consistent and clear Word of God that is applicable in all situations (Bebbington, 1989). Christians on YouTube have been observed using different portions of the scripture to interpret other parts of the Bible (Pihlaja, 2013b, 2016b), a practice that Malley (2004) has also observed in the reading of the Bible in physical, local contexts. What readings count as legitimate or not favor certain second-order discourses (Foucault, 1981) that are viewed as authoritative for different groups. Feuerstein's use of the Bible to represent "what Jesus said" as authoritative, factual reporting highlights his own assumptions about the nature of the Bible and doesn't recognize different beliefs about the Bible that might be held by others, particularly Muslims who don't accept the authority of the text. By aligning himself with "what Jesus says," he positions himself as an authoritative figure.

This is highlighted in Fontain's response which makes clear that Feuerstein's reading of the passages is a particular interpretation. Fontain says, in response to Feuerstein's statement that Jesus is the way, the truth, and the life.

> as a Muslim
> we have no problem
> it doesn't contradict Islam
> Jesus is the way
> the way we follow
> Jesus is the truth
> we believe he was truthful
> he's the life
> we have to follow him in this life
> no one can get to him
> no one can get to God
> except through believing in him
> no problem
> it's your interpretation
> that now
> from
> somehow from this verse
> you're you're interpreting that Jesus is claiming divinity
> (2014.06.01 JFo Video)

Fontain points out that the statement itself doesn't necessarily contain the claim that Feuerstein seems to present. By offering a second interpretation, Fontain problematizes the implicit argument in Feuerstein's video, which combines post-hoc beliefs about the scripture to interpretation. Fontain places the blame for the faulty argument solely on Feuerstein's "interpretation" of the Bible, highlighting that Feuerstein has taken the claim from a particular verse and extrapolated a larger theological point from it. Feuerstein, from Fontain's point of view, has taken a flawed English translation of the Bible and made assumptions about it, assumptions that are rooted not in truth or understanding of God, but in his own misconceptions.

Interpretation of the text does not, however, feature heavily in Feuerstein's talk either in his video targeting "Mr. Muslim" or in general. Indeed, the topic is almost entirely absent in Feuerstein's videos except when referring to it in a pejorative way: "You can't pick and choose what the Word of God says. The truth is not a democracy." Feuerstein presents "what God says" as clear and undisputed. His belief in the Bible downplays the role of interpretation and assumes, again, a "common meaning," one that true Christians and believers understand but non-Christians and non-believers cannot access. His lack of response to Fontain and his presentation in his initial video shows that the video is not, as he claims, intended as a way of addressing Muslims, but rather asserting a long-standing theological point to his Christian audience, without genuinely engaging with Muslim theology.

This point is made clearer as the video progresses. Feuerstein goes on to then refer to other parts of the Bible that also are used in apologetics to support the claim that Jesus is God, stating:

> think about that
> that when he looks at his disciples
> he makes claims of divinity such as
> if you have seen the
> me
> you have seen the father
> the father being Allah in your religion
> if you have seen me then you have seen the father
> for I and the father
> are one
> before Abraham was
> I am
> think about these words of Jesus Christ as he begins to claim divinity
> and now
> here is my question to you
> if Islam is true
> then how could Jesus say these things
> because he was either a liar and a lunatic
>
> (*Dear Mr. Muslim*, JF Video)

Feuerstein's argument relies heavily on the supremacy of the Bible, and reporting on passages that, when taken together, might suggest that Jesus made a claim at divinity, particularly John 14:7 and John 8:56–58. Feuerstein presents these claims, however, as though they are facts without question and does not relate them at all to the source material, in this case taken from the Gospel of John. Feuerstein's conclusion to this argument, that Jesus must either be a "liar or a lunatic" is again a revoicing of a common Christian apologetic argument, originating in the 18th century (Hopkins, 1863) and popularized by the Christian writer and apologist C. S. Lewis (Lewis, 1952). By describing Jesus as either "was who he said he was" or a liar or lunatic, Feuerstein positions the audience in a storyline where an explicit choice must be made about Jesus. This storyline, however, is one that Muslims reject because of its assumption that the Bible clearly teaches that Jesus claimed to be God and the assumed authority of the Bible as reporting what Jesus actually taught.

As with the video on evolution, Feuerstein does little to address any actual arguments against the deity of Christ made by Muslims and instead repeats a gross simplification of the Muslim position, that Jesus was just a "good man" rather than God. He also does little to address the belief system of Islam, and challenge any particular beliefs that "Mr. Muslim" may hold. Instead, the argument follows the same pattern as his address of "Mr. Atheist," projecting a simplified argument on the person being positioned, and then presenting his own belief as a move to retain the "last word" as he did with theamazingatheist. The video does not ask any genuine questions of a Muslim audience or invite dialogue. Instead, it is presentation of Feuerstein's belief as it relates to Muslims, one that seems oriented toward an audience of believers who appreciate and understand the arguments to which he appeals.

Feuerstein goes on to repeat a simple description of Christian belief in the ending of his video, saying:

> and so I propose to you
> that Jesus Christ was the king of kings
> the alpha the omega the beginning the end
> the author and the finisher of our faith
> the lion of the tribe of Judah
> the lily of the valley
> he was the beginning the end
> he is everything in the middle
> he is God
> that is what I propose to you
> and I propose to you that not only do I love you
> but he loves you as well
> and that he died on a cross for your sins
> and shed his blood
> for your sins
>
> (*Dear Mr. Muslim*, JF Video)

Feuerstein's language falls into Evangelical Christian register, referring to Jesus in different ways taken from the Bible and which emphasize Jesus as a special figure, someone who is not simply "a good man." The response highlights key tenets of Christian belief about the death of Jesus on the cross as an act of propitiation, intended for the forgiveness of sins. At the center of the message is Feuerstein's focus on his "love" for the audience, one that mirrors the love of God. By positioning himself as acting out of love for others, Feuerstein can deflect criticism for any message he puts forward, even aggressive messages, because they are presented as being motivated by his own compassion. By stating his "love" for others, he can also implicitly position himself with God, as he does in this video. Feuerstein loves the viewer, and so does God.

The specific Christian register suggests that like his video aimed at atheists, he is actually addressing a Christian audience and presenting an apologetic case for the deity of Christ to other Christians rather than to a Muslim audience. Particularly by using phrases like "shed his blood for your sins," he is revoicing language from the Bible and taking its authority through quoting it. Users without an explicit knowledge of the Bible or Christian register would not find the phrases "the alpha and omega," "king of kings," "the lion of the tribe of Judah," or "the author and the finishers of our faith" to hold a particular reticent meaning. Instead, for viewers in the shared sociocultural context of Feuerstein, these phrases echo with the words of praise songs and sermons built up in shared experience. They are more than theological statements – the phrases have specific and important significance within the shared repertoire of American Evangelical Christian culture and are affective for a particular audience who share the same faith. Christian register may then serve as one way Feuerstein can deal with the context collapse in which a mixed audience of users are watching his videos. They mark him as a member of the Evangelical Christian community, complete with specific theological beliefs, and reflect important epistemologies about the nature of the world and how Feuerstein views himself. This belief can be recognized by users who understand the concepts behind the Christian register without Feuerstein explicitly having to state his belief. The theology is implicit in the way Feuerstein talks about himself and others in the world.

The video doesn't invite a response from Muslims. Instead, Feuerstein's approach is to present his belief to his audience and use analogy or an opposing position to highlight what he already believes. The video is decidedly a one-way message, with Feuerstein speaking out to an audience. There is no meaningful way "Mr. Muslim" could respond. Instead of an invitation, the video ends with a specific "challenge" to accept the Christian message:

> so I challenge you today
> to meet the Jesus that I know
> the Jesus that will revolutionize you
> the Jesus that will walk into your heart
> and give you love compassion peace hope and joy
> that is my prayer
>
> (*Dear Mr. Muslim*, JF Video)

Feuerstein presents an invitation to Christianity to his "Muslim Friends," again using the language of Evangelical Christianity, one that focuses on Christ walking "into your heart," an important Christian metaphor for a "relationship" with God, another difference between Christianity and Islam that is highlighted in "outreach" to Muslims by Christians (Parshall, 2003). Feuerstein positions himself as offering something different and better to the Muslim audience, one that will "revolutionize" them. Like *Dear Mr. Atheist*, the message focuses on the experience of individuals and coming to know Jesus within their "hearts." The language of the "challenge" suggests that despite Feuerstein's positive positioning of "Mr. Muslim" at the outset, Feuerstein implicitly suggests that Muslims should become Christians, a positioning fits into a larger storyline that Christians believing in Jesus come to know God, while Muslims do not. It encourages and reinforces the belief Feuerstein's Christian audience would already hold about Muslims and Islam. Although Feuerstein does implicitly challenge the validity of Islam as a path to God, he doesn't directly confront a Muslim user. Instead, he very carefully "proposes" a statement to the audience, without making any demands. Like many of Feuerstein's calls to action, he makes a suggestion and "challenges" people to change their behavior. This tactic contrasts with a more heavy-handed approach that might state explicitly that Muslims should become Christians. There is also little recognition of what Muslims might already believe or an attempt to bridge the gap between the two faiths. The call to faith further supports an argument that Feuerstein is using his social media platform to primarily encourage like-minded users and to reach out to users who already have a shared cultural understanding that may allow them to understand the message of "salvation" as he has presented it.

The video did result in a response from the Muslim user, John Fontain, who like Feuerstein did not generally respond to other users specifically on his YouTube channel prior to this video. His response, however, *Dear Joshua Feuerstein Muslim Response John Fontain*, is a direct message to Feuerstein, one that is carefully produced with Fontain replaying key parts of Feuerstein's video in a carefully edited response. Fontain begins the video with a playful parody, wearing a backward baseball cap, saying, "Welcome to video" and then:

> I'm not racist against Americans
> you know
> I have many American friends
> I don't mind Christians
> I used to be one
>
> (2014.06.01 JFo Video)

Fontain's short parody of Feuerstein is markedly less aggressive and negative than theamazingatheist, highlighting Fontain's softer, more conciliatory approach to the presentation of his faith. The video is not about attacking Feuerstein, but looking for common ground between the two, something that is a recurring theme in his videos overall, particularly as his message relates to Christians. While theamazingatheist mocked Feuerstein, Fontain positions himself in a much more friendly way, playing Feuerstein's quote from the *Dear Mr. Atheist* video that "Evolution is not a science; never has and never will be" and giving a smiling thumbs up without saying anything. Like Feuerstein, the presentation of the words and beliefs of the other is first shown in a way of affiliation, both of which are implicitly critical of evolution, and by extension, atheism. These moments within both Feuerstein's and Fontain's videos attest to the importance of considering how discourse builds as an event. The affiliation in not consistent throughout the video, but it plays an important role in what follows and how viewers understand the position of the content creator in relation to them.

Like Feuerstein, the initial positioning is key to what follows in the video. Christians and Muslims are starting from the same place and despite what differences they might have, there is shared common ground in their belief. This is the beginning of a storyline in which Islam is a more consistent and truthful depiction of what Christians already believe, a storyline that appears in other videos in which Fontain speaks to Christians while doing "street dawah." In one video, Fontain is speaking with a Christian woman and says to her, when she agrees with him that there is only one God, "You are Muslim. Your beliefs are Muslim. They are not Christian." For Fontain, the distance between Christianity and Islam is not as significant as Feuerstein has presented. Fontain does make the important theological distinction that believing Jesus is God is a mistake. However, instead of mocking or attacking them, he presents Christians as simply misguided and much closer to Islamic belief than they might initially think. Fontain, responding to Feuerstein's claim that Jesus is "the way, the truth, and the life," says,

> as a Muslim
> we have no problem
> it doesn't contradict Islam
> Jesus is the way
> the way we follow
> Jesus is the truth
> we believe he was truthful
> he's the life
> we have to follow him in this life
> no one can get to him
> no one can get to God
> except through believing in him
> no problem
>
> (2014.06.01 JFo Video)

Unlike Feuerstein who makes a simple concession to Muslim belief and then moves on to positioning Christianity as different from Islam, Fontain's tactic is the opposite, using the majority of his video to position himself and his belief as the same as Christians. Fontain positions his belief in Jesus as "the way," accepting what Feuerstein has presented as a key tenet of the Christian belief. By aligning himself with the statement that "No one can get to God except through believing in [Jesus]," Fontain positions himself and Feuerstein and

Feuerstein's audience in the same way, as followers of Jesus moving toward God. In this storyline, there is no difference between Christians and Muslims – they both believe and want the same thing.

Positioning himself in this way, as affiliated and in agreement with Christians, is a recurring theme in Fontain's videos, showing that Christian belief and Islam are not in conflict with one another. Fontain regularly refers to a dawah book that he has published called *Jesus and the Injeel* which argues that Jesus, in his ministry was actually preaching the "injeel" which is mistranslated at "gospel" in the Bible and actually refers to a revelation from God to Jesus as a prophet, similar to the message given to other prophets. The argument attempts to deconstruct the Bible as an authoritative source and suggest that Jesus preached the same message from Allah as preached by other prophets. Instead, the argument holds, the message was consistently misinterpreted throughout the years, leading to the Bible being an inconsistent record of "God's word." While the argument positions the Bible in a negative way, importantly, it does not reject Jesus as "the way, the truth, and the life." Fontain asks users to share his video including the point that the "injeel" presented to Jesus is one of the five proofs of Islam, saying, "Share the video. Share the knowledge and convey this new point of evidence in a brotherly way to our cousins in faith." By positioning Christians as "cousins" to Muslims, Fontain makes clear that the message he is spreading is not inconsistent with the dominant belief of Christianity.

Finally, Fontain turns Feuerstein's argument against the atheists against Feuerstein, and he challenges Feuerstein's claim that Jesus is God saying,

> where is your evidence
> your evidence is in the Bible
> now the same way
> in your atheist video
> you refused to except evolution as a fact
> on the basis that it's not been observed
> then I also will present this to you
> how can you accept the Bible
> as a holy book
> when it has not been observed
>
> (2014.06.01 JFo Video)

Although Feuerstein had focused his criticism on the belief that Jesus is not God, he presented what he believed to be authoritative evidence: the Bible's words as he presented them. For Fontain, this evidence is not sufficient, and he asks and answers the rhetorical question "Where's your evidence?" challenging the Bible in the same way that Feuerstein has challenged evolution in his video aimed at atheists, by claiming that the Bible as a "holy book" has never been observed. Like Feuerstein's criticism of Islam and the assertion of the deity of Christ, Fontain's challenge of the Bible as an authoritative text is also a recurring theme in Christian-Muslim debates (Watt, 2013) and one that, in my observations, features regularly in discussions among Christians and Muslims on YouTube. For Fontain, questioning the Bible as an "observed" holy book implicitly challenges it as an authority.

Like Feuerstein's positioning of atheists as illogical, Fontain's challenge of Feuerstein makes an appeal to logic and evidence. It also suggests that Feuerstein is being inconsistent in his belief by rejecting evolution based on its lack of evidence but not applying the same criteria to the Bible. Fontain doesn't challenge the Bible explicitly or state that it is inconsistent, but he positions himself as questioning and asks Feuerstein to produce evidence in support of his claims. The argument puts the onus on Feuerstein to produce further evidence in support of the Bible. Fontain's challenge back to Feuerstein and the lack of a response suggests that Feuerstein is actually uninterested in dialogue with a Muslim audience. Although Feuerstein engages in apologetic arguments from time to time, the way he uses his social media presence does not favor having a long, measured discussion of the validity of the Bible.

Although Feuerstein and theamazingatheist appeared to target specific audiences, Fontain's audience is less clear. In 2014, he was a relatively new YouTuber using the site to promote his book. The approach to Feuerstein in the video suggests that Fontain, more than Feuerstein and theamazingatheist, is appealing to a third audience beyond those who share the same belief system. With the challenges on Christian religion being specifically focused on the lack of logic and intelligence, Fontain's presentation here and elsewhere of the logic of Islam and the consistency of the Qur'an in contrast to the Bible appeals to an audience beyond Christians and Muslims. By positioning himself as a free thinker and truth seeker, Fontain aligns himself with the atheists attacking Feuerstein. However, many of Fontain's interactions are with Christians, which he shows in his street dawah videos. While Feuerstein uses social media to present his own message without response and theamazingatheist uses response as a way of producing entertaining content, among the three users, Fontain seems the most interested in dialogue with whom he disagrees. In his videos showing himself doing street dawah in a variety of situations, this same positioning of himself as seeking truth and eager to engage in meaningful conversation is a recurring theme, with a storyline that positions all humans as seeking truth and understanding, and on the same path to knowledge of truth as it is presented in Islam.

While Feuerstein did not respond to Fontain, arguments in the comments show that Fontain's video attracted interest from Christians, Muslims, and atheists, all eager to argue different aspects of Fontain's claims. The comments show that there is indeed a diverse group of viewers engaging Fontain's content, including the diversity of issues that appear in this video. The longest thread of conversation includes a Christian questioning the authority of the Qur'an and a reasoned argument about specific claims with it, with polite comments from both sides including from a Christian responding to a Muslim: "Thank you for clearing that up [NAME]." and a Muslim responding to a Christian, "Hey [NAME]! I respect your thoughts and am going to adress all your points God willing." The discussion follows a genuinely positive path, although no users appear to change their minds.

However, despite these positive comment threads and Fontain's focus on Feuerstein's argument about similarities between Christians and Muslims, the comment receiving the most thumbs up (at 95), states: "Islam is the most dangerous religion today." This leads to an extended argument and a relatively reasonable discussion about the role of religion in inspiring violence, despite not occurring in the video. Unlike Feuerstein and theamazingatheist's videos, the larger sociopolitical context of Islam in the West appears to play a role in how the arguments develop and what topics are addressed by the users. The comments on the video also show the limitations that Fontain faces in presenting Islam in a social media context where users are often antagonistic toward religion generally, and quick to discuss the role of religion, and particularly Islam, in the propagation of violence. While the video focuses on positioning Christians and Muslims together, the comments suggest that the effect of this positioning is limited. Users push back against the notion of religion, generally, with users writing, for example, "All religions are rubbish built from fear and ignorance" and "Hey Joshua and John; fuck you; your both retards; you BELieve in the adult version of Santa Claus!" Fontain's interest in appealing to Feuerstein and affiliating with Christian belief provides an affordance for users to reject both religions together as equally illogical.

Users, when responding to each other in videos, are always positioning themselves in relationship to their audience. Who might be included in that audience is complicated by popularity and users' nominal roles as leaders in their different communities. This doesn't mean, however, that users are unaware of to whom they're speaking – Litt, and Litt and Hargittai (2012; 2016) have worked with Goffman's notion of the "imagined audience" to investigate how users think about audience when posting on social media, concluding that users are actually quite aware of their audiences. Litt and Hargattai (2016) write, "Even though users often interacted with large, diverse, and invisible audiences, they coped with the audience challenges by thinking about a general abstract audience or by thinking about a more targeted audience as they posted" (p. 9). Despite the context collapse of social media, users can and do cultivate specific audiences for specific content.

Feuerstein, Fontain, and theamazingatheist do this discursively, appealing to particular audiences through the way they talk about themselves and others. Limiting one's audience isn't, of course, always possible and users can't control who watches their videos. Cameron (2015) writes that "every aspect of a situation that we investigate and theorize is connected to other aspects of the situation" (p. 9). How these connections emerge on different scales, with different aspects of the interaction affecting the outcomes is highlighted in these two cases of conflict, one which marked by antagonism and another which is marked by a much more conciliatory tone. Clearly, painting any sort of description of "religious talk online" with broad strokes is unwise. At the same time, the patterns for interaction that we have observed have precedence in arguments about theology and religion more generally, be they patterns for representing evolution or discussions about the deity of Christ. The positions that users take and respond to are both specific to the local context and part of larger storylines about themselves and others.

What is common in the interactions is how users respond to others and present their own beliefs as responses to the beliefs of others, assuming a discursive relationship. This relationship goes beyond a dialogue, real or imagined, with other users. It also includes an ongoing conversation with the audience, with the content producers positioning themselves in an authoritative way, and viewers affirming the positioning explicitly in their comments and implicitly in viewing, "liking," or sharing the video. This affects not only the presentation of beliefs, but also the potential development of communities around users, who become spokespeople for particular beliefs. At the same time, little of this seems to be based on explicit appeals to identity-based communities. Instead, users are more likely to make individual arguments and avoid language that explicitly positions "we" against "them." Rather, users assert their position as correct and make an invitation for others to agree with them.

Discussion of religious topics initiates opposition and creates an environment where user response to the messages of others results in opportunities for content creation, a historical feature of argumentation (Billig, 1996). This content can be the basis for building affiliation among users, who find the videos and agree with the position taken by the content creator. Unlike e-churches or other online religious communities where shared belief is the starting point of the community (Hutchings, 2007; Estes, 2009), the videos we've so far examined are built in part on the back-and-forth of argumentation and the actions of others without a direct appeal to users coming together in any way behind a particular idea or belief. As a complex, dynamic system, unexpected components and influences can spur change, reflected in language use as users react to specific, disparate audiences (Androutsopoulos, 2014). The affiliation of Muslims and Christians in a shared distrust for evolution serves as a good example of this, one that appears to be unexpected for users in the data set, including Feuerstein. The result is a new series of affordances, providing further opportunities to present one's beliefs.

3.4 Conclusion

In the videos, conflict and antagonism have different effects, particularly when users are engaged in arguments with others who may not share the same beliefs as them. Conflict provides an affordance for users to present their own beliefs and build support, by positioning themselves as being attacked by others. Feuerstein's positioning as a religious and moral authority includes a positioning of Muslims and atheists as illogical, providing chances for new positionings to emerge in responses. These include positioning Feuerstein as either ignorant (by the theamazingatheist) or as misguided and unenlightened (by John Fontain). Through opposition and attempts made to silence other users, responses allow for the development of new positions in the changing social context. They respond to positionings and are subsequently given the opportunity to challenge the positioning with a new one. Social media interaction can then benefit from conflict, regardless of how negative it might be, as it gives content producers a platform to broaden their audience and reevaluate and remake previous positionings. At the same time, the constant conflict can lead to users taking more entrenched positions that are much less hospitable as the arguments continue. The following chapter will look more closely at how users position themselves with larger storylines to make sense of the conflict.

4 Stories and Storylines

4.1 Stories and Sacred Texts on Social Media

Storytelling is an essential part of sharing personal experience on social network sites (SNS). While some might wonder about the value of posting pictures of food and dismiss self-disclosure online, SNS work to include others in a narrative or story about the user's life. These stories can be episodic updates as they happen in real time (Page, 2010, 2013) and connect the lived experiences of friends and family in social circles. These stories can have different levels of importance for different users, but for religious users for whom lived experience often has an important spiritual dimension, status updates, pictures, and comments are sites to perform and enact faith, to show who they are and what they believe. Beyond status updates and tweets, stories can be used by figures like Feuerstein to create engaging creative content to be shared with others. All of the users in this study engage in storytelling in one way or another, whether it be talking about their own life and experiences, or stories about what they think is right or proper conduct. This chapter traces the different ways that stories are used throughout the data set, including the stories that the users themselves tell, such as Feuerstein's face-to-camera method of talking directly to the user, or in interviews with others, as John Fontain often does, asking people to tell him their story of reversion to Islam.

Stories and narratives have long been of interest to discourse analysts, with different definitions for what does or does not constitute a narrative (Ritchie, 2010). While storytelling can be understood as simply the telling of a string of events (Abbott, 2008), classically, Labov's (1972a) work on inner-city narratives has been influential in studying narrative, particularly looking at templates for storytelling and how regularities emerge. Labov (1972b) presented a model of storytelling that included steps of "complicating actions" and "evaluation" which give structure to the reason a person is telling a story – people tell stories because they have a point, and the point reveals something about how the storyteller understands the world. Labov's work was particularly important because it saw storytelling as a site of social interaction. The story was a way to construct and enforce social realities, beyond conveying information to others or serving a purely entertaining purpose, and stories and their regularities were important ways to encode cultural experience and relate one's own experience.

The telling of particular stories, in particular places, at particular times is a fundamental part of positioning, revealing key aspects of the teller's and listeners' social contexts. Bamberg's (1997) description of positioning is particularly useful to consider in tandem with the structures of stories for this reason – the stories give insights into how users are interacting with their social world. Stories also become an important way that religious users relate to those around them because the stories provide a way of embedding theological positions in lived experience, be it the teller's own experience, the hearer's experience, or by using stories which appeal to people's common-sense understandings of the world. The story is not only a way to share information, or to describe how one sees oneself in the social landscape, but stories also are a part of social action, of creating a social world. The three levels look at the position of the story characters, storyteller, and story hearer within social space.

On the first level, there are the positions allocated to characters within a given story. Who these characters are, and how they relate to context of the storytelling, differs depending on the kind of story that is being told. Given the variety of ways that they users employ social media, there is not a single kind of story that is told across the data set, but some patterns do emerge. This chapter focuses on stories told from sacred texts, stories told by users about their own life or experiences, and the stories users tell of others, recounted or revoiced on social media. Each of the different types of stories offers different opportunities for users to exert control over the elements of the story, with the fictional stories offering the most opportunity, in theory, for creativity. These stories, however, are relatively rare in the data set, with only Feuerstein using them at times. Much more regular are stories where users are recounting their own experiences or the experiences of others in a way that is purported to be factual; that is, the users make a point of presenting stories as things that have *actually happened*, something that is particularly important in the recounting of stories in which God or Allah is positioned as a character orchestrating the events. The stories of others also often occur in this same way, with the user telling another's story (or facilitating another story through an on-camera interview) and focusing on the factual nature of the story. For both Josh Feuerstein and John Fontain, focusing on the factual nature of the stories is of particular importance in attempts to persuade viewers about the value of what they present.

Stories from sacred texts, particularly the Bible, are an important part of religious talk online and can provide parameters for moral teaching. Feuerstein uses biblical stories that include fixed characters and storylines, so their retelling is limited by the text and the events and characters they include. However, the retelling of biblical stories includes interpretation. While the characters and stories can be taken from the text in the first instance, this doesn't necessarily mean that the content of the story must remain fixed. Instead, the telling of biblical stories often includes an element of hermeneutics, or the task of uncovering the meaning of a text (Thiselton, 2009). Hermeneutics can also be the site of collective meaning construction and community engagement, as research into reading groups has consistently shown (Allington, 2007; Allington and Swann, 2009; Peplow, 2011, 2016).

Reading texts with others involves complex interaction between different individuals' lived experiences: their own personal context, their collective and individual cognitive contexts, and the physical context in which the reading takes place. As Malley (2004) shows, the reading of sacred texts can be a part of community development, with readers meeting together and relating their own personal experiences to the message. Stories can also be a powerful way for authority figures to exercise power, particularly in the use of "second-order" discourses which appropriate the language of the sacred text to the words of individuals (Foucault, 1981). In online settings, the telling of stories, particularly stories from sacred texts that are well known, can play an important role in building a shared context and signaling beliefs.

Sacred texts provide a good example of how the context, the characters, and narrative of a story have a relationship to the context in which as story is told. In Bamberg's (1997) model, the second level is the positioning of the speaker and the listener as a story is being told. When a story is told – and especially in the case of stories told from sacred texts – the telling of the story places the teller in a position of moral authority and positions the hearer as a recipient of instruction coming from the text. Whenever a story is told, there is a reason for telling the story in the context it's being told. Any story told positions the teller and hearer depending on the reasons a story is being told and what a storyteller might be attempting to do in and with the telling of a story. The positions that come up in this second level could be explicitly intended to position the speaker and hearer in specific ways, which we will see in Feuerstein's clear linking of the hearer to the content of the story.

The Bible plays an important part of Feuerstein's presentation of himself and his beliefs, with 12 of his 27 videos including some reference to the Bible. By avoiding expository teaching (where the Bible is read and the meaning is explained), the stories can appeal to a general audience who don't necessarily need to have a comprehensive biblical knowledge to understand the meaning of the story. Instead, Feuerstein paraphrases and retells stories, only touching on main points as they come up, with little attention to the details. The stories are told to connect the contemporary world to the world of the text, with a clear point of application. In one video, for example, Feuerstein tells the story of the prophet Hosea marrying a prostitute named Gomer from Hosea 1. The description of the video reads "SHOCKING CONFESSION: I'm A Preacher . . . But I Love Prostitutes! #SHAREifyouCARE." Feuerstein begins by asking viewers, "Many of you guys know that I'm a preacher, but what if I told you I was in love with a prostitute?" The question is provocative and builds suspense about how it will be resolved.

Feuerstein then describes Gomer, saying:

> she's a hooker
> she's a ho
> she's a prostitute
> she's all of these things
> but God says [to Hosea]
> I want you to go
> love her
> so Hosea goes
> and takes her as his wife
> and
> he loves her
> and yet it was that she still had
> a love and a desire to kind of have the things of the world
> and so she chases all of these other men
> then sure enough she's sleeping with them
> and she's cheating on him
> and every time that she leaves him
> he goes
> and loves her again
> and he goes and pulls her out of the arms of other men and
> he just continues to love her over and over
> she cheats on him
> one two three four five six seven times
> I mean just keeps cheating on him and yet
> he keeps
> loving her
>
> (2014.04.15 JF Video)

Feuerstein loosely recounts the story of Hosea, drawing on the main points of the biblical story and establishing the positions and storyline: a godly man who is repeatedly cheated on but continues to love his wife despite her not deserving his love. Feuerstein does nothing to offer more historical context about the Israelites, but instead isolates and extracts the story a very specific purpose, as we will see below. The use of the scripture in this way shows Feuerstein's own belief about the text, that an individual story can be taken from the Bible and read without an understanding of a historical social context, a common belief about the Bible as being mutually comprehensible and applicable (Malley, 2004). Every story from the text, however obscure, is useful for understanding how God interacts with humanity.

Using the provocative question as a starting point to generate interest, Feuerstein then pivots to the second-level of positioning, moving beyond the characters in the Hosea story to the context of the viewer. Feuerstein says,

> you see it was that God told us that that was his love story
> for us
> he was using it as a way to
> somehow describe
> take this
> Jerry Springer situation and describe to us
> how much he loves us
> so right now
> you might be feeling like you've messed up too many times like
> you've failed over and over
> and that there's no way that Jesus can ever love you
> but I want you to know that where sin doth abound
> Christ doth much more abound
>
> (2014.04.15 JF Video)

The address of "you" marks Feuerstein's shift back to the second level of positioning, moving the viewer from the story to its application in the contemporary context. The characters from the story are then mapped on to the viewer's own experience. Feuerstein says the story is meant to describe "how much [Jesus] love us," drawing a comparison between the characters of the story and the viewers as "sinners" who are regularly pursued by God, in the same way as Hosea pursued his prostitute wife. The empathy the viewer has built in the initial part of the story for Hosea is then transferred to God and the anger and judgment of Gomer, the prostitute, is directed back at the viewer themselves. Moreover, given the video description and Feuerstein's own provocative question at the beginning, the story seems to be chosen for its sexual content. While the story of Hosea is potentially a lesser known Bible story, Feuerstein places it in a contemporary context, using words like "ho" and "hooker" and calling the story a "Jerry Springer situation"[1] that relate the characters and their difficulties to the viewer.

Feuerstein's language shifts markedly from a colloquial register in the final lines of the extract above with the phrase "Where sin doth abound, Christ doth much more abound." The verb "doth," an archaic form of the third person

[1] Jerry Springer was a well-known American talk-show host who exploited guests' often outrageous relationship problems to produce conflict on air.

present "do," appears to be taken from the register of the King James Bible where "doth" is found regularly. However, the words that Feuerstein says are not quoted in the text, but instead, Feuerstein appears to be a paraphrasing Romans 5:20 (KJV) in which the Apostle Paul writes: "But where sin abounded, grace did much more abound." The shift in register offers an implicit suggestion that Feuerstein is quoting the Bible, even though there is no mention of the text and the phrase isn't actually found in the Bible. It suggests the authority of the Bible in a second-order discourse (Foucault, 1981) which was present in Feuerstein's response to Fontain above about Christ's deity – it includes traces of the text and its interpretation without actually quoting it.

The effectiveness of the story requires the viewer to see themselves in some way related to the story of Gomer, tying their own personal narrative to a larger one from the Bible. Gibbs (2011) usefully describes this process as "the 'allegorical impulse' fundamental to human cognition, in which we continually seek to connect, in diverse ways, the immediate here and now with more abstract, enduring symbolic themes" (p. 122). The symbolic themes create "diverse, rich networks of meaning that are both metaphorical and often deeply embodied" (Gibbs, 2011, p. 122). These symbolic themes can also be observed in narratives about religious experience and conversion (Richardson, 2012) and are not arbitrary. They can be embedded in beliefs about sacred texts and lived experiences within communities holding a shared belief about a text. The text is not only a place to develop true belief about God, but scripture, and stories from it, can be used to "make sense" of lived experience in hermeneutic activity, particularly among Evangelical Christians (Malley, 2004). This is also something I have observed on YouTube as part of my own research (Pihlaja, 2013a). Biblical language and the stories taken from the Bible activate and mobilize networks of beliefs and provide theological support for interpreting lived experience in particular ways.

The story, therefore, proves particularly useful for Feuerstein, first by involving characters and a story that is salacious, and second, by relating the story back to a key message: that all people are sinners and are in need of God's salvation. In the third level of positioning – which describes how the speaker views themselves beyond the context of the story being told and in the larger social world – Feuerstein's telling of the story shows his belief that God plays an important powerful role in the world. God is a personal entity who tells people to do things, in the same way that Hosea is told to marry the prostitute. This positioning is often implicit. Feuerstein's approach and the stories he tells have coherence when considered in light of an ideology that places an understanding of God as omnipotent. The Bible is the literal Word of God at the center of understanding the social world, grounded in an American, Evangelical Christian context. Looking beyond the videos that make an explicit religious claim will, in the analysis, help us further understand how Feuerstein sees and experiences the world, not simply in terms of a religious ideology, but a larger sociopolitical worldview.

The biblical stories that Feuerstein tells do not necessarily require a belief in biblical authority to have impact, however. Feuerstein, for example, tells the story of Noah in one video with the description "The Beauty in The Storm! MUST WATCH for anybody going through a dark season! #SHAREifyou-CARE." Feuerstein prefaces the story by saying,

> hey guys
> Josh Feuerstein here
> have you ever been going through a situation
> particularly a storm in life
> where it just seems like the wind and waves
> just constantly pound and pelt against you
> well check this out
> not all not every storm is a curse
> some can actually be a blessing
>
> (2014.04.22 JF Video)

Feuerstein goes on to tell the story of Noah, who built an ark to weather a flood sent by God to destroy the world, but the story is framed initially using an experience that is shared by anyone, regardless of their belief: being caught in a storm. The "storm" of life is positioned as a difficult challenge, something that causes the viewer difficulty. This mapping of "storm" onto a "difficult situation" is not specific to the biblical narratives, but rather a common conceptual mapping. While this might be understood as a conceptual metaphor (Lakoff, 1987; Lakoff and Johnson, 1980), Grady (1997; 1999) describes these kinds of metaphors as "primary" – they develop from a basic connection between abstract experiences and concrete ones. Regardless of whether or not one knows the story of Noah, most viewers will have a basic experience of storms as negative.

Like the previous video including the story of Hosea, Feuerstein shifts between the character positions in the story and the viewer's position. Unlike the Hosea story, however, Feuerstein begins with a direct address to the viewer with the question "Have you ever," which positions the viewer as the focus of the narrative. Later, he brings in the story of Noah:

> not every storm is a curse
> some can actually be a blessing
> in fact
> check this
> when it was that
> when Noah built the ark
> well he was in a valley

he built the ark in valley
in a low place
in a desert land
but when he goes through the storm
well the storm takes him
and rests him on the mountaintop

(2014.04.22 JF Video)

Feuerstein's telling of the story of Noah and the ark pays little attention to the specifics of the story in the Bible (see Genesis, chapters 6–9) which doesn't mention a valley or desert land. Instead, the story of Noah told by Feuerstein infuses a "timeless, symbolic" (Gibbs, 2011) depth to the story, while at the same time appealing to viewers who might know the story of Noah based on non-specific knowledge about the Bible. Like Feuerstein's vague rewording of Romans 5:20, the specifics of the text are less important than the overall message of the video – troubles enter life not to persecute you but to help you come to a mountaintop. The story of Noah serves as a kind of authoritative backdrop to a larger narrative about the experience of individuals facing difficult circumstances in their lives. What is important is not the specifics of the story but the fact that it does not contravene the "common meaning" of the Bible.

The story doesn't contain any difficult theological concepts and ends on an encouraging note, with Feuerstein saying:

there's time in your life
that God can allow you to go through a storm
but it's not to persecute you
and it's not to punish you
it's actually to elevate you
to take you to another level
so that
I want you know
and be encouraged today
that God has a strategy
in the storm

(2014.04.22 JF Video)

More important than the specifics of the story of Noah and its theological implications is a larger storyline about the relationship between humanity and God. In this third-order positioning, Feuerstein's video is establishing an apologetic argument around the problem of evil, one that sees it as part of a larger plan. Even difficulty is good because it ultimately leads to better situations for believers. This use of the Bible shows Feuerstein's awareness of his audience, which could include Christians and non-Christians. Unlike the examples of Feuerstein using words specific to Evangelical Christian register, the telling of the story of Noah is potentially more open to a variety of audiences who might not necessarily share his faith. It does not assume a belief, or make belief a precondition of a user hearing the message and applying it to their lives.

The response to the video suggests that there is no concern with Feuerstein's application of the story in this way, and the comments are almost entirely positive. Users write, for example:

God Bless, thank you (2014.04.22–2 JF Video Comments)

thanks Josh I needed this reminder (2014.04.22–2 JF Comments)

yep Big storm, thanks so much Josh (2014.04.22–2 JF Video Comments)

I thank jesus for helping me get through ea and all of my storms. God knows til I wanted to change I went through many of them and even asked god why? But now I know it was to make me stronger for my future and his son seen me through the storms and is right by my side today. Thank you jesus for ghe stregnth u have given me to walk dwn them lonely dark rocky paths just to c me be a better man than I was at the beggening. Amen!!! (2014.04.22–2 JF Video Comments)

The majority of comments are simply thanks to Feuerstein and tags of other users, with little arguing with or further explicating the story. Instead, Feuerstein's stated goal of encouraging users appears to be effective, insomuch as users are eager to show their appreciation. Longer comments, like the one above, also show how users relate the story to their own lives, including the metaphor of "storms" in describing the troubles that they have overcome. Feuerstein is effective in positioning the viewer in the place of Noah. Users agree with and accept Feuerstein's narrative about their experiences and use the comments section to praise him.

Although Feuerstein regularly refers to the Bible and makes use of it in many of his videos, one video features a story that doesn't make explicit reference to the Bible or God, beyond Feuerstein's regular sign off of "God bless." In a video with the description, "To Those Surrounded by Negativy! [sic] #shareifyoucare," Feuerstein tells the story of Aaron Rowston, a hiker who was trapped while hiking and had to cut off his own arm to escape being trapped. The story was made into the film *127 Hours*, which Feuerstein uses as an analogy for being "trapped" by other things in life:

> is there a relationship or a friendship
> or maybe you're just tied to the memories of your past
> maybe there's something in your life
> that you need to cut away from today
> maybe there's something that's holding you back
> maybe there's something that has you handcuffed
> that you're not able to grab ahold of your destiny
> and your future
>
> (2014.05.02 JF Video)

Again, Feuerstein tells a well-known story to position the viewer as being able to overcome their difficulties, including rich metaphors that compare spiritual experience to physical experience. The story highlights that Feuerstein's message does not necessarily require an explicit biblical explanation, although the story does relate to Jesus's teaching that one should cut off a hand if it is causing sin (Matthew 18:10). The story fits into a larger storyline that people are "held back" or "handcuffed" by negative experiences and the viewer must "cut the dead things out of your life." The video follows the same structure of positioning the viewer in a place of negativity and using a story to highlight how the viewer might overcome the negativity in their life.

The video illustrates Feuerstein's position as a positive and encouraging voice rather than a theologian focused exclusively on biblical exposition. Like other evangelists – notably mega-church pastor Joel Osteen (2004) whose book *Your Best Life Now: 7 Steps to Living at Your Full Potential* illustrates a "self-help" approach to Christian theology – many of Feuerstein's videos are not fundamentally about teaching theology but encouragement. The Bible, in this context is meant as a kind of guidebook for people, one that helps viewers "grab ahold of your destiny and your future." While the Bible is regularly present in Feuerstein's videos, his ability to present the same message without the text suggests that while it rhetorically is important to the message, in practice the specifics are not, and the messages can be applied to a variety of stories.

Although Feuerstein does not regularly read directly from the Bible, throughout the comments sections on his videos, users can be observed using Bible verses to support one another and as a source of authority. An example of this can be seen in a comment on Feuerstein's video with the description, "Do you feel like you are CONSTANTLY UNDER ATTACK? Thieves don't break into empty vaults! 90 seconds to change your life!" A user responds to another comment attacking Feuerstein and says,

> Yet another Scoffer! Mr. Scoffer, do you realize that you are fulfilling 2 Peter 3:2??! Also, if anything, your comment only makes Joshua feel worthy for being persecuted for the Lord! Matthew 5:11 "Blessed are you when people insult you, persecute you and falsely say all kinds of evil against you because of me." Good day to you, Mr. Scoffer! (2014.07.30 JF Video)

The use of scripture in this comment represents the implicit power the Bible has for users on Feuerstein's page. The citation of 2 Peter 3:2[2] without any reference to what the verse says shows the user's belief that not only the point of the text is clear and obvious, but that its application in this specific situation is also obvious. Ironically, the reference itself is inaccurate, as it appears the

[2] "I want you to recall the words spoken in the past by the holy prophets and the command given by our Lord and Savior through your apostles."

user intended to quote the following verse three, "Above all, you must understand that in the last days scoffers will come, scoffing and following their own evil desires." Ironically, the reference to Matthew 5:11 has a clearer message, suggesting that anyone who attacks "Joshua [Feuerstein]" is only proving his point, that he is doing the work of the Lord.

Despite the consistent presence of the Bible in Feuerstein's talk, a similar presence of the Qur'an is not as prominent in John Fontain's videos. Instead, Fontain only makes passing reference to the text of the Qur'an, quoting it to Feuerstein in his response to *Dear Mr Muslim*. Fontain states,

> because the Qur'an says
> [Allah] begets not
> nor was he begotten
> and there's nothing like him
> so God
> does not beget children
>
> (2014.06.01 JFo Video)

This reference to what "the Qur'an says" is presented as a direct quote from the text, although Fontain does not repeat the sura in Arabic as others do. The reference is an attempt to produce evidence for a contrary claim made again by Feuerstein: that Jesus is God. Fontain contests this point, but he chooses to appeal to the text for his reasoning. The text then gives him authority for the claim, but in a way that also assumes an interpretation of the text. The phrase in English "Allah begets not nor was he begotten" is not an explicit response to a Christian belief in the deity of Christ. Rather, it is mobilized as evidence against Christian belief. By doing this, the verse takes on an apologetic function not as a way of crediting Muslim belief, but discrediting Christian belief. Fontain follows this up with a rejection of a Christian metaphorical representation of God as father, saying "God does not beget children." The importance of this different conceptualization of God, not as father, is asserted not as a positive argument for Islam, but as a means to differentiate it from Christianity, a common difference in Christian and Islamic theology that Dorst and Klop (2017) have also affirmed in their research with Dutch Muslim teenagers.

Other Muslims, however, can be observed at times supporting claims using the Qur'an or hadith (the collected stories and sayings from the Prophet Muhammed), but there are no examples in Fontain's videos, or the comments sections of any of the users, of stories from the Qur'an or the hadith being used in similar ways. There are examples of individuals that Fontain interviews reciting from the Qur'an or hadith to support a point. This happens, for example, when a "sheik" that Fontain is interviewing recites a verse of the hadith to support the point that not only he was born Muslim, but all people are born Muslim. In another instance, while interviewing an American Muslim in

Chicago, the interviewee recites the Qur'an without any reference in English to the sura or location of the text:

> you know
> beware of Allah
> you know
> he's going to burn you
> <Quotes Qur'an in Arabic>
> literally
> Allah's going to burn you
>
> (2014.04.08–2 JFo Video)

The assumption is then a shared knowledge of the meaning of not only the Arabic but the meaning of the verse. The quoting of the Qur'an in this instance adds credence to what could be a potentially controversial statement, that Allah would "literally" burn you. This use of the text to support a potentially controversial claim – and the specific notion of a literal hell – can also be observed in Christian discussions about literal readings of the Bible on YouTube (Pihlaja, 2014a), and seemingly protects the speaker from a criticism that their claim is in some way unnecessarily antagonistic. The recitation of the verse in Arabic also adds authority to their statement, rather than necessarily clarifying it for the casual listener, as it assumes a specific knowledge of the text, similar to the recitation of Bible verses without clarifying what the text actually says. We will return to this discussion of the use of Arabic in the next chapter.

The difference in the use of the Qur'an (or the absence of its use in Fontain's videos) and the Bible underscores the key point that the two texts are fundamentally different in constituency and they play different roles in their respective beliefs. That said, the context collapse of social media creates a situation in which sacred texts can become conflated, and the use of each can come to resemble the other, particularly in the comments sections in which users quote from texts to support arguments and attack one another. Rather than the videos, then there is evidence of the quoting of the Qur'an both by Muslims and opponents of Islam in the comments sections of other videos, particularly in arguments on theamazingatheist's videos. Responding to claims about Islam, particularly an argument put forth that early Muslims fought back against slave masters, a non-Muslim user cites the Qur'an as evidence the claim is false.

> That is so much bullshit. The idea that the Muslims fought defensive warfare is utterly refuted by any map of the early expansion of the Muslim imperialists. The early Muslims fought their neighbors to expand Islam to establish the global caliphate. Read Sura al-Anfal to get an idea of how they thought about this. You"ll see plunder being described as "Gifts from Allah" and enslaving women after murdering all the men in surrounding tribes was perfectly fine. The Sura even states that Mohammed is to have a 20% cut of the plunder. (2014.10.15 AA Video Comments)

The Koran advocates for self defense and not aggression for no reason, as well does christianity. (2014.08.27 AA Video Comments)

In the first example, a user is responding to a historical claim made by a Muslim, one that is meant to refute the storyline that Islam has historically been a religion of the "sword," an argument we have seen in the previous chapter as having long been used to criticize Islam (Ernst, 2004). The reference to "Sura al-Anfal" signals a knowledge of the Qur'an by the commenter, but one that repeats a common argument made against Islam: that because the Qur'an includes instructions about military operations and in particular, the "Spoils of War," Islam is intrinsically violent in its worldview. From a comparative perspective, the use of the sura in this way ("Read Sura al-Anfal to get an idea of how they thought about this") shows that the commenter sees the meaning of the text as obviously clear, without any need for further explanation. The assumption is then that the text will speak for itself and other users do not need any context for the sura to understand its meaning.

The second comment, however, shows how an opposite argument can be made, again appealing to the Qur'an as an authority. Neither of the arguments is strictly correct or incorrect but representative of citing textual evidence more generally. In discussing the different positionings above, I discussed how claims and counterclaims – *logoi* and *anti-logoi* (Billig, 1996) – are reflected in responses. Truth claims seem to reflect less the content of the texts and more on how the user is oriented to the text. Claims using or contravening the text are means to position the user either in a narrative where the text has authority and should be believed, or the text is not authoritative and instead represents evidence of dangerous belief. This use of the Bible against Christians in making a truth claim can be observed in theamazingatheist's video, *Religion: Does Anyone REALLY Believe It?* in which he argues that Christians do not actually believe in the Bible because they do not, as far as he sees, actually follow its teaching.

> like the Bible says
> we gotta stone homosexuals to death
> we gotta stone witches to death
> we gotta
> uh
> stone Sabbath breakers to death
>
> (2014.08.26 AA Video)

Like Feuerstein's vague quotation of the Bible and Fontain's appeal to what the "Qur'an says," theamazingatheist shows that the same strategy can be used to attack Christian belief. In the case of both the Qur'an and the Bible, the text itself often becomes the source of contention, if not anything specifically taken from it. The phrase "the Bible says" occurs 225 times in the full corpus, with the phrase appearing in the videos and comments of all the users. The phrase was used by both Christians and non-Christians alike, in attempts to offer evidence both for and against Christian belief, showing its plasticity and functionality as resource for users in arguments about religion in a context in which the Bible is seen as the key sacred text.

While the uses of sacred texts I have so far discussed see the Bible and Qur'an as right or wrong, good or bad, the Bible plays a more complicated role in the discourse of John Fontain, particularly in relation to how the Bible should be addressed by Muslims when attempting to speak to Christians about Islam. Rather than use the Qur'an, the Bible and Jesus as a religious figure play dominant roles in Fontain's discussions about how to talk about Islam, often to the exclusion of discussion about the tenets of Islam. The Prophet Muhammad plays a less prominent role in the videos, with Fontain saying in one video, "Jesus is mentioned in the Qur'an 25 times. So the name Jesus is in the Qur'an, is more frequently mentioned then the name Muhammad" (2014.07.14 JFo Video). For Fontain, the discussion of the Qur'an is not a main part of the work he does on the site. Instead, to succeed at dawah in the contexts he presents, the teaching must be oriented toward the Bible and Christian beliefs about Jesus.

The orientation of Fontain's ministry toward Christian faith is seen from his first video, *Jesus & the Injeel – John Fontain* which is a presentation of his booklet, intended to be used in street dawah and particularly focused at Christians. The video and the booklet argue that Christians have a misconception of what Jesus preached. Instead, Fontain argues, the original teachings of Jesus were a revelation from God, similar to the revelation to other prophets. He highlights that word "gospel" is used in the Bible, is actually referring to the "injeel," a revelation from Allah, not the "gospel" as is has come to be understood by Christians as the message that Jesus died for the sins of the world (John 3:16). Fontain's book is supported by a website (www.jesusandtheinjeel.com) which makes the same claim. The video does not quote directly from the Bible. Instead, refers to the different New Testament books by name, and reiterates his point about that the term "good news" or "gospel," is actually a reference to the "injeel." For Fontain, it is wrong for Muslims to say that they believe in the Bible, but they should say instead that they believe in the "injeel."

Fontain also published a second video (13.12.09 JFo Video) to further clarify this point. When arguing with Christians, Fontain suggests, Muslims practicing dawah might "use the contradictions with the Bible," but he disagrees with this tactic. He says,

> You've either got someone who stops believing in a creator
> because you put him off
> by pointing out all the problems of his Bible

you get someone who leaves religion
or now you get the Christian
which now
blindly follows his belief
because you're showing that the Bible is not
uh
a sense of proof
for his faith
so now he uses his feelings as proof
and this is very dangerous
okay
because feelings are not proof
for your belief

(13.12.09 JFo Video)

Fontain's use of the Bible is clearly intended to build on a belief in a creator. For Fontain, a key part of presenting Islam to a Christian audience is building on common ground between the two. We observed this in Fontain's video directed at Feuerstein, which first praised Feuerstein for recognizing the goodness of Muslims and saying that he had no issue with the claim that Jesus was "the way, the truth, and the life." The strategy is not to undercut Christian belief and delegitimize it, but to instead draw a shared common ground and make an argument that true belief in Jesus and his message is actually a belief in Islam.

This orientation of Islam to Christianity contrasts with concerns about Muslim radicalization online which see Islam in online settings as unrelated to other forms of faith expression (Bermingham, Conway, McInerney, O'Hare, and Smeaton, 2009; Edwards and Gribbon, 2013). Although social media has been seen as a radicalizing force, Fontain takes a much different stance toward the role of Islam and Muslims in the world. He argues for a more integrated engagement, one that recognizes the dominant position of Christianity in the West. Fontain's positioning of himself, other Muslims, and Christians establishes a non-oppositional storyline, in which Jesus and the fundamental parts of Christian belief are conducive with Islam.

This can be seen most clearly in Fontain's videos showing him talking with Christians while doing street dawah. Fontain is explicit about his strategy in targeting Christians and using their beliefs to create openings for Islam. In the same video, describing how to use his booklet *Jesus and the Injeel*, Fontain says to the viewer:

if you say to a Christian
can you believe Jesus was given a revelation called the Injeel
from God
they would say no
in Mark

Chapter 1 verse 14
okay
he says
now after John was arrested
Jesus came to Galilee
preaching the gospel of God
[. . .]
when you go to the oldest Greek scriptures of the Bible
subanallah
it says
after John was arrested
Jesus came to Galilee
preaching the injeelian of God
subanallah
all the Christian scholars accept
the New Testament was written
after Jesus
okay
and this is written by Matthew Mark Luke John and Paul and
various different authors
and it's speaking about
in the time Jesus
so this word injeelian was used

(13.12.09 JFo Video)

Fontain's use of the Bible and the authority of "Christian scholars" shows an eagerness to affiliate with others who "believe in a creator." By establishing a position of "believers in a creator," Fontain is able to construct a storyline here Muslims and Christians are fundamentally the same. This position is made possible by the presence of atheists because the position is only meaningful when it contrasts with "non-believers in a creator." By drawing lines of affiliation in this way, Fontain rejects Feuerstein's claim that the deity of Christ is the defining issue, but rather seeing God as the creator is more important to their identities as "believers." In this storyline, Muslims and Christians share the same core belief in God – the "Abrahamic Ummah" (Shafaat, 1991) – and this shared history can and should be used to encourage Christians to revert to Islam.

The quotation of Mark 1:14 also shows a willingness to engage with the biblical text in the same way as Christians, although the use of the Bible does cause some problems for Fontain in that he does not, as I showed above, profess a belief in the Bible. Instead, what Fontain does seem willing to do is accept the Bible as a starting point for discussion about Jesus and God and their relationship to Islam. Like Feuerstein, the Bible is a resource for reaching out to Christians because of its place as an authoritative text in Christian belief. By pointing to the inclusion of the "Injeel" in the biblical text, Fontain orients the conversation away from the specifics of the biblical message and toward a Muslim understanding of the world.

While this does ultimately include rejecting the Bible as God's word, as Fontain shows in a conversation with a Christian woman whose husband is Muslim, he does not present it as a precondition for becoming a Muslim.

Fontain's use of the Bible in street dawah shows how belief adapts to context, particularly in spreading faith to diverse audiences. Fontain is not making the point that the Bible is ultimately reliable but that parts of it can be exploited for particular purposes. While the argument contradicts itself (the Bible is unreliable as a source/the use of "injeel" in the Bible shows that Jesus was preaching the message of Islam), it is effective in a moment of argument with a Christian. The use of the argument, however, has larger implications because it treats the Bible as partially true when it is convenient, but also rejects it as a reliable source of information about Jesus.

This approach to Christianity and the Bible contrasts directly with theamazingatheist's approach to discussing the Bible. In his video, *EVOLUTION DISPROVED AGAIN! STUPID ATHEISTS!* he describes the Bible as:

> an ancient book
> that people have been fighting about for two thousand fucking years
> a book
> uh of nonsense
> full of contradictions
> full of immorality
> full of shit
> the Bible
> um
> it's interesting
> sure as uh
> as mythology
> but that's all it is
> a book of myths
>
> (2014.06.16 AA Video)

Throughout theamazingatheist's videos, there is no credibility afforded to faith of any kind. The description of the Bible here and elsewhere includes none of the attempts at bridge-building seen in Fontain's videos, but rather a complete hostility toward it, with perhaps the very small concession that it is "interesting" as "mythology." This positioning of the Bible as completely lacking credibility is then used to position Christians negatively, as theamazingatheist describes the beliefs as "once . . . believed by a primitive people." Belief in the Bible is a sign of ignorance, implicitly positioning theamazingatheist as informed and knowledgeable. If the Bible is full of contradictions, by opposing it, theamazingatheist takes a position of consistency.

However, like Fontain's use of the Bible to convert Christians, the use of the Bible as a force to oppose in society, and indeed the position of "atheist," assumes an oppositional role, and a storyline that positions theamazingatheist as a kind of antihero against the dominant belief. By taking this position, theamazingatheist requires an opponent, rather than presenting his own coherent epistemology beyond a generic appeal to "science." This storyline sees the position of the atheist as primarily oppositional to dominant beliefs. theamazingatheist is then consistently positioning himself in oppositional storylines, even when they have little to do with questions of religious belief, such as rejecting feminism.

The different approaches to the Bible are worth considering in the context of a social media, where Fontain is working to maintain a public face of Islam in front of a variety of audiences, one which includes both the opponent in an argument and also a larger audience. Fontain's presentation of the Bible and his treatment of it assumes a context in which he is spreading dawah, often on the street in Christian majority countries such as the UK, USA, and Brazil, and attempting to engage Christians in the message of Islam. theamazingatheist by contrast makes no attempt to reach out to people of faith, but his videos also assume a dominant Christian ideology which he presents himself as opposing. Although he presents his atheism as a rejection of God as a concept, in practice, his atheism is a rejection of a Christian God. The focus on the Bible, rather than other religious texts, reinforces whom he presents himself opposing.

4.2 Conversion, Reversion, and Change

In Chapter 2, I discussed the different ways that changes in belief have been described in the literature and by different people of faith including "conversion," or coming to personal faith (Bebbington, 1989), for Christians, "reversion" (the preferred Islamic description of coming to Allah) (Justdawah.org, n.d.), and "coming out" (Cimino and Smith, 2011) as atheists (although this refers particularly to the moment of publicly identifying as an atheist rather than a time when a person comes to disbelieve or recognizes their own disbelief). For Fontain, Feuerstein, and theamazingatheist, why people believe what they do, and how beliefs can shift over time, were recurring themes.

Because Fontain's channel focuses on dawah, many of the videos also include stories of people coming to Islam. These occur either in the interviews with other Muslims, presentations of or stories about successful dawah encounters, or Fontain's own story of coming to the faith, which he tells in different ways and at different times. In addition to the biblical text, Christianity also plays an important part in the narrative of John Fontain, as a revert from Manchester (UK). Fontain's own story of reversion comes up in his videos and stories of reversion and how a person "came to Islam" serve as starting points for subsequent videos that follow. These stories of reversion frame how the Islam faith is presented. In Fontain's discussions both with

Muslims he interviews and in his interaction with people while doing street dawah, the individual's own experience is often the starting point for conversation.

Like Fontain's approach to dawah in general, the stories of reversion often include an explicit rejection of Christian belief, particularly the Bible. Fontain, however, never positions Christians in an explicitly negative way, with the exception perhaps of missionaries going to Sierra Leone and "bribing" the natives with food. Instead, the Bible is positioned negatively, not as the result of any one individual's mistakes but the process of translation over time. The problem, according to Fontain, is not that Christians have been dishonest or wrong, but that they have been misled by a false belief in a flawed text. In telling the story of his reversion in his video *Christian Accepts Islam – Magic, Diamonds And Music [MUST WATCH]*, Fontain focuses on his own relationship with Christianity as a young man and positions himself as never fully accepting of Christian belief, even from a very young age. He says:

> I was brought up in a Christian family
> so we would go to church
> every Sunday and
> from a very young age
> like
> I knew that
> Christianity was not
> what I believed in and
> one of the first instances which I remember was
> I was actually in church and we had to
> write a song about
> God
> and my song was
> Jesus and God
> this was my
> it was like a little rap
> and
> I remember the pastor came over to me
> grabbed the piece a paper
> and scribbled it out and said
> no
> Jesus is God
> and it's from this moment
> maybe I was about seven years old
> when I realized that Christianity is not
> it's not for me
>
> (2014.05.26 JFo Video)

Fontain imbues his understanding of Allah on what appears to be a simple childhood memory. He begins by talking about his own understanding of the world as a child and identifies an early experience where he is corrected for saying "Jesus and God" rather than "Jesus is God." The pastor in the story is positioned in a negative way, as correcting the young Fontain and attempting to instill in him a false belief about God. In this story, Fontain portrays himself as being aware, even from the age of seven that "Christianity is not for me," suggesting a kind of unique knowledge which positions himself in a positive way to Muslim audiences.

For Fontain as a Muslim man, this simple experience serves as evidence of his own awareness of truth as a child, to which he "reverts" as an adult. It positions him as skeptical of Christian belief from a very young age and, in some way, more authentically Muslim than Christian. This storyline is particularly important for Fontain who receives criticism for being a white British Muslim and is seen as a "traitor" by some in the comments. Fontain rejects a notion that he was ever really a Christian but instead held the belief from a very young age. The story also positions Fontain as especially bright, being able to tell that the theological position that "Jesus is God" is untenable. Like stories of conversion, Fontain's reversion story which he discusses in this video also includes an important backstory wherein he experiences a worldly or sinful lifestyle, and attains a degree of success as a jazz singer, but ultimately realizes that the life he is pursing as a recording artist will not bring him peace and that Islam is the truth. Fontain positions himself as rejecting both Christianity and worldly success. Key to the story is Fontain's choice to reject his music career in favor of becoming a Muslim – he suggests that leaving of the music industry was not a failure, but a choice he explicitly made. The choices that he makes throughout his life make sense in terms of an overall storyline about his own Muslim identity, one that is his true nature.

For Fontain and other Muslims that are interviewed on his channel, reversion to Islam does not occur in a moment but is rather a part of a "journey" or a "path" that gradually leads to a more pious lifestyle. The process of becoming a Muslim is explicitly an "achieved identity" (Peek, 2005). While Fontain emphasizes the importance of people saying the shahada (the Islamic declaration of faith), in at least one instance where he compels a woman on the street to say it after convincing, it is not seen as being a transformative moment, but rather a start to a more pious life. Fontain's own story of reversion also stressed the process by which he came to Islam, slowly coming to practice it more. In the same way, an interviewee in one of Fontain's videos states,

> at the age of 24 25
> I said to myself
> by the time I'm 30
> I must stop all the nonsense
> and have a

and and
during that transition
of
5 6 years
I started slowly
you know
dropping and leaving behind
nonsense

(2014.04.08–1 JFo Video)

The interviewee still offers a negative evaluation of his life prior to becoming more serious about his faith, but the word "nonsense" and the timescale of six to seven years suggests a lack of urgency for what he was leaving behind. Instead, the process of becoming more pious is related to growing up, with the age of 30 being seen as a cut-off point for the end of the "transition." It is not seen as a moment of salvation or immediate change, but something that the speaker came to over time and at their own volition.

This notion of agency and making a choice to become a Muslim is key for understanding Fontain's approach to dawah, and a decoupling of Islam from cultural contexts where it is the dominant force. While both stories of Christian conversion and Muslim reversion focus on the emptiness of a "worldly life," Fontain and the other Muslim voices he highlights include a second element of rejecting other faiths, often Christianity, showing again the context in which they practice their faith. Fontain's story of reversion also focuses on his experience of Muslim community and the hospitality of Muslims, something that is implicitly contrasted with Christian communities, which are absent in his story about his experience as a child. The videos position Islam not as an organized religion, but rather submission to the way of the creator. Islam and Christianity are implicitly contrasted, with the negative aspects of religion identified with Christian belief, and the positive aspects of faith attributed to Islam.

Stories of conversion and reversion are not limited to Christians and Muslims in the data set, and the importance placed on one's childhood experiences and being aware from a young age is also part of theamazingatheist's rejection of Christianity. In theamazingatheist's video *Religion: Does Anyone REALLY Believe It?*, theamazingatheist tells the following story:

most of the atheists here on YouTube
are former believers
they were once pious
devout faithful people
and I've never been that
you know
maybe I was a believer when I was
a wee lad and no bigger than this

and I was naive
and I believed in Santa Claus
and the Easter Bunny in the Tooth Fairy
and God
but uh
you know
once I stopped believing in Santa Claus
and the Easter Bunny
and the Tooth Fairy
around the age of
I don't know
six
I also stopped believing God
because
just like those other things
I saw no evidence for him

(2014.08.26 AA Video)

theamazingatheist's story of "stopping" belief in God, compared to Fontain's story of reversion is far less complicated. theamazingatheist presents himself as having grown up skeptical of God and the Bible from a very young age. God is positioned with Santa Claus, the Easter Bunny, and the Tooth Fairy as things that he "saw no evidence for." The story is, however, prefaced by an acknowledgment that many atheists, particularly atheists on YouTube had some history within Christian faith, and were in some cases "pious, devout faithful people." His attempt to disassociate himself with these stories of rejection positions him as aware of the truth from a very young age. Like Fontain, theamazingatheist reports the moment he stopped believing as the result of his own logic: "I saw no evidence for him."

Key to theamazingatheist's story of rejecting belief in God is a positioning of faith as similar to other childish beliefs, ones that are particularly focused on children being given things as presents. The notion and use of "belief" here, where theamazingatheist describes himself as "maybe I was a believer when I was a wee lad" and in the phrase "and I believed in Santa Claus" positions belief in an especially negative way, equating belief in God with belief in magical things. By comparing these kinds of belief, "believing in God" is devalued. Belief is instead contrasted with "evidence," which includes an implicit positive valence when compared to belief in the "Tooth Fairy." Without explicitly attacking faith, he positions religious belief as ignorant and childish, and lack of belief – and particularly his own lack of belief – as intelligent and mature.

The implicit comparison of God to Santa Claus, the Tooth Fairy, and the Easter Bunny is taken up explicitly in the comments, as users employ it to explain their own lack of belief in God or their inability to understand Christian belief. Stories of users who believed and then ceased to believe are present in the comments sections of theamazingatheist's videos, and in particular the video on whether or not Christians actually believe in the Bible or not. One particularly clear example comes from a user who responds directly to the question posed in the video *Religion: Does Anyone REALLY Believe It?*:

> Yes. I used to believe all of that magic stuff in the bible and I grew up on Chic Tracts (shudder). Dragons, unicorns, and faeries were silly, of course, but talking snakes and donkeys, the Garden of Eden, the Flood, water into wine, the multiplication of the loaves and the fishes, et al were true because it is in the bible. To not believe the bible was QUESTION GOD, to listen to Satan, to put your soul into eternal damnation, to hate Jesus. I was also taught that while the bible was the true and inerrant Word of God, it also had its little "hiccups." I just had to have faith in the Word and believe in Jesus.
>
> When I became a teenager I began to read the bible from cover to cover and to read it critically. I also shopped around, trying on Pentacostalism (RIP album collection) and becoming a Roman Catholic as well as studying other religions. During this time the "miracles" seemed less and less credulous, the Binding of Isaac (well, the entire OT) more horrifying. But I couldn't let it go and the reason I couldn't let it go was because of fear. Fear of Hell because I couldn't believe any of it anymore. Once I acknowledged THAT I was finally free. It was like I could see colors differently. I could breathe.
>
> My family is still religious and some more so than others. I have not told them I am an atheist. I have told them I am a Buddhist (true) and for some of them, it's the same thing. While no one has confronted me about it, there is a special point about prayer and the "Reason for the Season" at family functions now. (2014.08.26 AA Video Comments)

There are some similarities in this story to theamazingatheist's uncomplicated story of coming to atheism. However, the commenter's experience falls more in line with stories of leaving Christian faith found in other research (Cimino and Smith, 2014; LeDrew, 2013; Smith and Cimino, 2012). They describe a much more complicated relationship between their religious identity and their social context. They position themselves as being ignorant when they were a Christian and believing in "talking snakes and donkeys," which are implicitly compared to mythical creatures like "dragons, unicorns, and faeries." The commenter then describes a period of doubt about the Bible, but being held back by fear. By acknowledging that Hell was not real, the commenter describes being finally "free," implicitly drawing an analogy between faith in God and bondage. The commenter also confesses to not being truly "out" as an atheist and one who continues to participate in family functions that appear to include some religious overtones.

Despite conversation playing an essential role in Evangelical Christian belief (Bebbington, 1989), in the data set, there are far fewer salvation stories. Feuerstein himself does not regularly appeal to his own story of salvation, although he does, as we've seen in his invitation to Muslims, offer the possibility that Jesus could "revolutionize" the lives of Muslims viewing his video. The absence of a personal conversion story seems, however, not to be a function of the belief system, but his particular use of SNS. Although Feuerstein does occasionally speak about his experiences, they tend to be only cursory references or used to set up a story of recovery from rejection, such as when Feuerstein alludes to a woman who left him (see 2014.05.20 JF Video). Instead, the nature of Feuerstein's short videos is to provide quick, clear, shareable messages in which knowing anything about him as an individual is not important to understanding the content. In every video in the data set, while Feuerstein is the dominant figure and his personality is important for animating the specific message, who he is, where he is, and what he believes exactly are of secondary importance to the message he is presenting.

While Feuerstein himself does not engage in any explicit story of his own conversion, they are not completely absent from the comments sections on his videos. Users revealed very personal stories in responses to Feuerstein's videos. One commenter writes:

> Having been with multiple people before I was married, and married before I was saved, I have to say that this is one subject that unsaved people just won't understand. Before I was saved, I was actually concerned that my wife had not had some of the same experiences that I had, I was concerned that she had not been able to experience things sexually that I might not have been able to provide her. I actually gave her permission to go out and try things.
>
> After having been saved I see what a mistake this was. Our household relations are supposed to be a reflection of God's to ours. Our marriage is supposed to be a reflection of Christ's to the church. Even the way we father (parent) our children are supposed to be a reflection of the way our Father parents us. (2014.08.29 JF Video Comments)

The story of conversion in this comment works as a way of realizing past mistakes and making amends for them. The story is simple in its reductive evaluation, describing a negative understanding of the world prior to conversion, one that is made clear upon being "saved." The story of salvation not only allows for a rejection of past negative thoughts and experiences, but a positive way of retelling the present, positioning "household relations" as a "reflection" of one's relationship to God. Even in this small story, the allegorical impulse (Gibbs, 2011) is present, offering structure and meaning to the day-to-day interactions of husbands and wives.

Comments can also imply stories. Users do not necessarily disclose specific events but suggest an event structure that matches the storyline that Feuerstein shares. These include personal stories of violence and abuse, particularly when Feuerstein discusses the domestic violence case of the American football player Ray Rice against his girlfriend. One user tags Feuerstein and relates a story of being physically and emotionally abused by a boyfriend before initiating a divorce. The commenter ends saying that she is "completely broken" before thanking Feuerstein for making the video. There are no likes on the comment and no responses, and the user does not appear to make any other comments. The recounting of one's own experience in light of the video, particularly when it is attached to a Facebook page and one's real name, suggests some viewers are encouraged to disclose their own struggles in a public setting. While there are no likes or replies to the women's story, other examples suggest that telling the story is not about getting help in any way, but speaking the truth about one's own experience in a public setting. The commenter affirms that their own struggle is validated by the video and they will not be attacked by others for sharing their own experience.

Because these comments are attached to users' names and public Facebook profiles, the disclosure of things such as personal sexual history and abuse are potentially quite damaging. The extent to which users are willing to reveal these experiences may suggest that users understand Feuerstein's page to be more private than it is, but this seems unlikely given their presence among other commenters. Instead, it appears that some users treat the comments on Feuerstein's videos as a safe space to share, one in which they may be unheard, but one in which they are likely to attract "hate" in the same way as one might on YouTube. The safety appears to reflect on both the platform of Facebook and Feuerstein's presence, which fosters a spirit of encouragement.

4.3 Positions without Stories

The multimodal elements of videos are an implicit part of positioning. These elements often complement spoken language project an implicit position, depending how a user relates to the camera and orients the gaze of the viewer. The framing and composition of Feuerstein's videos in particular are essential for understanding how he builds rapport with viewers. The videos regularly feature only his face, shot in a portrait orientation – the picture looks out of place on a desktop computer but is instead meant to be viewed on a phone, face-to-face with Feuerstein as he speaks directly to the viewer. Feuerstein addresses "you" in a way that Fontain and theamazingatheist do not, and he builds rapport with the viewer by targeting users who are in vulnerable circumstances and producing videos that serve as kinds of individual pep talks. The format also favors short, direct videos, as it is would be difficult to conceive of listening to Feuerstein speak with the same energy and immediacy for longer than several minutes.

Despite the immediacy and off-the-cuff informality of Feuerstein's videos, they do appear to have elements which are scripted. The lack of fillers in his talk and the direct, specific objectives of each video suggest that Feuerstein has done some scoping and planning prior to filming. Feuerstein does not ramble or chat but often makes clear that he has a specific message or word for the user. Most of the videos start with a similar greeting of, "Hey guys, Josh Feuerstein here" and a line immediately following which sets up a clear agenda for the video. Feuerstein's videos have a specific message with clear and defined structures and clear applications. The unpolished production allows for a disciplined, specific message that appears personal, friendly, and immediate even if the actual content is not genuinely being planned and produced in real time.

From a visual perspective, theamazingatheist's videos represent a higher level of production value. Shot in landscape orientation in high definition with an external microphone and lighting, theamazingatheist takes more care to present his content in a professional way. Like Feuerstein, theamazingatheist speaks directly to the camera, but at a further distance, making his upper torso visible to the viewer. theamazingatheist also consistently stands in his videos, adding a performative energy to the videos and reinforces the sense that he is responding to confrontation and creating a distance, particularly when compared to the "selfie," portrait style of Feuerstein. For theamazingatheist, there is an added legitimacy to the quality of the video production, one that is more common among "professional" YouTubers whose production value sets them apart from amateur users. The higher quality of production presents him in a more professional way, particularly in contrast to Feuerstein, whose videos lack the same quality.

John Fontain's videos show a much more diverse variety of locations and approaches to video editing. When speaking directly to the camera, Fontain sits and addresses the viewer, but often makes videos outside, showing himself doing street dawah. His videos also frequently include a "bumper" – a computer generated introduction sequence with sound effects and titles. Fontain also posts videos of himself appearing on various TV shows, which have a higher production value and offer a further legitimacy to his online presence by showing he is not simply a YouTuber. This is particularly clear when Fontain uploads videos from "The Deen Show," which takes place on what appears to be a television studio set, and has a clear sense of professional production beyond Fontain's own presentation of himself. Again, the production value and the sense that Fontain has been invited on television adds an additional authoritative positioning.

These approaches to making videos again underline the differences in how users represent themselves and their beliefs online. There is no single style, and how a user presents themselves physically affects how they are perceived. Fontain's approach, like Shabir Ally, moves away from the face-to-camera approach of many vloggers, and by interviewing people he presents as authorities on Islam and dawah, there is an implicit appeal beyond the world of YouTube or Facebook. Fontain presents himself in the real world, doing dawah on the street in physical locations. This contrasts with Feuerstein, who does not frequently interact with others in his videos, but works to position himself in a much more intimate and personal way. The approaches result, as we have seen, in viewers responding to them and their content in different ways.

Multimodality is also present in the responses to videos on Facebook, which includes the ability to respond to videos with images. Text responses make up a larger majority of the responses to Feuerstein's videos, but images do attract attention, particularly when attacking Feuerstein or Christian beliefs more generally. One such example includes a photo of a Bible with the caption "Proof that God exists" next to a Spiderman comic, with the caption, "Proof that Spiderman exists." The images, by and large, represent attacks on Feuerstein's arguments, with themes that mock Feuerstein and his supporters. The Bible and Spiderman post leads to a thread of responses with users deducing an argument made from the image: the Bible is an unreliable source for claim in the existence of God. While the image itself is not especially provocative compared to other images containing profanity and vividly mocking religious symbols, users do respond negatively, writing for example: "you are truly one sick, lost, perverted, confused COWARDLY individuals ... I will pray for you." Other users respond to the image with websites linking to information about the Bible and responses challenging the assertion of the image, as in the comment:

> Actually bro, there's 25,000 manuscripts that have been found and cited supporting the New Testament. That's the most in history. If you don't believe me I challenge you to look it up, you'd be surprised at the evidence I'm sure. (2014.08.28 JF Video Comments)

Responses like this one suggest that the photo is presented in a way to make an argument, one that can be responded to with an opposing viewpoint. However, the original poster does not return to argue the point, and one commenter writes, "I propose we just ignore all the stupid comments made by the atheists. Not the ones asking questions but the stupid comments." As the commenter observers, the user posting the image is seemingly not interested in debate, but the debate continues on without them. Like the arguments presented in the previous chapter, the argument does not resolve disagreements, but continues with users posting back and forth, as in the case of the exchange around calling Feuerstein "fat," without any clear progress of resolution.

While YouTube in 2014 did not allow the posting of pictures in the comments sections of the video, images searches of theamazingatheist also bring up similar content, with screenshots from videos taken and given captions with the purpose of mocking theamazingatheist (see, for example, Know Your Meme, n.d.). Indeed, theamazingatheist has also been the object of remixing and editing of photos, including videos that have been subsequently removed from YouTube and other images used to embarrass him. Like theamazingatheist's character "Josh Moronstein," the remixing of images is one of the practices of social media use, where different patterns and forms of meaning – in this case "memes" – have salience and are recognizable to other users. These are not exclusively from users with an opposing ideological position, as some of the "hate" that is directed at theamazingatheist in these images and in the comments sections of his videos has little to do with his position as an atheist, but more in users disliking him as a public personality.

Considering the multimodal elements of the videos, it becomes clear that the videos themselves are not simply presentations of arguments. The person delivering the message and how they present it influences how users respond to the message and, over time, can create a particular style around a user. When a user clicks on a video by Feuerstein or theamazingatheist, there is little variation in what one can expect. The users have honed specific styles that appeal to a particular set of viewers and lead to predictable results. The responses follow predictable patterns that differ between users, but the type of comments that appear on each users' video do tend toward certain consistencies, which we will explore in the next chapter.

4.4 Conclusion

The interaction among Fontain, Feuerstein, and theamazingatheist, at least in the initial instance, arose from conflict around belief, but the practices that we have observed in this chapter are not entirely motivated by conflict. Sacred texts were particularly important resources for meaning-making and claiming authority among all the users, regardless of religious affiliation and could be used to position oneself and others, either through the telling of stories from the texts, or quoting parts of the texts to others. Personal stories were important for presenting an authoritative, authentic position, and that stories of conversion, reversion, or deconversion use the process of change to describe how they came to a positive place. Authority is then drawn from religious texts and religious authorities as well as the user's own personal experience, providing evidence for why users believe or do not believe what they do.

5 Themes

5.1 Themes and Keywords in Videos

Facebook founder Marc Zuckerberg has compared presenting oneself online to presenting oneself as a brand (Vogelstein, 2009) – a user is not only representing their personal experience, they are creating an image for themselves. As social media personalities, Fontain, Feuerstein, and theamazingatheist all exhibit traits of "micro-celebrity," a term used to describe users on social media who produce their identity in a manner to be consumed by others for social and/or economic benefit (Page, 2012). They have followers and fans on social media who treat them as representatives of particular positions, and each of them benefit both in social and financial capital from their prominence online. This position of influence, regardless of whether any of the users claims to be a leader, can be seen in how their respective audiences respond to them, be it explicitly praising a video, or tacitly repeating and developing their ideas in comments.

The investigation of storytelling showed how videos shape conversations, be they around issues like evolution, stories about the work of Allah in the world, or encouragement of individual users. Among the three users, the videos are often focused in their scope and aim, suggesting that they prepared before they recorded a video and, in some cases, edited it after it was recorded. All of the users are attempting to do some persuasion and their presentation of their beliefs or their attempts to interact with other users includes an appeal to agree with them. The effectiveness of these appeals and the influence that each user has on discourse of their respective audiences is then focus of this chapter. What users say in the comments and how the discourse is shaped by these three video makers can show the extent to which the users do shape what their audiences talk about.

Initially, thematic analysis looking for recurrence, repetition, and forcefulness in the videos and comments (Owen, 1984) was useful for gaining a general sense of the differences among the users. However, to provide a more robust, empirical approach to the data, we will now turn to descriptions of language use from a macro-perspective, with the goal of both describing individual users and comparing and contrasting them with one another. In a previous chapter, I briefly touched on the notion of "keywords" in discourse and their usefulness for beginning to describe key topics in discourse and differences in registers and themes in different kinds of discourse. Scott (1997) describes a keyword as "a word which occurs with unusual frequency in a given text. This does not mean high frequency but unusual frequency, by comparison with a reference corpus of some kind" (p. 236). This unusual frequency can be then described as "keyness."

In Chapter 2, I described how I collected and transcribed data for the study, noting that given the different approaches to social media and the different levels of fan and community engagement and popularity of the users, the corpora differed greatly in size. The goal of the data collection was not to compile representative corpora of different users, but to capture interaction at a particular point in time. This focus limits the use of keyword analysis in this project and requires that specific questions be asked using the corpus linguistics tools, particularly addressing how individual words show differences in not only the topics which are discussed in the videos, but how they are discussed.

Taking all these points into consideration, I've adapted a corpus-assisted discourse analysis for this study (described in Chapter 2), using keyness to aid in describing the global or macro-patterns in the discourse. Differences between video pages from different users is of particular importance in this study – for example, comparing comments from theamazingatheist's videos to the comments on Feuerstein's videos. This gives us a way to look for differences in the comments that might not have been picked up by the positioning analysis. Additionally, in the following analysis, I use the sampler reference corpora available in WMatrix (Rayson, 2008) taken from the British National Corpus (BNC) (both spoken and written). These reference corpora are meant to represent a norm of language use, but what the "norm" should be in this study, is not necessarily clear. The Facebook and YouTube data includes a variety of different speakers and writers of English interacting in specific online contexts about specific topics. This specific topical nature of the videos means that while different reference corpora did not always rank keywords in the same way, they all revealed similar differences in the themes and registers that I discuss below.

There are also several challenges in using statistical measures in this study and before engaging in analysis that involves keywords, it's important to make several caveats. The corpora in this study are very small and the keyness of any individual word must be considered with the number of occurrences, as a raw number and as a normalized frequency. This is particularly important when thinking about words that do not occur in the reference corpus. For example, in comparing the video talk of John Fontain, a speaker of British

English, against the BNC sampler corpus, there are 96 occurrences of "dawah" in Fontain's talk and no occurrences in the BNC sampler (and indeed, none in the full British National Corpus at the time of this publication). Where there are no occurrences of an individual word in a reference corpus, comparison is difficult and grows more difficult when words regularly occur in one corpus but not in another (like John Fontain's talk compared to the BNC spoken sampler). Further, a list of keywords does not take into account how a given keyword is used. While a word like "God" might be key in both Fontain and Feuerstein's talk, compared to the reference spoken corpus, what they mean by "God" in might differ based on the context.

As a starting point to investigate the themes in the each user's talk, I will compare the corpus of video transcripts to the BNC spoken sampler provided in WMatrix (Rayson, 2008) to produce keywords lists as an opening for discussion about the larger themes on the channel and comparing and contrasting the findings to the discourse analysis that has preceded. First, we will consider the top 100 keywords and multiword entries in the corpora of each individuals talk using WMatrix. In cases where more than one word held the 100th spot, I included all words at the cut-off point. While 100 words is an arbitrary cut-off point, it does provide a substantial overview of the most significant differences between two corpora and gives us a starting point for talking about the differences and similarities of the topics in the videos. From that, I will consider themes in the keywords and relate them back to the close discourse analysis that I have thus far presented. I will also compare corpora against one another – for example, Fontain's talk compared to theamazingatheist and Feuerstein – to identify other differences that might be present.

The top 100 keywords from John Fontain's videos provide a useful example of how keywords can give a sense of the overall topic. The top 100 keywords, the number of occurrences, and normalized occurrences (per 1000 words) are presented in Table 5.1 (e.g., Islam – 210 occurrences – 7.1 occurrences per 1000 words)[1]. WMatrix also groups multiword phrase as a single unit, so they appear as well, joined with an underscore (e.g., "music_industry"). The talk from John Fontain's videos amounted to 29,490 words.

This table, with the top 100 keywords in columns from right to left, reveals some predictable results – the list is full of words related semantically to Islam including, "Islam," "Allah," "Muslim," "prophet," "Mecca" and Arabic phrases including "subanallah," "inshallah," "hamdallah," and "alakbar" which I will discuss in more detail in the following section on register. The inclusion of "Jesus," "Bible," "Christian/Christians" suggests that there is a

[1] The log-likelihoods for all top 100 keywords in this Table and all subsequent tables fell above 6.63 or $p \leq 0.01$. Keywords are arranged in descending order by keyness.

Table 5.1 *Keywords in John Fontain's Videos*

Islam	210	7.1	brothers	30	1.0	brother	27	0.9
Muslim	124	4.2	cause	33	1.1	Mecca	9	0.3
dawah	101	3.4	sister	25	0.8	accept	26	0.9
God	145	4.9	mosque	16	0.5	believed	14	0.5
Allah	88	3.0	booklet	20	0.7	guide	14	0.5
Muslims	74	2.5	to	750	25.4	England	19	0.6
believe	132	4.5	so	318	10.8	basically	30	1.0
Jesus	93	3.2	my	173	5.9	given	34	1.2
Koran	61	2.1	Christianity	17	0.6	Manchester	13	0.4
subanallah	60	0.2	this	308	10.4	Abraham	11	0.4
prophet	59	0.2	atheists	14	0.5	rap	9	0.3
Muhammad	51	1.7	Ali	15	0.5	revelation	13	0.4
inshallah	50	1.7	and	1047	35.5	rappers	8	0.3
hamdallah	36	1.2	you_know	147	5.0	non-Muslims	8	0.3
Bible	46	1.6	Africa	21	0.7	five_times_a_day	8	0.3
pray	38	1.3	Brazi	12	0.4	UK	8	0.3
shahada	30	1.0	Injeelian	11	0.4	everyone	28	0.9
religion	32	1.1	hadj	11	0.4	came_to	18	0.6
Christian	40	1.4	deen	11	0.4	sisters	14	0.5
dua	26	0.9	nation	16	0.5	Moses	9	0.3
message	40	1.4	is	467	15.8	final	18	0.6
worship	24	0.8	sister	25	0.8	Arabic	8	0.3
messenger	24	0.8	videos	18	0.6	website	7	0.2
people	186	6.3	upon	26	0.9	tawhid	7	0.2
life	59	0.2	music_industry	11	0.4	cassava	7	0.2
Christians	28	0.9	beliefs	11	0.4	alakbar	7	0.2
Sierra_Leone	22	0.7	Ramadan	10	0.3	claim	17	0.6
creator	21	0.7	belief	14	0.5	purpose	16	0.5
Injeel	21	0.7	many	64	2.2	world	30	1.0
assalamualaikum	20	0.7	from	141	4.8	story	19	0.6
know	273	9.3	accepted	20	0.7	Brazil	12	0.4
peace	26	0.9	in	473	16.0	show	29	1.0
actually	127	4.3	prophets	10	0.3	me	157	5.3
YouTube	17	0.6						

clear orientation in Fontain's language toward not only Islam, but some basic elements of Christianity and words like "Abraham," "creator," "God," "believe/believed/beliefs," and "pray" are neutral words that does not necessarily denote one belief or another. This is particularly noteworthy in considering the use of "God" and "Allah." Fontain and the people shown speaking in his videos favor "God" over "Allah," with 145 and 88 occurrences, respectively. There is also a focus on religious works and actions in the keywords, with words like "pray," "dua" (prayer), "hadj" (pilgirimage), "five_times_a_day," and "deen" (religion). While "believe" and "belief" are keywords, there is a unique focus in Fontain's videos compared to Feuerstein and theamazingatheist on the actions that one does as a Muslim, rather than what one thinks or believes. This highlights the focus in discourse on Fontain's channel on what individuals do, and how they come to be Muslim or follow Allah. The emphasis in the stories of reversion we have discussed above is not on what a person believes, or the moment when they come to believe, but the actions that are a part of that belief. Those actions suggest a kind of progress toward practice, something Fontain emphasizes in his practice of dawah.

The high occurrence of the words related to Islam might also show a weakness in the reference corpus, as many of the words simply do not appear in the BNC spoken corpus, including the word Islam. A search of the full BNC reveals only 11, 11, and 2 occurrences of "Islam," "Muslim," and "Allah." Comparing Fontain's talk to Feuerstein and theamazingatheist, however, reveals high occurrences of many of the same words related to Islam with "Islam," "Muslim," "Allah," and "dawah" still occurring in the top 10 keywords when compared to the other users. Perhaps unsurprisingly, Fontain speaks about Islam much more than the other users.

The keywords show further evidence of what discourse analysis in the earlier chapters revealed – Fontain, and people shown speaking in his videos with him, discuss Christian belief with a similar frequency to words and phrases related to Muslim belief. "Muhammad," for example, appears 51 times in comparison to "Jesus" which is said 93 times. Of the 93 occurrences of "Jesus" in Fontain's talk, all have a positive or neutral valence; there is no instance of Fontain speaking negatively about Jesus. This same positivity, however, does not relate to mentions of "Christianity," which occurs 16 times to a neutral or negative valence, for example, as something to "leave" as seen in the statements "I left Christianity because of the Bible" and "now you can leave Christianity . . . you believe in one God." The stories of reversion are about leaving the false belief in the Bible and turning to Allah, which implicitly are critical of Christianity.

The semantic domain of "kin" also emerges from Fontain's talk, seen in the keyword list as "brother/s" and "bro" (which occurs 60 times cumulatively in the spoken corpus). The use of "brothers" and "sisters" in the language is regularly metaphorical, relating to fellow Muslims, while "father," "mother," "grandfather," and "grandmother" often occur in talk about families and their relationship to the Muslim faith, particularly when it comes to talking about conversion stories. The use of familial metaphors serves as a collectivizing strategy and Dorst and Klop (2017) show that conceptualization of fellow Muslims as brothers and sisters is common in Muslim discourse. Similar to the description of fellow believers as "brothers" and "sisters" in Feuerstein's talk, but unlike Christian descriptions of God as "father," there is no metaphorical description of Allah in terms of familial relationships, something that relates to larger differences in the conceptualization of God and religious communities in Christianity and Islam (Dorst and Klop, 2017).

The list also includes keywords that are the result of very specific topics that come up in videos, such as the discussion of "cassava" leaves from a discussion that Fontain has with one woman while doing street dawah. With a small dataset like the video talk corpora, a short talk about a single topic that is not present in the reference corpus can crop up, showing how knowledge of the dataset is particularly important. The keywords, when taken from a relatively small sample of videos, will always skew toward less common words, particularly if they are picked up in a particular passage of a conversation. Moving between scales of analysis becomes particularly important to identify if any keyword requires further investigation or if it is an outlier.

Compared to Fontain's videos, Josh Feuerstein is far more direct and to the point, with videos rarely lasting over two minutes and often very specifically scripted. In total, Josh Feuerstein's 27 videos in the dataset combine for 12,140 words. The top 100 keywords, the number of occurrences, and normalized occurrences (per 1000 words) are presented in Table 5.2.

Unlike Fontain's keywords, Feuerstein's keyword list includes far fewer words related to his own belief in Christianity, although this may again say less about Feuerstein's talk and more about the BNC and the frequency of talk about Christianity in the corpora compared to talk about Islam. That said, words related to Christianity still place on the list, including "God" in first place, "Jesus Christ," "Bible," "pray/prayer," "Christians," and "Holy Ghost." The keywords make it clear that Christian belief is key part of Feuerstein's talk and it plays an explicit and frequent role in his videos, something that was clear already in the discourse analysis of Feuerstein's videos. Despite the relatively small number of words, the overwhelming message of his videos being related to Christian themes is evident in the keyword list.

The keywords "click/clicking," "please," "share," and "moment" highlight the consistency with which Feuerstein implores his audience to share his videos and highlights Feuerstein's focus on the spread of his videos on Facebook. While both Fontain and theamazingatheist also make similar requests (theamazingatheist more consistently than Fontain), the relative length of Feuerstein's videos (usually around two minutes) emphasizes the consistent tag for his videos, encouraging users to share the video more significant. This is also true of the word "bless" which occurs 58 times in the dataset and which is also a key part of Feuerstein's regular sign-off, "God bless you." This phrase is one that is repeated in the comments regularly and relates to a larger Evangelical Christian register that I will discuss below.

The keywords in Feuerstein's talk also highlight the positive nature of many of his videos. Words like "beautiful," "life," "love," "encouragement," "peace," "joy," "promise," "treasure," and "truth" carry a positive valence, and

Table 5.2 *Keywords in Josh Feuerstein's Videos*

God	130	10.7	begin	12	1.0	evolution	5	0.4
bless	58	4.8	name	25	2.1	somebody	24	2.0
click	50	4.1	please	32	2.6	ever	18	1.5
guys	44	3.6	feeling_like	8	0.7	treasure	5	0.4
video	50	4.1	encouragement	9	0.7	prostitute	4	0.3
beautiful	44	3.6	Jesus	15	1.2	Feuerstein	4	0.3
moment	44	3.6	Jesus_Christ	10	0.8	relationship	8	0.7
life	58	4.8	trash	7	0.6	joy	6	0.5
share	48	4.0	this	136	11.2	awareness	5	0.4
Facebook	21	1.7	newsfeed	6	0.5	impossible	7	0.6
challenge	26	2.1	destiny	6	0.5	promise	6	0.5
Josh_Feuerstein	19	1.6	in_fact	22	1.8	hey	11	0.9
friends	33	2.7	clicking	7	0.6	my	65	5.4
below	25	2.1	science	10	0.8	truth	11	0.9
you	511	42.1	sex	9	0.7	man	20	1.6
your	131	10.8	realize	9	0.7	America	9	0.7
comment	27	2.2	peace	9	0.7	very	61	5.0
on_the_side	21	1.7	going_through	11	0.9	always	28	2.3
day	43	3.5	dark	12	1.0	preacher	4	0.3
today	48	4.0	let's	26	2.1	joy	6	0.5
timeline	12	1.0	rejection	7	0.6	because	55	4.5
world	32	2.6	loves	11	0.9	marry	5	0.4
Bible	17	1.4	Christians	8	0.7	needs	15	1.2
that	433	35.7	simply	14	1.2	pain	7	0.6
take	52	4.3	already	22	1.8	get_back	9	0.7
message	17	1.4	reality	9	0.7	circumstance	4	0.3
love	30	2.5	sexuality	5	0.4	most_of_all	3	0.2
friend	21	1.7	atheist	5	0.4	Holy_Ghost	3	0.2
hear	29	2.4	prayer	6	0.5	cave	3	0.2
maybe	31	2.6	to	307	25.3	brokenness	3	0.2
bottom	21	1.7	broken	10	0.8	amen	3	0.2
top	24	2.0	storm	6	0.5	Allah	3	0.2
pray	10	0.8	stolen	7	0.6	AKA	3	0.2
right_now	13	1.1	Islam	5	0.4			

words with a negative valence like "brokenness," "pain," and "storm" are things that one is "going through." These topics represent a marked difference from the language of Fontain who focuses on particular ways of practicing Islamic faith. By contrast, Feuerstein's keywords suggest a more general focus on positivity (such as "destiny"), one that, when put in the contexts of his videos, is often related to Christian religious practices. The keyness of "Jesus Christ" (occurring 10 times) compared to "Jesus" (occurring 15 times) without "Christ" shows one way in which Feuerstein's language implicitly suggests an Evangelical alignment – Fontain refers only to "Jesus" rather than

"Jesus Christ." At the same time, the word "save" is almost completely absent from the spoken corpus in all its forms with only one occurrence of Feuerstein referring to Jesus as the savior of the world. The word "sin" in all its forms is also largely absent from the corpus, with only ten occurrences and is not in the top 100 keywords.

The high occurrences of "you" and "your" (which are also keywords compared to both Fontain and theamazingatheist's videos) reflect the nature of Feuerstein's talk as oriented specifically toward the viewer in a direct way. While this might be a more regular feature of vlogging in general, the fact that Feuerstein employs it more in comparison to the other users in the dataset highlights his approach to religious talk online. Feuerstein's multiword expressions in the keyword list also give an insight into his idiolect and importantly the ways he addresses his audience. "Right now," for example, shows how Feuerstein attempts to speak to viewers' immediate circumstance, in the same way that he uses "today" which also appears in the Top 100 keywords:

> so maybe you're going through a situation right now
> that you're facing adversity
>
> (2014.04.15 JF Video)

> so I want you to know that today
> with Jesus Christ
> you have hope
>
> (2014.05.04 JF Video)

This is markedly different from Fontain's approach to making videos, which treats the audience in a general way and does not attempt to make a one-to-one connection with particular users. Feuerstein's appeal to the individual is most clearly seen in a video with the description "heeeeeeey . . . YOU . . . shhhh . . . Listen to this secret . . . #youarebeautiful" where he presents himself as speaking secretly to the viewer to tell them that he thinks they are beautiful and values them. The vertical orientation of the video suggests that the video is made specifically to be viewed privately on a mobile phone, with Feuerstein speaking face-to-face with the viewer. The content is meant to be theologically sound, without a theological focus, something that appeals beyond a narrow focus of Christians and expands the audience.

At 30,638 words, theamazingatheist's content is similar in length to John Fontain's. The top 100 keywords, the number of occurrences, and normalized occurrences (per 1000 words) from his 19 videos are presented in Table 5.3.

While "atheist" and "atheism" appear in the top 100 keywords, unlike Fontain's and Feuerstein's keyword lists, other markers of atheism in the list are ones that are recognized topics that correlate with non-belief, particularly the words related to "science" (including "evolution/evolutionary," "knowledge," "universe" science/scientific," "theory," "math," and "gravity") and words that represent the

Table 5.3 *Keywords in theamazingathiest's Videos*

God	127	4.1	Noah	13	0.4	bunch	11	0.4
atheist	61	2.0	human	19	0.6	Christianity	11	0.4
rape	55	1.8	Christian	22	0.7	understand	35	1.1
believe	103	3.4	like	229	7.5	stupid	23	0.8
fucking	91	3.0	let's	52	1.7	feminism	13	0.4
evolution	46	1.5	feminists	15	0.5	complex	15	0.5
universe	42	1.4	joke	19	0.6	movies	9	0.3
video	57	1.9	tooth	18	0.6	costume	9	0.3
science	43	1.4	math	11	0.4	big_bang	9	0.3
amazing	44	1.4	Islamic	11	0.4	Hollywood	9	0.3
shit	49	1.6	gravity	11	0.4	scientific	10	0.3
fuck	43	1.4	Starfire	11	0.4	fantasy	10	0.3
atheists	22	0.7	Josh_Feuerstein	11	0.4	penis	8	0.3
kinda	23	0.8	accident	21	0.7	creator	8	0.3
women	52	1.7	bullshit	13	0.4	I_believe	11	0.4
Christians	25	0.8	this	296	9.7	woman	26	0.8
feminist	26	0.8	Jesus	25	0.8	story	21	0.7
jokes	23	0.8	believing	13	0.4	sex	12	0.4
guy	36	1.2	gender	12	0.4	knowledge	16	0.5
raped	18	0.6	evolutionary	12	0.4	tv	8	0.3
theory	24	0.8	anyone	33	1.1	Islam	8	0.3
guys	22	0.7	somehow	17	0.6	I_guess	8	0.3
created	25	0.8	Internet	10	0.3	victim	9	0.3
Bible	23	0.8	Ebola	10	0.3	exist	14	0.5
fairy	16	0.5	atheism	10	0.3	moron	7	0.2
because	153	5.0	accidental	10	0.3	magical	7	0.2
even	68	2.2	comic	12	0.4	gay	7	0.2
NFL	13	0.4	peace	15	0.5	evolved	7	0.2
videos	20	0.7	sexual	13	0.4	elevator	7	0.2
life	41	1.3	earth	22	0.7	douchebag	7	0.2
Wiles	12	0.4	sexist	10	0.3	deep_down	7	0.2
comics	12	0.4	hit_on	9	0.3	cosmic	7	0.2
Kevin_Sorbo	12	0.4	Josh_Moronstein	9	0.3	YouTube	7	0.2
Greta	12	0.4						

opposing point of view (like "accident/accidental," "created/creator," "magical," "fantasy," "believing," "tooth" "fairy," and "story") showing hallmarks of both scientific and humanistic atheism (LeDrew, 2012). Knowing the background of the conflict, these words are not surprising given the nature of the videos in the dataset being aimed at Feuerstein and his criticism of "evolution" as science (with "science" and "evolution" also appearing in Feuerstein's keywords).

Many more of the words, including "Greta," "feminist," "jokes," "raped," "Kevin_Sorbo," "[Rick] Wiles," and "NFL" reflect the topic of specific videos. More than Feuerstein and Fontain, theamazingatheist's videos address specific issues that arise in the news or online, and the responses reflect the content of the news story on which theamazingatheist is commenting. For example, "Kevin Sorbo" is a celebrity who criticized atheists, and whom theamazingatheist responded to in a single video. This approach to making videos is a key part of being a professional YouTuber, particularly one whose channel is not about their daily life. theamazingatheist's videos addresses topics that are likely to drive traffic to his videos, including stories that are in the news and are potentially related to his persona as someone who challenges Christianity and popular culture in general. This means less consistency in topics video to video, and videos that might draw interest from the audience in and of themselves. Unlike Fontain, there is not an overarching mission and message to his work.

Compared to Feuerstein's talk, there is a marked difference in words with negative valence, reflecting what discourse analysis has already showed. His interaction with others, particularly with Feuerstein, is marked by negativity and insults, revealing the persona that theamazingatheist performs in his videos. He is aggressive and antagonistic and part of his appeal is his ability to attack others. This seems to be particularly successful when he focuses on Feuerstein, given the comments on videos addressing or mocking Feuerstein. Unlike Fontain and Feuerstein, the main focus of theamazingatheist's videos appears to be less on making arguments for atheism and more on engaging viewers on a variety of different topics from a particular ideological perspective.

Swear words are also prevalent in theamazingatheist's talk, particularly compared to Feuerstein and Fontain's talk who do not swear seemingly as a part of their performance of religiosity. For theamazingatheist, the use of swear words contributes to his persona of irreverence. By swearing, he draws a clear contrast between himself and the religious users and positions himself as an antihero, someone who rejects cultural norms and expectations. This effect is heightened when speaking to religious communities and about religious topics. At the same time, because YouTube does not place restrictions on the use of swear words in videos, the effect is perhaps diluted in his videos in a larger context where swearing is not uncommon.

While these lists of keywords show deviations among the users, they also show a substantial amount of overlap. This is unsurprising, given the nature of the data collection, which focused on gathering videos of users interacting with each other. Users, in their responses, do not stray far from the topics of the videos to which they are responding. Rather than using their responses to stage completely new arguments, they serve the purpose of refuting what the first user has said. The content of the first video is treated as an invitation for the presentation of a counter point, and though the user might take an opposing position, the content of the response is still bound by the previous video. A Christian response to an atheist video must, in some way, engage the topic of evolution. The result is an increased centrality of science in interaction between users.

5.2 Themes and Keywords in Comments

Building on the keyword analysis, patterns can be observed in how and when different topics emerge and what this shows about the discourse. Keyword analysis focuses on what is present in the discourse, but what is absent can often raise certain questions about why users are creating the content that they are and to what effect. For John Fontain, his presentation of an Islamic outreach message can be seen in the keywords which relate to Islam and, in particular "dawah." However, what he almost exclusively avoids is a discussion of a political perspective on Islam, with the word "terrorist" only appearing two times in the videos in the dataset, in comments about how his own perception before reversion that all Muslims were terrorists and perceptions from his parents that he would become a terrorist if he reverted. In both cases, the topic of terrorism is not addressed beyond this, and Fontain's videos avoid the topic as rule. Instead, there is a clear attempt to present Islam in a positive light, with statements like, "If we truly believe that this is the final message from Allah then we have to share this beautiful religion" (2014.07.16 JFo Video). The emphasis is on the positive nature of following Allah, with little focus on judgment or negative descriptions of humans without God.

Looking at the whole of the comments corpus does, however, mask that some videos received more comments than others. Figure 5.1 shows the distribution across Fontain's videos from the dataset, with one representing the oldest video in the dataset and 21 representing the newest (see Appendix for full list of videos).

As Figure 5.1 shows, a majority of Fontain's videos received less than 100 comments, with only seven videos above 100. The two videos receiving the most comments (2,161 and 867, respectively) are *BRITAIN FIRST Invade Manchester Mega Mosque! – ITS GONE TOO FAR! – John Fontain*, and *Dear Joshua Feuerstein Muslim Response John Fontain*. In *BRITAIN FIRST*

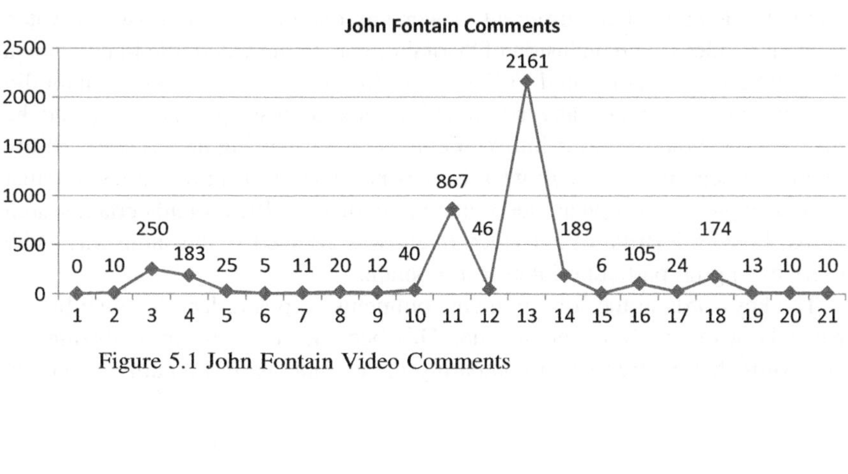

Figure 5.1 John Fontain Video Comments

Invade Manchester Mega Mosque! – ITS GONE TOO FAR! – John Fontain, Fontain pretends to be a member of the far-right British political party "britain First" who enters a mosque in Manchester to expose Muslims as being anti-British but is instead welcomed by a Muslim man who invites Fontain back to his house for curry. It parodies in some ways a viral video that appeared around the same time, which showed two white British men driving through a Muslim-majority neighborhood in the UK and referring to it as a "no-go" zone. Fontain's video was posted on May 16, 2014, and as a parody is meant to represent that fear of Muslims by Britain First as unfounded and show that British Muslims are warm and welcoming to white British people.

Between the two videos, they represent 72 percent of the comments on the dataset and create a challenge in interpreting the keywords analysis. Fontain regularly does not receive large numbers of comments, but when touching on issues that could be seen as controversial, many more commenters appear. His *BRITAIN FIRST Invade Manchester Mega Mosque! – ITS GONE TOO FAR! – John Fontain* video is not explicitly an attack on Britain First, but an attempt to position Muslims as warm and welcoming to everyone. The positioning of Muslims in this way, however, subsequently positions Britain First members as ignorant, angry, and full of unfounded suspicions. Although Fontain presents his portrayal of Britain First as a kind of parody, it is a malignant positioning that encourages others to treat the members of Britain First negatively and discount their opinions.

For Fontain, his appearance as a white British man, and particularly his red hair, becomes a way of mocking him in the video comments as well, with the word "ginger" appearing 66 times in the comments, 54 occurring on the parody video of Britain First. For the commenters, Fontain's commitment to Islam as a white British man makes him a "traitor" to Britain, with users writing "Shut up you traitorous ginger wanna-be arab!" and "a ginger Muslim, you should be ashamed of yourself." The overwhelming negative response is surprising given the lack of the same level of negativity on other videos. The responses suggest that the video attracted a different viewership, one that does not usually watch Fontain's videos. The inclusion of "Britain First" in the video title likely drew a different audience compared to Fontain's other videos. Moreover, Fontain did not subsequently make any additional videos addressing this topic, and he manages to avoid the same influx of comments suggesting he has some ability to control negativity through what is or is not discussed. In the same way that theamazingatheist's topical videos attempt to drive traffic around certain search terms, Fontain's Britain First video likely was affected in the same way, with users having no particular interest in Fontain.

The keywords in the John Fontain comments corpus reflect this distribution and take a markedly different tone. This becomes clear when analyzing the keywords that emerge when comparing the comments on Fontain's videos to the video transcripts. Looking at the top 100 keywords compared to the reference corpus, the comments on Fontain's videos have a clear sense of the negativity that does not exist in the video transcripts. The 4,196 comments collected from the 21 YouTube videos that are included in the dataset comprise 227,797 words. The top 100 keywords, the number of occurrences, and normalized occurrences (per 1000 words) are presented in Table 5.4.

This table, showing the top 100 keywords in columns from right to left, includes verbs like "hate" and "kill" as well as number of examples of profanity that don't occur in Fontain's videos. While Fontain generally keeps a positive

Table 5.4 *Keywords in John Fontain Comments*

you	5326	23.4	religions	149	0.7	pbuh	80	0.4
Islam	1142	5.0	that	3146	13.8	how	482	2.1
God	1474	6.5	Christian	214	0.9	kill	147	0.6
Jesus	990	4.3	science	162	0.7	NAME	83	0.4
Muslims	772	3.4	does	451	2.0	says	246	1.1
Allah	609	2.7	Jews	170	0.7	NAME	77	0.3
Muslim	615	2.7	who	1079	4.7	video	133	0.6
u	615	2.7	NAME	118	0.5	ignorant	84	0.4
religion	624	2.7	ur	121	0.5	guys	88	0.4
your	1538	6.8	Fontain	108	0.5	evil	111	0.5
do	1672	7.3	Islamic	139	0.6	cant	73	0.3
Quran	412	1.8	son	267	1.2	killed	154	0.7
is	4552	10.0	stupid	145	0.6	NAME	71	0.3
Bible	396	1.7	faith	152	0.7	they	1409	6.2
prophet	342	1.5	NAME	104	0.5	heaven	85	0.4
Muhammad	293	1.3	fucking	131	0.6	religious	139	0.6
believe	525	2.3	if	974	4.3	Satan	69	0.3
not	2275	10.0	NAME	100	0.4	NAME	69	0.3
people	971	4.3	Christianity	133	0.6	NAME	69	0.3
I	3055	3.4	hate	141	0.6	verses	74	0.3
what	1164	5.1	fuck	111	0.5	me	702	3.1
Christians	254	1.1	prophets	94	0.4	etc	116	0.5
so	1075	4.7	all	1120	4.9	man	382	1.7
lol	206	0.9	im	95	0.4	peace	214	0.9
are	2331	0.2	am	300	1.3	thats	67	0.3
evolution	215	0.9	respect	133	0.6	book	229	1.0
say	529	2.3	read	211	0.9	Pentecostal	69	0.3
why	499	2.2	them	757	3.3	Mohammed	69	0.3
know	557	2.4	shit	101	0.4	idiot	73	0.3
John	216	0.9	saying	200	0.9	heaven	85	0.4
like	773	3.4	worship	117	0.5	about	683	3.0
truth	255	1.1	no	787	3.5	true	215	0.9
because	540	2.4	Quran	80	0.4	slaves	72	0.3
just	684	3.0						

tone and avoids political arguments, the comments section often returns to more negative themes. This is confirmed when comparing not just the keywords, but the key semantic fields in WMatrix including Violent/Angry, Crime, Dead, and Unethical appear in the top 10 fields. There is also an interesting collection of words related to argumentation and science, including "evolution," "fact/facts," "science/scientific," "respect," "ignorant," "idiot," "against," "false," "ignorance," "clearly," and "lies." While Fontain presents his videos as an invitation to or description of Muslim life, the commenters respond with arguments for and against certain points, including issues that are only marginally mentioned in the text. For example, Fontain's brief gesture of giving a "thumbs up" when responding to Feuerstein's comment that "Evolution is not a science" results in arguments about the validity of evolution as science in the comments section of the video. The topic itself is almost completely absent from Fontain's video discourse, but "science" is a keyword in Fontain's comments.

Despite the language of violence in comments, the discussion does not explicitly orient toward terrorism. When the focus of the comments is on violence, it is about violence in general in religion and in Islam specifically. Terrorist attacks are mentioned by name in the comments, including "7/7," "9/11," and "Lee Rigby" (a British solider murdered by a terrorist), but none of the specific terrorist events become the topic of discussion in the comments. Instead, they are represented as iconic examples of violence. This may, however, show the effect of the video topics, and Fontain's focus on dawah. The audience that his videos attract are more focused on the topics that Fontain himself addresses in his videos. At the same time, "dawah" is absent from the comments keywords, despite being in the top ten keywords in Fontain's talk. Commenters do not use the comments to discuss dawah more broadly or share their own experiences of dawah.

"Religion" and "religions" occur a combined 773 times in the comments and represent a focus on the negativity of religion generally, not just Islam. The majority of the 773 uses in the comments are negative, while Fontain tends to speak about "religion" with a positive or neutral valence. When the commenters are positive, they are often in response to negative depictions of religion in general or Islam in particular. For example, when one commenter writes "Religion is poison . . . " a second user responds, "Islam is peace." The comments continue with the first commenter responding and a third user joining in:

User 1: Evidence doesn't support your statement, friend . . .
All religions claim "Peace" . . . None of their track records support that and the fundamental doctrines of Christianity, Judaism and Islam divides people . . . Peace isn't compatible with bronze and iron age bullshit where the main character of their fictional "holy books" is a war god . . .

User 3: Atheism is a poison. What do you expect from some creatures who deny the mercy of Allah who created them? They don't even confess that there is a creature! I don't blame them all, but I put the blame of some people who attack others who love ALLAH! Okay NAME! What is your evidence that God does not exist? (2014.04.08–2 JFo Video Comments)

The comment "Religion is poison" and its explication show a lumping together of all religions into the same category. The counterpoint to this is not that religion is good and useful, but that atheism is actually "poison." The structure is symmetrical. Importantly, these comments don't all appear to be the result of users simply "trolling" the video – that is, leaving antagonistic comments without any orientation to the topic of the video. It is a genuine discussion with users arguing back and forth over particular points.

The responses to Fontain in his Britain First video and Feuerstein's lack of further engagement when Fontain responds to the *Dear Mr. Muslim* video suggest that the conciliatory tact is not necessarily effective in leading to more positive interaction between Muslims and non-Muslims. Even though Fontain positions himself and other Muslims in a non-violent way, users respond by making the opposite argument, claiming that Islam is not in fact peaceful. This pattern can also be seen in the following exemplar comments, one promoting Islam as a "religion of peace" and one challenging the same assertion:

we are very much thankful to ALLAH that HE Has made us Muslims that too from the ummah of prophet Muhammad (peace and blessings of ALLAH be on him). Islam is a religion of peace. it gives solutions to every problem with which man is grappling right now and as well as through history and future as well. (2014.08.30 JFo Video Comments)

Over 18,000 terror attacks in the past 10 years in the name of allah
Yea, religion of my peace my ass. (2014.06.01 JFo Video Comments)

These two comments show how claims and opposing claims are made with evidence to support them. The arguments that follow reveal that Fontain's videos attract a mixed audience of viewers, including Christians, atheists, and Muslims, all of whom are present in the comments. Fontain attempts to present Islam in a particular way, with a focus on dawah and generally positive descriptions of the faith which avoid discussions of terrorism or more controversial issues. When he does touch on the topic, the result is a deluge of criticism with users engaging in larger sociopolitical issues about the role of Islam in the UK and the perceived threat on British culture that users supporting Britain First present. The two comments above highlight again the difficulty of moving conversations forward in these arguments where users respond point-by-point with set counternarratives that, in the case of attacks on Islam as a religion of violence, go back for centuries.

While Fontain makes a clear effort to avoid topics like extremism in his videos, other Muslim personalities on YouTube are less reticent about addressing the topic. Shabir Ally often speaks about political issues, including terrorism specifically, on his TV show *Let the Quran Speak*. There has been increased interest in the role of social media in radicalization, but users like Fontain, by not addressing the issue, explicitly position themselves in a storyline that does not include violence, either in opposing or supporting it. Ally's teaching and representation of Islam follows a more holistic approach, addressing issues of citizenship in particular as they relate to Canadian life, where he is based. Fontain, however, is more focused on spreading dawah, which he represents as international and universal, posting videos from a variety of international locations, and speaking to people in Sierra Leone, the UK, the USA, and Brazil, all with the same message.

How commenters respond to Fontain reveals some of the preconditions of talking about Islam as category of belief on social media in 2014. This can be seen, for example, with the appearance of "Jews" and "Israel" in the keywords list. While Fontain makes only two passing references to people as Jews and makes no comments about the State of Israel, "Israel" appears 93 times in the comments of Fontain's videos, while "Jew" and "Jews" combine for 225 occurrences. These comments suggest that the video topic does not necessarily guarantee that the content of the comments will follow this same topic. Instead, the comments, particularly when the videos address controversial issues, can reveal preexisting concepts and feelings about Islam and its role in the world.

The analysis highlights another way in which context collapse on social media problematizes user's imagined audience. Content creators must appeal to a diverse audience, with a multiplicity of actual viewers, while at the same time maintaining their own voice and vision. While Fontain might want to avoid discussions of religious extremism and violence, they come up in the comments, particularly when he makes an effort to challenge an entity that is politically opposed to him (like Britain First). Fontain does very occasionally respond in the comments section, but they again reflect his overall mission of spreading dawah, asking users to message him with questions and explicitly telling users he will not respond when it is clear they are not arguing in good faith.

While Fontain's themes and comments suggest attempts to avoid controversy, theamazingatheist, as we have so far seen, readily courts it. The topics of his videos have a less consistent thread, owing to his interest in creating popular content that can be picked up in searches of current events. theamazingatheist's model requires engagement with his videos to increase his visibility and ultimately, his revenue on the site. As a result of this greater visibility, his videos attract more interest with higher viewership and more

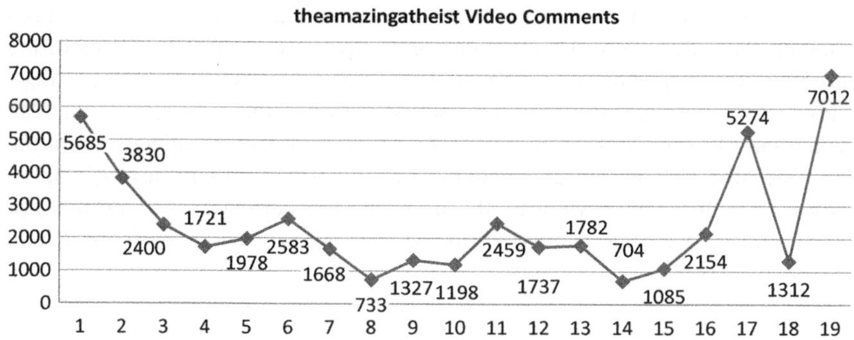

Figure 5.2 theamazingatheist's Video Comments

commenters. theamazingatheist also benefits from his antagonistic approach when it comes to driving interest in his videos, as taking a controversial stance is likely to draw negative attention from at least one audience, leading to more comments on the video. Whether or not these comments are positive is of little importance, particularly in cultivating an image as an antagonist to people in power.

The distribution of comments on theamazingatheist's videos is therefore more consistent when compared to Fontain, with fewer outliers, as seen in Figure 5.2.

Unlike Fontain's videos, there is a smaller deviation between theamazingatheist's comments, with 1,198 comments on the least commented on video and 7,012 on the most. The top three videos include responses to Feuerstein, showing that for theamazingatheist, as he says, attacking Feuerstein is good business and plays importantly into his "brand" of theamazingatheist, one that he explicitly cultivates and maintains. As a longtime, professional YouTuber, theamazingatheist takes more care in the consistency and quality of his uploads and does not have, like Fontain, videos with a wide range of scenery and formats. His videos are much more disciplined, with either scripted or semi-structured content keeping him focused.

The result, the comments count show, is more consistent engagement. Although some videos do better than others in terms of views and comments, how and why videos come to be successful is something theamazingatheist specifically discusses, as he does in talking about the usefulness of Feuerstein for him as a figure to attack. This contrasts starkly with Fontain and Feuerstein who, to a certain extent, avoid explicit discussion of generating interest in their videos and do not appear to want any attention drawn to their own popularity. Nonetheless, Feuerstein over the six months of observation and following his videos about theamazingatheist appeared to have grown more consistent in the types of content he developed.

Given the comparative consistency of the comments, the corpus of theamazingatheist is less skewed toward one or two particular videos in terms of the numbers of comments, although as the analysis of keywords in the videos showed, the absence of a specific word or words in the reference corpus can potentially lead to some false flags. The 48,414 comments collected from the 19 YouTube videos that are included in the dataset compromise 2,355,873 words. The top 100 keywords, the number of occurrences, and normalized occurrences (per 1000 words) from the comments corpus are presented in Table 5.5.

Table 5.5 *Keywords in theamazingatheist's Comments*

you	51994	22.1	about	9089	3.9	did	5825	2.5
I	46039	19.5	actually	3100	1.3	comment	1283	0.5
do	19561	8.3	Christians	2180	0.9	amazing	1115	0.5
God	10707	4.5	fuck	2022	0.9	Christianity	1152	0.5
that	44759	19.0	stupid	2197	0.9	person	1879	0.8
just	12214	5.2	evidence	3036	1.3	am	2596	1.1
is	45846	19.5	universe	1952	0.8	Josh	983	0.4
people	11117	4.7	say	4709	2.0	belief	1223	0.5
it	37241	15.8	Christian	2379	1.0	bullshit	897	0.4
because	8275	3.5	really	3614	1.5	proof	1219	0.5
believe	5972	2.5	theory	2264	1.0	scientific	1154	0.5
your	11868	5.0	wrong	2658	1.1	can	9456	4.0
evolution	4007	1.7	someone	2375	1.0	logic	1027	0.4
religion	4041	1.7	saying	2504	1.1	feminist	909	0.4
atheist	3452	1.5	lol	1444	0.6	beliefs	1000	0.4
does	6789	2.9	get	4121	1.7	im	828	0.4
what	11846	5.0	something	3554	1.5	videos	1044	0.4
if	12949	5.5	religious	1954	0.8	feminists	927	0.4
not	21081	8.9	exist	1791	0.8	feminism	829	0.4
video	3457	1.5	argument	1742	0.7	read	1672	0.7
like	8843	3.8	rape	1430	0.6	yeah	1090	0.5
science	3143	1.3	faith	1611	0.7	trying	1720	0.7
why	5698	2.4	thing	2712	1.2	true	2052	0.9
fucking	2913	1.2	things	3089	1.3	Big_Bang	773	0.3
so	10344	4.4	they	14680	6.2	hate	1078	0.5
how	7178	3.0	no	7957	3.4	reason	1755	0.7
know	6156	2.6	Jesus	1500	0.6	idiot	805	0.3
Bible	2858	1.2	atheism	1187	0.5	life	2977	1.3
think	5510	2.3	want	3406	1.4	prove	1309	0.6
shit	2413	1.0	Islam	1178	0.5	real	1898	0.8
are	21788	9.2	even	4407	1.9	anything	1780	0.8
atheists	2258	1.0	understand	2040	0.9	anyone	1381	0.6
guy	2375	1.0	me	7085	3.0			
TJ	2140	0.9						

Compared with the keywords in theamazingatheist's videos, there appear to be fewer key differences between the comments and video content. Keywords related to religion and theology (e.g., "God," "believer," "religion," and "atheist") are present, along with technology and science (e.g., "evolution," "science," and "universe"), swearing (e.g.,"shit," "fucking," "fuck," and "bullshit"), insults (e.g., "stupid" and "idiot"), and argumentation (e.g., "evidence," "theory," "wrong," "argument," and "prove"), all of which are also key fields and topics for the whole of the comments corpus. These findings support the earlier suggestion from the discourse analysis that theamazingatheist's representation of himself and atheists as logical, sane, and based in science is a position held and maintained by his viewers. The commenters as well take up this same mantle of logic and argumentation.

Several outliers in the keywords also give a sense of the topics of the videos. One that I alluded to above, when looking at the keywords for theamazingatheist, included the keywords "Greta," "feminist," "jokes," and "raped." Keywords related to this topic also appear in the comments, with particularly high occurrences of "rape" (1,430) and "feminist," "feminists," and "feminism" (909, 927, and 829, respectively). These reflect comments on two of theamazingatheist videos *Rape, Feminism, and The Amazing Atheist* and *Not A Feminist, Not A Sexist* (which had 2,459 comments and 1,327 comments, respectively). Moreover, "rape joke/s" occurred 199 times, reflecting the very specific argument that occurred among commenters about whether or not theamazingatheist's "joke" about the raping of a feminist critic was appropriate or not.

The inclusion of swearing in the top keywords does suggest that commenters on theamazingatheist's videos are potentially more antagonistic and negative, although the presence of swearing is not always negative in online discourse (Pihlaja, 2016a) and may also say more about the absence of swearing in the reference corpus. However, compared to the Feuerstein comment corpus the words "fucking," "shit," "fuck," and "bullshit" are still in the top 100 keywords and their use regularly carries a negative valence with users employing profanity to attack others' positions as in "this guy is a fucking idiot" and "Oh my fucking god. This Josh guy is fucking special." The use of profanity in this way does, however, seem to be a function of YouTube comments and my earlier work has also found similar patterns in YouTube comments section (Pihlaja, 2014a). The comments on Feuerstein's videos on Facebook have simply far less profanity and when it is present, it can garner responses like, "You should apologize to the public and restrain from making comments if you're going to use profanity. God bless you."

The inclusion of words related to the theme of "science" is also interesting in comparison to Feuerstein's comments corpus, the user whom theamazingatheist addresses most in the dataset. While "evolution" is not in the top ten keywords compared to the BNC, it is the top keyword when compared to the

Feuerstein comments, occurring 4,007 or .17 times per 100 words compared to 5 or .01 times per 100 words. This suggests a difference in focus in discourse around religious belief between theamazingatheist and Feuerstein, with the comments on theamazingatheist's videos focused on evidence and science as it relates to religious belief and Feuerstein's commenters focusing more on religious experience and the practice of religious faith.

Like theamazingatheist, Feuerstein's comments are also more consistent than Fontain's, with the most commented video receiving 941 comments and the least comments a video received at 61. The increase in video comments over time also reflects the growing interest in Feuerstein's page, beginning around the time when Feuerstein first engaged theamazingatheist around the end of May and beginning of June 2014 (Videos 9–11 in Figure 5.3). The videos collected in the dataset then show a steady increase in Feuerstein's viewership, with Feuerstein's most commented on video in the dataset occurring on September 29, 2014 with the description "Wow!!! Some SCARY SCARY truth about why we as Americans are not really free and why the world could END for us TOMORROW!!!!" Like Fontain, the engagement with a controversial political issue (in this case, food supply and policy) draws more interest than his more positive videos.

Like Fontain's most commented on video, Feuerstein is also successful in attracting views through engaging in political discussions, in this case discussing food supply and arguing that a single corporation controls the ability to produce food. The video highlights Feuerstein's political interests, which unlike Fontain's video parodying "Britain First" does not appear to have an explicit religious message, but instead focuses on the importance of the "free society" for Americans and saying, "Let's start doing something about this.

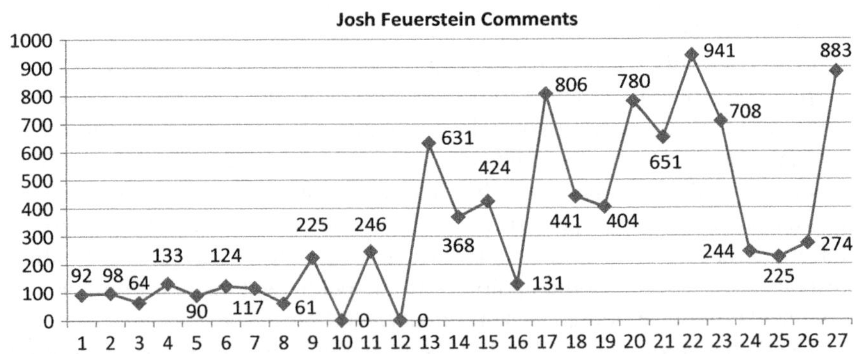

Figure 5.3 Josh Feuerstein Comments
NB: the videos that received "0" comments were from re-uploaded videos which did not appear on Feuerstein's own page.

We have to change the world." What this action is, however, is not clear, and the specific issue of food security does not appear to be a recurring concern for Feuerstein, either in the dataset or in subsequent videos. Instead, it represents a broader political position about "freedom."

The 8,278 comments collected from the 27 Facebook videos that are included in the dataset compromise 185,936 words. The top 100 keywords, the number of occurrences, and normalized occurrences (per 1000 words) appear in Table 5.6.

Table 5.6 *Keywords in Josh Feuerstein's Comments*

you	4863	26.2	word	289	1.6	someone	176	0.9
God	2002	10.8	that	2730	14.7	need	359	1.9
amen	1358	7.3	is	3072	16.5	weed	88	0.5
I	4901	26.4	does	437	2.4	prayers	99	0.5
thank_you	1062	5.7	really	344	1.9	wrong	188	1.0
your	1556	8.4	hear	269	1.4	how	431	2.3
love	820	4.4	am	331	1.8	amazing	95	0.5
bless	560	3.0	because	450	2.4	bro	76	0.4
do	1565	8.4	please	244	1.3	keep	211	1.1
Bible	529	2.8	it	2596	14.0	if	777	4.2
u	500	2.7	like	617	3.3	things	248	1.3
Josh	406	2.2	Christian	182	1.0	lord	199	1.1
Jesus	434	2.3	ur	119	0.6	person	170	0.9
me	1147	6.2	religion	148	0.8	read	168	0.9
so	1152	6.2	praying	121	0.7	Joshua_Feuerstein	68	0.4
thanks	369	2.0	truth	193	1.0	marijuana	72	0.4
my	1243	6.7	life	369	2.0	get	303	1.6
needed	452	2.4	atheist	109	0.6	heaven	81	0.4
just	819	4.4	sin	118	0.6	dude	66	0.4
this	1930	10.4	smoking	129	0.7	are	1531	8.2
what	1008	5.4	Christ	130	0.7	seeds	82	0.4
Joshua	195	1.0	pray	253	1.4	heaven	81	0.4
know	565	3.0	im	103	0.6	thats	62	0.3
pot	206	1.1	wow	105	0.6	good	366	2.0
people	774	4.2	prayer	142	0.8	shall	200	1.1
videos	227	1.2	why	356	1.9	preach	68	0.4
message	264	1.4	true	249	1.3	science	86	0.5
awesome	191	1.0	say	361	1.9	Iraq	78	0.4
Christians	204	1.1	thank	127	0.7	all	871	4.7
video	232	1.2	faith	133	0.7	sharing	91	0.5
brother	332	1.8	not	1447	7.8	bad	141	0.8
believe	341	1.8	man	391	2.1	words	191	1.0
lol	158	0.8	lord	199	1.1			
guy	176	0.9	right	348	1.9			

The theme of "gratefulness" emerges in the top 100 keywords, with phrases like "amen," "thank_you," and "thanks" occurring in comments praising Feuerstein and thanking him for his videos. The words "message" and "word" and "words" relate to positive evaluations of Feuerstein's videos as do "awesome," "amazing," "good" and "wow," which shows that positivity can be extended from the video content to the video comments, including the word "bless" which Feuerstein regularly repeats. Like theamazingatheist's commenters who match the negative tone of many of his videos, the commenters on Feuerstein pages match the encouraging tone of the video, with few attacks on others and a clear trend toward positivity. The inclusion of "needed" also shows how users describe Feuerstein's message as something they "needed to hear." The keywords suggest that the anecdotal evidence of positivity and thankfulness for Feuerstein is shared by many users.

As with the other videos, there is also the presence of words related to topics specific to video content that might seem otherwise out of place, namely "weed," "marijuana," and "smoking" which come from the final video in the Feuerstein corpus with the description: "POT SMOKING ATHEIST turns CHRISTIAN and BAPTIZED in JESUS NAME! #60seconds #churchofchampions #boom #GODSNOTDEAD." With the focus on both atheism and smoking pot, a large number of comments addressing the issue and challenging Feuerstein appear, providing further evidence that when controversial topics come up, users are more likely to engage in arguments. These controversies are also more likely to attract users who might take an opposing view, particularly when a specific group (like atheists) are explicitly called out in the title or description of the video.

Different grammatical forms of "pray" occur a cumulative 628 times and show a focus on the action of "praying" and requests for prayer by the commenters on the videos. The collocation of "I pray" is often followed by a specific goal for prayer, as seen in the following comments taken from the Feuerstein comments corpus:

> I am praying for you, and for the ones that are so blind. I pray their eyes will be opened. I pray their eyes will be opened.
> I pray for [Iraqi Christians] every day.
> I pray you are encouraged
> I pray that the holy spirit imparts wisdom
> Please pray for are troops every where
> I have a wonderful man, I pray that every woman finds her wonderful man!
> I pray to God every night to save this world!

For these commenters, prayer has a clear focus and goal (for encouragement or imparting wisdom) and/or is regarding specific people or issues (for Iraqi

Christians or "our troops"). The goals of the prayers are often nonspecific and do not necessarily have clear outcomes. Instead, like Feuerstein's videos, they often address difficulties in a general way. Asking for and receiving prayer represents a unique practice in the Feuerstein comment corpus and a similar practice is not present in Fontain's comments or discourse, although "prayer" is discussed in general terms and Fontain encourages users to "make dua" (the Arabic word for prayer) to discern the will of Allah.

Users also offer prayers of support for others in the comments:

User 1: Joshua my sister has been mass uo [messed up] on pill for a couple yrs now and last night she got arrested she has really hit rock bottom bad can you please pray for her
User 2: Prayers of healing and guidance. I pray God will change her habits and heal her spirit. in Jesus name I pray, amen.
User 1: Thank you so much my nephew is having a hard time in kife he is only 7 and father in prison for 15 yrs and no mother basically I don't know what to do (2014.09.26 JF Video Comments)

In this exchange, the first commenter appears to be asking Feuerstein to pray for their sister. Instead of Feuerstein, a second commenter responds praying for the woman. Within an hour, the specific request is met with a specific response, with the user following typical spoken prayer structure in her comment. The response both meets the need of the first user and publicly displays empathy toward User 1, and User 1 subsequently responds with a further request that had received no response at the time of data collection, despite the comment suggesting that the user was in need of further support. There appears to be little ongoing interaction between users on Feuerstein's Facebook page that might constitute a community in the way that might be seen in other online contexts.

The engagement with Feuerstein's videos is both affected by Feuerstein's decision to post them on Facebook and Christian practices around prayer. The users on Feuerstein's videos are engaged with the message and demonstrate affiliation with the message. These practices for affiliation are similar to offline practices of offering words of support or praying for one another. The keywords, however, fail to capture an important element of Feuerstein's comments: the tagging of other users. Throughout Feuerstein's comments, users regularly type the name of other users ("tagging" them) so that a notification will appear when they access Facebook and their attention will be drawn to the video. Tagging other users is a prevalent practice on the page, with the comment tagging a user often then being "liked" by the tagged user, suggesting that they have seen the comment. These can also develop into interaction in the comments sections, with the "tagged" user offering thanks to the user who has tagged them.

This practice of tagging other users serves a function similar to that of saying that one is praying for another user. It allows the user to show empathy for another and do so in a public way, which the tagged user can then acknowledge by "liking" the comment. By tagging others, the viewer performs care for others and draws attention to the video, serving Feuerstein's purposes and further publicizing the video. The videos are also regularly shared, with comments and likes appearing on the shared video of other users and generating more interest and views for the video as it moves across Facebook. Commenting then serves the further purposes of Feuerstein, by spreading the content to new users, and commenters, who gain social capital for displaying concern and empathy for their friends without necessarily displaying the video in their own newsfeed.

The one-off responses and the lack of responses when users state specific needs (as in the user above not knowing what to do in the face of difficulty) suggests that while users might display affinity for and affiliation with Feuerstein's message, little meaningful engagement occurs beyond one-off comments and minimal engagement with others. Importantly, Feuerstein himself is not involved in the comments sections and there is no suggestion from the site that Feuerstein is doing anything more than reading the comments (which he reports doing). While users ask specifically for Feuerstein's prayers or support, it is not clear that he ever explicitly offers it to his viewers, and maintains a clear one-to-many relationship with his viewers through a focus on making videos and sharing links, rather than responding to users publicly. There is also little evidence that Feuerstein is privately responding to users as he makes no mention of communicating with his viewers and the viewers in the comments do not regularly suggest that they have spoken with him privately. Instead, the comments serve a purpose for users to thank Feuerstein and share the video with friends, occasionally engaging in further interaction.

This use of comments contrasts with the evidence from the YouTube pages. Although users on theamazingatheist's videos do praise his videos, there is not a function of tagging others in the comments, beyond responding to people who have already commented. theamazingatheist's approach to making videos, without addressing the individual viewer or attempting to speak to their experience, leads to comments sections that are much more oriented toward the topic of the video. The kinds of comments that follow from a video appears to then be a mix of topic and approach to video production, as well as the platform where the video is posted. Both the nature of the platform and theamazingatheist's use of it do not encourage similar displays of support.

While the data suggests a great deal of overall positivity on Feuerstein's pages, this does not always appear to be the case when clicking on the comments section of a video. Often, negative comments can rise to the top of a section (which features the most "liked" comment first) and while a majority of the comments might be positive, if one negative comment appears and is liked by several users, it can gain prominence. Users respond to this hate, however, with comments like "Why are people hating on this message.? It's not bashing atheists so why are you still here? Obviously you don't have a life" which garners supportive comments like "As for Atheists, I think they're so desperate to prove themselves right that they attack anything they can in anyway the can." The comments can and do draw attention, but Feuerstein's supporters are quick to respond with messages supporting Feuerstein, leading to their prominence when looking at the whole of the comments corpus.

The analysis of keywords and themes provides a macro-snapshot of the different channels. However, given the nature of the data collection, topics from specific videos and inconsistencies in the numbers of comments lead to false flags, including uncommon names or word types that are underrepresented in the reference corpus. This is particularly an issue when it relates to discourse about Islam, where words that appear in Fontain's keyword list – particularly the Arabic phrases – simply do not appear in the reference corpus. While they appear as especially "key" given their relative prevalence in the videos, the keyword analysis also shows the underrepresentation of Muslim speakers in the reference corpus.

5.3 Registers

The keyword lists showed how Feuerstein's and Fontain's language makes use of words and phrases from Christian and Muslim belief, respectively. While in all three spoken corpora, the semantic domain of "religion and the supernatural" had a high keyness when compared to the Spoken BNC, this provides little insight into how the language of religion is used. Indeed, keyness analysis shows how the same words (e.g., God) can appear across the different corpora, sometimes with very different meanings. The clearest and most striking example of a community-specific register occurs throughout John Fontain's videos. Fontain regularly uses Arabic phrases, as do the people that he interviews and this becomes an important part of how he represents himself and others in his videos. These phrases include inshallah ("if God wills), subanallah ("glory to God"), alhamdulillah ("praise be to God"), and mashallah ("God has willed it"), all of which appear in the top 100 keywords when compared to the BNC spoken corpus and Feuerstein's and theamazingatheist's videos.

These so-called Allah expressions (Piamenta, 1979) permeate Arabic language and interaction (Morrow, 2006), and Clift and Helani's (2010) study of "inshallah," for example, shows how the phrase can be used in Arabic talk to signal topic-transition sequences. These phrases act as discourse markers in Fontain and other Muslim's discourse when they are talking with one another. The use of the phrases position the speakers both in terms of their semantic value which shows an orientation to Allah and his will, and as discourse markers, ordering what is being said and showing affiliation and agreement with others. Clift and Helani (2010) citing Abboud (1988) and Gilesnan (2000) suggest that in Arabic, these "Allah expressions" do not necessarily denote religious affiliation because they cannot be avoided in Arabic. In the context of English language conversation, however, their use can mark affiliation and religious faith.

In Fontain's videos, Arabic phrases routinely occur at the end or beginning of clauses and act a way of signposting what has been said or what is coming. Fontain uses it when describing how his own life and dawah are guided, saying, for example,

> I went into the shop
> to get some more books
> and subanallah
> there is a sister looking at the Qur'ans
>
> (2014.06.14 JFo Video)

In cases like this, Fontain uses "subanallah" (glory to God) to mark that what proceeds and follows in his talk has a theological significance, that what occurs is not happenstance but has been brought about by the will of Allah. The phrase is inserted into the talk and like Fontain's Arabic greetings at the beginning and end of his videos, it does not necessarily provide an essential semantic place – the viewer can understand the content of the story without understanding the precise meaning of the words. Instead, it shows Fontain's orientation to the event in a way that other Muslims will recognize and appreciate. It also marks his own piety, showing that in his day-to-day life he is oriented toward the will of Allah, something that is a key overarching message in his videos.

Arabic use increases when Fontain is interviewing other Muslims, further highlighting its role as a discourse marker when Fontain or the interviewee are speaking in unstructured ways, seen in the following example where an interviewee is recalling his life story:

> well hamdallah
> I mean
> being from a Turkish-Cypriot background
> you know people'd
> people would ask me
> uh
> were you born Muslim?
> I mean
> no
> every child is born a Muslim
>
> (2014.04.08–1 JFo Video)

Here, "hamadallah" (thanks to God) serves as a topic marker, showing that what follows is something that the speaker is thankful for, in this case simply being born. The phrase, following "well," also works as a kind of filler, buying the speaker time as he starts to construct his life story in the interview and decides where he should begin. Co-occurring with the fillers "well" and "I mean," the phrase represents a kind of thinking that, again, is oriented toward Allah and his will. The phrase positions the speaker as a member of the Muslim community implicitly, particularly in the interview setting where he is being asked to orient himself toward a story of his own reversion. The phrase constructs a discourse event that is centered on an explicitly religious narrative, one that is specific to a Muslim orientation to the world. When using Arabic rather than English, the speakers are able to speak to a community in the natural prosody of their speech.

Examples of Arabic use in Fontain's conversations with the Muslims he interviews appear throughout the dataset and can sometimes act as a kind of back channeling. In Fontain's interview with a blind man in Chicago, Fontain asks the man about himself and how he came to Islam, using Arabic throughout the interview to back channel and to fill his turn, as in the following example:

INTERVIEWEE:	I love going with
	all the brothers and
	you know England
	you do everything by train
FONTAIN:	yeah
INTERVIEWEE:	so you get to actually
	go and experience the whole country
	mashallah
FONTAIN:	hamdallah

(2014.04.08–2 JFo Video)

Here, the affiliation between the two users is facilitated by the use of Arabic, with both Fontain and the interviewee using Arabic phrases to mark the end of a topic-sequence, in the same way as "inshallah" (Clift and Helani, 2010). The phrases orient the conversation back to a storyline about the will and pleasure of Allah, an important focus in Islam and one that reinforces the explicit stories about reversion and being guided by Allah. In Fontain's final "hamdallah" (thanks be to God), the Arabic phrase consists of the complete turn – which Clift and Helani (2010) call the "inshallah turn" – and offers a potential end to the topic. Fontain does this repeatedly throughout the interview using "subanallah" in particular to fill his turns.

The same use of Arabic is mirrored in the comments. Although Fontain's videos attract negativity and antagonism from various commenters, the use of Arabic always carries a positive valence in the comments. "Mashallah" and its variations occur 84 times in the comments and different spelling variations of "subanallah" occur more than 20 times in the comments. Examples of these Allah expressions include:

SubhanAllah. He is fantastic men. I like him. (2014.04.08 1 JFo Video Comments)

Mashallah i love this brother for the sake of Allah SWT (2014.07.20 JFo Video Comments)

AlhamduLillah. May Allah make u firm on deen & make it easy for u. (13.12.20 JFo Video Comments)

The use of Arabic in this way also allows for shared experience and language beyond English. It engages in the same "shared repertoire" beyond the English-speaking community. Importantly, the use of Arabic signals Fontain's affiliation with the global Muslim community, the *ummah*. The comments here suggest that Fontain's viewership reaches beyond the English-speaking audiences and reveals a further context for his videos. Fontain subsequently re-uploaded some of his videos with Arabic titles and descriptions as well as Arabic subtitles, further targeting an audience beyond the English-speaking world.

Not all of Fontain's videos contain Arabic in the same way, and a clear contrast in register can be seen in Fontain's videos "*Revealed* John Fontain – Jesus & the Injeel and Dear Joshua Feuerstein Muslim Response John Fontain." While Arabic regularly appears in Fontain's talk, in the video addressing Feuerstein, Fontain begins with an Arabic greeting, but does not, in the video that follows, use any Arabic. In both of these cases, Fontain is explicitly targeting a non-Muslim audience, and the absence of Arabic shows that Fontain's use of the expressions unlike speakers of Arabic in conversational settings, is motivated by his audience. While they might build camaraderie with other Muslims, when addressing Christians in a Western context, Fontain's language is focused on the message of Islam as it relates to Christianity, rather than Muslim-majority contexts.

Feuerstein's register shows some similar traits of shared register, in his case coming directly from Christianity. The repeated use of "God bless" both by Feuerstein and his commenters exemplifies this, as does "amen" in the comments corpus, appearing 1,607 times. "Amen" serves as a holophrastic response in Feuerstein's videos that, like the Arabic phrases in Fontain's videos, orients the commenter toward Feuerstein. The language of family and familial relationships is also present in the discourse of both Feuerstein and Fontain, referring to "brothers" and "sisters" in their discourse as a way of marking affiliation and represent metaphorical categorizations of others that are nonspecific. The boundaries of who is or is not a brother or sister is not necessarily clear. Similarly, both users avoid labels that might be applied to denominations or sects of their faiths, with neither specifying their own beliefs beyond the very broad categories of "Christian" and "Muslim." While one might be able to make some assumptions about their affiliations based on the positions they take, both work to avoid these labels and instead represent themselves inclusively. This positioning of themselves as open and accepting of others downplays the possibility for disagreements among their users, something that theamazingatheist as we have seen does not attempt.

An "atheist register" is more difficult to identify. There is a more regular use of profanity in both the videos and comments, particularly the words "fuck" and "shit," which are completely absent from Fontain and Feuerstein's spoken discourse. Profanity does stick out in the language of theamazingatheist but it's difficult to generalize further about its salience as marker of atheist discourse. The use of profanity does feature more regularly in the videos of the atheists rather than Christians, but this might be the effect of Christians being aware of "policing" by other Christians (Pihlaja, 2014b). For content creators and particular Christians in visible roles like Feuerstein, there appears to be less incentive for using profanity. That is not to say that people reporting to be Christians do not use profanity in comments, because there is evidence of this, particularly in arguments in the comments on theamazingatheist's page. Users can be seen insulting theamazingatheist with equally offensive language, for example:

> LOL TJ, Amazing atheist . . . . first of all, you need to get a life. While Joshua is living a happy meaningful life you're here sitting and watching each and every one of his videos. I never understand why an atheist would waste their time in these debates if you think your time alive is limited. Secondly . . . Even your evolutionist preach Richard Dawkins admits that the human body is intelligently designed because of the complexity and whatever. . you can search it up yourself . . You fat useless cunt. (2014.10.22 AA Video Comments)

This comment provides an exemplar case of how profanity and antagonism cut across positions on YouTube. In this sense, antagonism and profanity, although abundantly present in theamazingatheist's videos and comments, are not a reflection of his ideological position, but rather his expert use of YouTube, which is known for its antagonistic content. theamazingatheist's use of profanity is less a reflection of his status as an atheist – indeed, many atheist users on the site can be observed making videos void of profanity – and more a reflection of his persona as a YouTuber.

5.4 Celebrities and Communities

The analysis of keywords in videos and comments shows a close relationship between the talk of the video makers and the commenters, with the comments mirroring the video content in many ways. Having looked at how users interact, the extent that communities emerge among the viewers, either in terms of their practices or a shared sense of belonging, is hard to judge. Religious communities both on and offline can be clear examples of communities of practice, as groups of people within regular contact and mutual engagement, joint negotiated enterprise and a shared repertoire of negotiable resources (Lave and Wenger, 1991). Often these communities, like online churches, have clearly defined ways of entering the community and taking part in the rituals and practices (Hutchings, 2007), analogous to offline communities. The practices I have so far analyzed suggest the possibility that similar communities might emerge around users like Feuerstein, Fontain, and theamazingatheist.

The clearest indicator of "community" from a community of practice framework is the "shared repertoire" of users from the same religious backgrounds. The frequent "subanallah" and "mashallah" in Fontain's videos and "amen" in Feuerstein's videos represent knowledge that goes beyond a shared "jargon" – the phrases have meaning that orient toward a particular faith community. What is more difficult to see, however, is the extent to which there is a joint enterprise around the videos, including mutual engagement and shared goals. The engagement takes many different forms, but is, perhaps with the exception of some comments in Feuerstein's Facebook, very rarely "mutual." The videos are transactional, with Feuerstein speaking a message to a large audience, and users responding to praise him. There is, however, very little engagement between Feuerstein and the commenters on his videos – he posts the videos and does not follow up or cultivate a sense of community among users. There are no instances of users referring to a "community" around Feuerstein.

Fontain also does not attempt to cultivate a community around himself and his videos. Given Fontain's focus on spreading dawah and equipping and informing Muslims, there is less mutual engagement, but rather a focus on how the work he does encourages specific users. Rather than developing into communities of users, Feuerstein, Fontain, and theamazingatheist are central figures and their presence is materially necessary for their channels or pages to exist – without the videos they post, there is not community around them. Instead, they are the focus of the videos with a focus on their own personalities as micro-celebrities. Considering the videos that Feuerstein, Fontain, and theamazingatheist make, the importance of their own "social benefit" in the production of the videos is a useful focus. Particularly in the case of the *Dear Mister* videos, all three users gained visibility from their interaction and benefited when more prominent users took notice of them.

What is difficult about the users I have analyzed, however, is how they attempt, particularly in Fontain and Feuerstein's cases, to focus attention on a clear message which they present as being larger than their own personalities.

While theamazingatheist manages his personality and channel in a way that is explicitly oriented toward his own social and economic benefit, Feuerstein and Fontain position themselves in a different way, focusing on goals that are not necessarily dependant on their specific personalities. For Fontain, the goal of spreading dawah is presented as a goal for every Muslim, and for Feuerstein, the goal of encouraging others and spreading his message is one that the viewer contributes to by sharing the video. In these cases, there is a need to downplay their own individual personality while still taking part in self-promotion similar to other micro-celebrities. Feuerstein is, after all, asking people to share *his* particular video in which he plays an integral role. It is impossible to decouple him from this message and the spread of personality with religious messages is certainly not unfamiliar, particularly in the USA where there is a history of personality-driven television focused on the marketing the gospel through particular televangelists (Schultze, 2003).

In all three cases, the users position themselves as leaders, albeit without explicitly claiming this position for themselves or telling others to follow them. Instead, by presenting themselves as authorities on belief, sacred texts, and logic, they are able to garner authority from viewers who are encouraged by them. Commenters on Fontain's videos write,

> Thanks we need people like you to make people to understand Islam. (13.12.09 JFo Video Comments)

> Thank you so much for showing us the way you divided the Holy Qua'an!! Such an amazing way to help us reach peoples minds and hearts and give Dawah in an easy way. (2014.07.14 JFo Video Comments)

These reflect the similar positive comments on Feuerstein's videos and illustrate how users interact with videos and understand their purposes. Particularly in the second comment, the use of "us" to describe the viewership seems to suggest the viewer imagining themselves a part of an audience of other Muslims who are learning from Fontain. This isn't evidence that a community has emerged around Fontain's videos but that the viewing of the video helps the audience orient toward a larger notion of "we." Hearing one's own views expressed in a public setting and the sense that a larger community exists helps to create a sense of affiliation and belonging, one that is more similar to Lundby's (2011) notion of community in the lived experience of believers. Fontain facilitates these feelings by standing as a public figure representing the belief.

While Feuerstein and Fontain don't, in the dataset, make explicit claims at leadership, their presence and encouragement of users to spread their content includes an implicit position of authority.

> One thing that I do not do here often on the amazing atheist channel
> is defend myself
> from criticism
> first of all
> I don't like to be put on the defensive
> I prefer to be offensive
> <laughs>
> second of all
> I prefer to talk about issues and topics larger than any one person
> including myself
> third of all
> it's just boring
>
> (2014.07.29 AA Video)

While theamazingatheist might be the best example of a "micro-celebrity" of the three main users – he explicitly makes a salary from this videos and crowdfunding sources, and has a large and active fan base – this comment suggests that he has at least a stated aversion to being the object of focus and an interest in "topics larger than any one person." He does, however, regularly become the topic of conversation and his approach, particularly his opposition to feminism, show how users aren't necessarily unified in support of him or each other. At the same time, his parodying of Feuerstein and the subsequent attacks that appear on Feuerstein's page show that users do follow his lead and even if he is not explicitly taking a leadership role, what he does is viewed and emulated.

Although Fontain nor Feuerstein don't foreground their day-to-day lives in the way that other daily vloggers might, their own experiences are often present in their videos, be it John Fontain talking regularly about his own experiences of reversion in Sierra Leone or Josh Feuerstein showing video of himself out with his children on a "daddy date." These videos play an important part in maintaining a social media presence, which values the appearance of authenticity and access. Even theamazingatheist who explicitly downplays his own personal life maintains a separate channel to provide more personal content. In terms of YouTube success, other users have grown significantly from allowing access to their personal lives in addition to their own produced content. Users like the popular fashion vlogger Zoella or the American filmmaker turned YouTuber Casey Neistat expand their audiences by providing content that focuses specifically on their personal lives and creating ongoing stories attached to these "daily vlogs." There is clearly interest on social media for content that does not simply focus on the discussion of theology, but includes some element of lived experience.

Because of the nature of micro-celebrity on social media, success without access in some way to an "authentic" version of oneself is difficult. Although Feuerstein does not daily vlog, his engagement with viewers contains an element of personal connection and care that goes beyond the preaching of the Bible. Users are genuinely engaged with the content that Feuerstein produces and he has a demonstrable impact on how users interact with the world, to the extent that commenters report on the positive effects of his videos and the encouragement they feel. This goes beyond a stated theology or the presentation of belief, but focuses on the impact of belief on the individual user's life, using social media as the way of reaching others. This is wholly unique compared to theamazingatheist and John Fontain whose videos might have the potential for this impact, but it is certainly not the focus of their work.

Looking at the overlap in keywords and the nature of the "mutual engagement" in the dataset, it may also be useful to conceive of YouTube communities beyond someone who creates content and the users who affiliate with them. Users do engage with one another across ideological lines, both in creating video content and in making comments on videos of users they both agree with and those whom they oppose. Despite the disagreements surrounding them, particularly the Christians and atheists who regularly watch and comment on one another's videos might usefully also be conceived of as a community in conflict. These users exhibit the features of a community of practice – they engage regularly with one another, they have a shared knowledge based of previous experiences on the site and the ongoing arguments, and they have a joint shared enterprise of argumentation. Playing the role of the "hater" in this community might simply be one way of interacting around religious topics.

It's difficult to see the outcome of these antagonistic interactions on the relationship between opposing sides. Although there is evidence that antagonism from opponents to one's ideology or faith can act as a kind of rallying cry for particular communities and work to unite affiliated users around a common cause, the effect on the individual users doing the antagonizing is difficult to measure. My previous research (Pihlaja, 2014a) has shown anecdotal evidence that users eventually burn out after focusing exclusively on attack videos. Users like theamazingatheist continue to make a consistent living of antagonistic interaction over years and years, but they appear to be the exception rather than the rule, with the focus of YouTube shifting more and more toward heavily produced content and YouTube celebrities who avoid overt political and religious orientations in favor of producing "positive" content.

Although the users in this study lead with their faith (or lack of faith) as a defining feature of their online personas, some users have followed a different path, in which their faith has emerged as topic of discussion over the time they have been present on social media. One example of this is the user Shay Carl, a former DJ from Idaho who began posting videos on YouTube in 2008 and grew into prominence as a "daily vlogger." On his channel, the "Shaytards,"

Shay and his wife and five kids posted videos regularly since 2008, following their rise from living in a small house in Idaho, to founding the YouTube production company Maker Studios, which was subsequently sold to Disney. Prior to a scandal around Shay's contact with a "cam girl" performer in early-2017, the Shaytards were often considered the "first family" of YouTube, with a community of users surrounding them. The Shaytards also happened to be Mormon, a subject they didn't hide in their videos, but one that did not feature prominently in their daily videos. Instead, they chose to present it as an important part of their lives, but not necessarily their YouTube videos.

The Shaytards (and other vloggers for whom faith plays a small part in their daily videos) suggest a possible third way for the presentation of faith one in which it is present, but not a dominant part of their day-to-day videos. This allows from a development of community around them which is not exclusive to users from a particular faith background, and one that does not provide clear opportunities for "trolls" and "haters" to attack their belief. Users, the Shaytards prove, can be both religious and popular among a diverse audience, provided their faith does not dominate their video content and therefore allows them to access a much larger, more diverse audience whose commitment is not contingent on their faith or lack of it, something that can't be said of any of the main users in this study.

These contrasting examples highlight an important maxim of religious interaction online: expressions of religious faith on social media, when they are public and are oriented toward outreach, may be met with derision. It appears impossible to present religious faith online without some amount of immediate, antagonistic response. While the patterns for argumentation are not necessarily new, this feature of digital communication is – users who enjoy some amount of exposure will likely be met with some amount of immediate resistance. Although this is not unique to expressions of religious faith (indeed, any famous social media personality is subject to some amount of trolling and "hate"), it does have consequences for how users present themselves and their faith and potentially consequences for how faiths develop in a digitalized world.

5.5 Conclusion

In this chapter, we've investigated how video discourse influences the content of comments using macro descriptions of the data. Looking at keywords and themes, meaningful differences between the different users' approaches to both their faith and their use of social media can be observed both in the ways they present themselves and how other users respond to them. Recurring themes were observed and could differentiate users from each other. The themes also suggested that users might orient to specific audiences by focusing on specific topics at specific times and using a specific register when speaking to one group rather than another. Shifts in registers also showed that users, specifically John Fontain, were adept at dealing with context collapse, by making content that appealed to different audiences at different times, depending on the message. Building on this work, I will now return to the larger questions that began this analysis and bring together the close discourse analysis of interaction with the keyword analysis to show how users present themselves and their beliefs and the effects this has on how users from different faiths or no faith interact in online contexts.

6 Evangelical Outreach: Arguing, Appealing, and Consoling

The rise of social media micro-celebrity has been the object of some derision. Online video, particularly in the early days of YouTube and Facebook, was often low on production value and scripted content. Anyone could, in theory, upload a video of themselves talking to a camera, or videoing their family life, or playing a video game. Why then should YouTubers become multimillionaires from simply talking to a camera? These complaints have grown less common as social media has become more ubiquitous and the difficulty of building and maintaining an audience has become clearer. Ease of access and production does not mean gaining and growing an audience is equally easy. Successful users must produce content that make sense and is engaging for the platform they choose, at the right time, and in the right way, to be seen by a large audience.

"Online" spaces have also come to affect "offline" spaces. Shabir Ally, the host of the TV show *Let the Quran Speak,* debating a British Christian in Birmingham in the UK illustrates the interconnectedness of online and offline spaces. Ally's popularity is due in part to his willingness to debate Christians, a practice which is particularly engaging in the context of YouTube. The debates occur in offline spaces, but YouTube is the vehicle that popularizes them and brings Ally's voice across the world. Like radio and TV before it, the Internet as a technology of dissemination and communication – and how it shapes interaction – has important social and theological consequences.

Religious Talk Online has so far investigated the effects of social media on religious discourse by considering the language use of a small set of religious users and considering what their interaction reveals about the effects of the medium on faith and its presentation. For those interested in the state of interreligious dialogue, this book does not offer an especially positive picture. Users were observed positioning themselves and others in fairly predictable storylines, some that have been told again and again both online and offline. John Fontain and Joshua Feuerstein are civil with one another, but a closer look at what they are saying shows limited critical engagement. Moreover, users like theamazingatheist and his followers show endless derision for people of faith, with very little to show in terms of mutual respect.

Users are compelled to respond to a broader social context and this engagement requires some adaptation at least in the presentation of belief. While Joshua Feuerstein may not have expected a popular YouTube atheist to respond to his Facebook video, the response influenced how he could interact with others on his own page. The analysis shows that interaction with opposing users is key to how and why different methods of outreach develop. How that orientation and focus on response to others changes the ways users present themselves and their beliefs – and indeed, if it has effects on the belief itself – will be the focus of this final chapter.

I've already noted that social media allows for a diverse range of voices to gain access to large audiences and to be heard and interact in a way that has not been possible before the popularization of the Internet. However, despite this sense of democratization, the Internet and the particular sites I have investigated in this book are not democratized. They are owned and operated by multinational companies that place monetary value on engagement and viewership. Subsequently, particular voices are favored over others, with users who are the most skilled at attracting an audience coming to the top. Moreover, viewers and users of social media do not come to content as blank slates, and the initial, Point Zero conditions of an interaction (Cameron, 2015), include previous ideas about what religious belief is or should be. Viewers are necessarily oriented toward these positions regardless of their own personal thought processes and arguments. Be they Muslim or Christian or atheist, dominant ideas about religion and faith and God dictate the available positions that users take. Religious talk on social media is then like religious talk in the offline world – it is oriented toward the prominent voices and ideas that have influenced the development of religious thought for centuries and the conflicts and histories of contact between groups.

These histories have consequences for how users present themselves and their beliefs to others. For users speaking in English, in the West, on US-based social media sites, the history means that the conversation is necessarily influenced by Christianity as the dominant faith system. Fontain, Feuerstein, and theamazingatheist positioned themselves in storylines in which Christianity plays a key role, whether their position be an antagonist to Christian doctrine, or a Christian preacher encouraging his followers, or a Muslim who speaks more about Jesus than Mohammad, focusing his energy on making Islam recognizable to a Christian audience. The moment Fontain says to a Christian woman, "Sister, you are Muslim!" Fontain is positioning himself and his beliefs as essentially the same as the Christian. The message permeates Fontain's work and is the direct result of speaking in a context where Christianity is the norm. He is presenting his faith as accessible to everyone, but particularly to Christians living in a world oriented toward Christian belief.

The users also targeted specific audiences with specific messages. While all their videos may be public, not all content attracts the same amount and quality of interest from each audience, and different groups can be targeted through posting particular content on particular sites (like posting encouraging videos on Facebook), by discussing particular topics (like dawah), or using specific language (like the register of a particular belief). Even when all of a user's content is public, discursive work can be done to either exacerbate differences (such as making attack videos directed at more popular users who subsequently respond) or consolidate and build affiliation (by focusing on one's base users and avoiding controversial topics).

Social media, however, does not have a monolithic effect on the presentation of belief. Instead, the medium of video and the sites (YouTube and Facebook) provide different affordances that users exploit in different ways depending on any number of known and unknown factors – audience, physical location of the users, the history of a particular belief, and the particular makeup of the site. The quick two-minute, easy-to-share video is effective for Feuerstein because it plays to his strengths as an energetic and fast-paced preacher. His success on Facebook rather than YouTube is not by chance nor by accident, but because his style becomes matched well to Facebook's affordances. He creates compelling content that his audience is happy to share with their friends. It's not simply that Feuerstein is good at making short videos – the medium shapes the content he produces.

YouTube's comparably long history of drama, of users attacking one another and arguing about religion, creates a different set of affordances that favor theamazingatheist's style, which revels in drama and attacking users he can portray as being stupid and particularly good examples of the ignorance of Christian belief. The history and environment of the site which theamazingatheist played a role in developing includes an audience that is sympathetic to his message and long-form videos "debunking" Christian arguments. The content is oriented toward an audience that is largely unsympathetic to Christians and share in his animosity, presenting Christians and Christian belief as unenlightened and silly in comparison to atheism when they comment. Like Feuerstein's videos, nuance gives way to producing content that is easy to consume and generates interest and views. Clear, consistent representation of particular belief systems is far less important.

The condition of the site and the users on it interact in a way that the two exert influence on one another. These affordances and their effects – presentation styles and content, and the interaction that follows – subsequently shape the way that belief is presented and lived out by the users. While two minutes might be a good timescale for presenting an encouraging message, Feuerstein's preaching about biblical stories, such as the retelling of Noah and the ark, often lacks an attention to detail that might be present in a longer form video or a written blog post. This leads to a simplification of belief and the stories that he draws on from the Bible to support his arguments reduce complex ideas to simple phrases or takeaway points. Serious discussions of theological points are absent from the comments section, replaced by users offering support from one another. In the same way, theamazingatheist's focus on antagonism and attacks becomes associated with atheism more broadly, with users repeating his attacks and treating Christians and Christianity in the same way.

Confrontation is not, however, a necessary feature of social media, despite the persistence of negativity and its interest to researchers. Among many popular YouTubers, a presentation of oneself as relentlessly positive is also a clearly tenable position. John Fontain is, perhaps, the least combative user in this book – he does not appear interested in making sensational content. Fontain presents himself as a friendly, knowledgeable authority both on Islam and Christianity. Still, the focus on confrontation and debate, which is endemic on the site, continues to play a role his videos, from the arguments on the street while doing dawah, to a video he posted in 2015 showing him confronting the evolutionary biologist Richard Dawkins at a book signing. His video attacking Britain First and subsequent lack of engagement in the same political issues suggests that certain forms of confrontation work better for him than others.

Presentations of belief are responses to the complex factors, and these factors change over time. They are emergent with achieved religious identities, despite the insistence of some users on their own faith's permanence and appeals to scripture as a definitive, unshaken authority. The presentation of beliefs changes as users speak to each other or different audiences, at different times, and on different platforms. The extent to which this is new, however, should be revisited in line with Herring's (2004b) question about mediated communication more generally: is technology changing the way people interact or is it reflecting something that was already present in social interaction? The question challenges us to place discourse in an even larger sociohistorical context and ask again what is unique, if anything, about the videos and comments in this book. Indeed, in the interaction between Christians and Muslims, many of the same arguments observed have existed for centuries. At the same time, the role of social media in the development of atheism might arguably be more novel.

While these questions are unlikely to lead to satisfying answers, we can say, considering the histories among these groups and what has been analyzed in this book that social media offers a uniquely transparent, public, and immediate view of how people talk about religion. It allows researchers to see and trace how ideas and the presentations of belief emerge and change, often quickly and in reaction to others, and it highlights the need to look at all the factors contributing to religious talk, many of them obvious and explicit, and many of them hidden and implicit. The presentation of belief is the sum of these factors and, as we have seen, a response to a specific context and audience.

The reactionary nature of the interactions among theamazingatheist, Fontain, and Feuerstein has recurred at every level of analysis, both in the implicit positioning of other users and the explicit arguments between users. *Logoi* and *anti-logoi* (Billig, 1996), the claim and counterclaim, came up repeatedly in videos and comments. The arguments are by-and-large not nuanced or critical because they are vehicles for establishing and reestablishing existing storylines. While dialogue and debate might be a means to change minds and critically examine one's own belief, there appears to be little evidence of that occurring. Instead, the presence of adversaries is an opportunity for users to retell their own storylines when challenged and to generate content for counterclaims which subsequently generate support among viewers with whom you are affiliated.

The content and themes of the arguments are not especially unique. Christian resistance to evolution has a long history, as do arguments about the deity of Christ, two major themes in the interactions among the Christian, Muslim, and atheist users. They revoice the arguments of established theologians, biologists, and religious thinkers that have circulated in some cases for centuries. They are scalable in a discourse dynamics description of interaction, with the initial conditions feeding into and through the discourse event and leading into stable patterns on the sites. The patterns become themes on different channels that orient toward the storylines that each of the users is cultivating: the atheist antihero, the Christian motivational speaker, and the Muslim apologist.

The specific content of each argument is situated, and the situated context determines how and why it develops. One cannot look, for example, at the development of Joshua Feuerstein as a micro-celebrity, the content he posts, and the responses he receives without understanding his history with other users, the nature of the platform he uses, and the sociohistorical context of his theological and political positions. As an individual user, Feuerstein makes videos that are provocative and this history of provocation establishes a particular context and storyline for him – every video he makes must be understood in the context. At the same time, he exists in a specific American Evangelical context, but one that is now regularly challenged by detractors. Understanding the nature of Feuerstein's presence on Facebook, his influence among his fans and the themes and beliefs that are recurring on his page, requires seeing it as emerging from the interaction of these factors. They include both his own strategic thinking about his audience and his role online, and how the context itself provides affordances for new positions, be they online in his interaction with other users, or the offline political context, as with his engagement with arguments about gay marriage laws or gun control in the USA.

How the users interact with their audiences problematizes the notion of context collapse which describes the difficultly social media users in conceptualizing their audience (Marwick and boyd, 2011). The users appear to have a well-developed notion of audience, one that includes like-minded viewers, users who are openly opposed to them, and users who do not necessarily have a specific affiliation. The challenge for the users is first, producing content which appeals to both a core audience of like-minded viewers and a broader audience of viewers who are potentially interested in the claims, ambivalent, or openly hostile; and second, responding to and effectively engaging viewers who fall along the spectrum of interest. When users run afoul of this, as Fontain does parodying "Britain First," the response can be swift and unrelenting. However, opposition is not an end point of interaction. Instead, it provides an opportunity to either double down on a position, as we saw in Feuerstein's response to theamazingatheist, which reasserted the main points of his initial argument. Alternatively, the user can continue with a different tactic, which Fontain seems to choose, not creating political content and focusing instead on dawah.

While appealing to different audiences at the same time is a difficult proposition in theory, in practice, users are quite adept at it. Throughout the analysis, we have seen evidence that audiences do not always overlap. John Fontain attracts a multitude of haters with his perceived attack on Britain First, but subsequent videos focused exclusively on dawah attract little or no attention from the same commenters. Fontain abandons political topics after the attacks, and manages to subsequently maintain an audience of seemingly like-minded users. Feuerstein, by contrast, after attracting the interest of theamazingatheist, continues to make videos in the same vein and indeed responding to the theamazingatheist directly. At the same time, subsequent videos in which he does not explicitly address issues that are of interest to atheists remain relatively free of antagonism. This does not appear to be a mistake – Feuerstein occasionally courts negative attention from atheists by making videos like *Dear Mr. Atheist.* The responses allow him to justify a storyline of persecution, where he can position himself as doing the will of God and being hated by atheists for the work that he is doing. He does not need to condemn the attacks of others or delete them from his page; they act as a reinforcement of the larger storyline. Negative attention is actually good for the brand, particularly when the attacks appear to be unnecessarily antagonistic, as in the case of theamazingatheist mocking him. Feuerstein and his viewers read it the same way – Feuerstein is suffering for his faith, for telling the truth, to an audience that is blinded to it. Like the work of Harré

(2000) on terrorism, the enemies in one users storyline are the heroes in another, and there is no shortage of users to position in any ongoing storyline and these enemies can be used to reinforce his own position.

Even more than Feuerstein, the position of "antihero" and antagonist is most naturally suited for theamazingatheist. Atheism remains a minority position particularly for viewers in the USA, whom his videos largely focus on. theamazingatheist is skilled at taking antagonism and using it to his advantage, with the expressed goal of driving interest in his channel through his attacks on others. For theamazingatheist, a storyline of persecution is needed to position himself as someone whom Christians are actively attempting to silence. This position of antihero and antagonist has larger implications for the development of atheism, particularly given the importance of social media in its increased visibility. As one key voice of atheism on YouTube, how theamazingatheist presents atheism has implications for its development going forward, particularly with the influence micro-celebrities have in leveraging responses on social media. While it is unlikely for figures like Feuerstein or Fontain to exert significant influence over the development of their respective faiths, theamazingatheist is in a different position. He is an influential voice on one of the main platforms that has driven the rise of the atheism in the public sphere in the early twenty-first century. What he says and how he behaves potentially matters more than users like Josh Feuerstein, who are competing against many larger, more popular voices in the Christian community.

Of course, describing how "Muslims" or "Christians" or "atheists" use social media simplifies the diversity of users and contexts, and that nuanced analysis of religious talk on social media must start with small scale analysis of individual users, rather than top-down descriptions. This book, however, has shown how positions and storylines within specific interactions can be traced to historical patterns. This is the case, for example, in the discussion of the deity of Jesus Christ among Christians and Muslims. How users position Jesus and Muhammad in their interaction with each other has implications for the social action they are attempting to accomplish and how they see themselves in the world. These storylines, as they have come up in the videos and the comments, are rarely unique.

The Internet and social media have democratized access to information about religion and practices for accessing and distributing it. In the same way that the printing press gave access to readers of the Bible, removing the Catholic Church as a mediating force in the Christian believer's experience of the sacred text, the Internet has also increased access to different kinds of information. Some of this, while relatively mundane, is worth noting because of its effect on the reading of sacred text, such as the ability to search by keyword and isolate and decontextualize certain parts of a text. While the practice of citing "chapter and verse" is by no means new to Evangelical Christianity in particular, this increased ability to isolate sections of the text facilitates and encourages searching the text for relevant passages, rather than reading the text as a whole and gaining and comprehensive understanding. Instead, bits of the text can be used and plugged into arguments to support both *logoi* and *anti-logoi* positions in arguments. In these argumentation contexts and indeed the uses of the text in Feuerstein's videos, the Bible is not something to be read and understood, but something to be used to affect change. These uses can be both positive, in attempts to encourage others, and negative, in attempts to curb or stop the actions of others through appealing to the text as an authority to support exertions of force.

In Harré's (2000) work on positioning as it relates to terrorism, he notes a symmetry in positions in narratives about the other's enemy – in the case of narratives about terrorism, George W. Bush's discourse about Osama bin Laden and vice versa. In the narratives of both, the other served an important purpose for justifying action and providing an ideological basis for attacks. Harré and colleagues (2009) expand on this notion in describing "just war" narratives writing: "The moral high ground must be seized and the enemy positioned as morally base. The narrative is always 'Good eventually triumphs over Evil'" (p. 9). This similar structure is seen when conflict arises in religious talk online, with the person speaking or writing taking the position of "good" and positioning the opponent as "evil" in any number of ways. This happens explicitly in narratives about the other, with both Christians and atheists explicitly calling the other "evil," and implicitly in narratives that position the other negatively, often as regressive (in terms of atheist storylines about Christian belief), or proud and ignorant (in Christian storylines about atheists). Both storylines also highlight the notion of eventually triumphing, with atheists pointing to the progress of scientific innovation, and Christians appealing to God's judgment. They are both zero sum – one side's losses are the other side's triumphs.

The example of Bush and bin Laden shows how opponents can be useful in presentation of belief. For theamazingatheist, his presentation of belief is almost always presented as an opposition to some other entity, be it Feuerstein's ignorance about science, the actor Kevin Sorbo's negative statements about atheism, or a feminist blogger's criticism of his approach. In all three cases, theamazingatheist uses others to position himself as morally superior, as a person responding to an ignorant, illogical attack and presenting his own response as logical and reasoned. In a storyline where the religious are positioned as regressive and ignorant, theamazingatheist needs Christians like Feuerstein to support his own storyline. The same holds true for Feuerstein who began his video entitled *Dear Mr. Atheist* with the statement "You know, the other day I had an atheist tell me that I was an idiot moronic and stupid for believing in God" (2014.06.02 AA Video). If atheists are arrogant, rude, and aggressive, quick to mock both Christians and God, the Feuerstein needs examples to prove his point and give him the moral high ground, positioning himself as motivated by love and avoid profanity and demeaning language. theamazingatheist provides an ideal opponent as well because he embodies many of the traits of the insulting atheists that Feuerstein addresses.

These storylines about the other exist in individual videos, but they are also constituent parts of larger patterns that permeate Christian and atheist talk about the other. Unlike interactions with long histories (as in Muslim-Christian relations), the talk occurring on social media following the growing presences of atheism in the public discourse about religion is mapping how the religious users (and in particular, Christians in the West) and atheists interact around issues of faith. As in any complex, dynamic system, the context determines how these different scales interact and how the interactions emerge as patterns over time. What shapes these interactions, where they happen, and how they develop is subject to the constraints and affordances of the technologies and each individual user's history. In 2014, stable patterns were beginning to emerge, but still very much in flux, with users like theamazingatheist taking political stances and continuing to define what it meant to be an atheist.

There are certainly positive models. Indeed, the debates of Shabir Ally and his interaction with Christians show both parties agreeing to respectful terms and apparently resulting in mutual respect and understanding at least on the face of it. At the same time, the good will and understanding that emerges from them is of secondary importance – both parties engage in the debate with the often-stated intention of winning an argument, and convincing the audience and their opponent that they are correct. Perhaps these interactions are favorable to some arguments where users insult one another and attack each other's beliefs. However, the notion that debating beliefs is necessarily transformative should also be scrutinized, particularly when debates are used to rally support for particular positions, as with videos by Christians and Muslims seeing and hearing what they want in a debate. Videos like *Shabir Ally's Argument on "Land of Israel" Is Destroyed by Dave Hunt* are met with counter videos like *Jay Smith Got Destroyed by Dr. Shabir Ally on the Trinity and the Christian Concept of the Atonement*. Who destroys whom is very much in the eye of the beholder.

The awareness of the "opposition" in the presentation of belief assumes both a plurality of religions and faiths, and a belief that one particular orientation is correct. Throughout this book, the implicit assumption of each user has been that their position is ultimately the most logical. Despite recognition of differing views, an ecumenical approach to faith does not necessarily follow.

Instead, an increased pressure to parse different worldviews has developed, with viewers encouraged to compare them and identify which one is "right" compared to the other. The focus on "debate" rather than dialogue has effects beyond social media, leading to actual debates like the one between Shabir Ally and the Seventh Day Adventist that I presented at the beginning of this book. Both participants implicitly begin with the premise that an individual must choose between the two positions – that one position is right and one position is wrong – and that debate will help people decide which is which.

From this point of view, the Internet serves as a kind of repository for ideas that a user can access and use to seek the truth for themselves – users need only hear the available positions to make a decision about which is correct. However, by reifying religious experience and faith, and treating them as positions to be defended in debates, they become decontextualized. One's faith, religious experience, or lack thereof must be either right or wrong, and it must be applicable beyond their own individual experience, something that can be defended when challenged. Where the sharing of religious belief and experience can be met with skepticism and antagonistic responses, there is no place for a lack of certainty about what one experiences or believes – a chorus of detractors and believers with fixed conceptions of these experiences are omnipresent.

What is potentially dangerous about this foregrounding of debate is the lack of critical engagement with sociohistorical context, and how different positions have emerged over time. Users like the ones studied in this book spend little time in their videos and commentary reflecting on the cultural context of their belief, the socioeconomic factors, ethnicity, or language – the myriad of different factors which constitute particular beliefs in particular times. While all three of the users take political positions, like their religious beliefs, they are presented in specific storylines with positions allocated and little critical engagement with how these beliefs have developed. Instead, claims and counterclaims are simply true or false, and their veracity is best deduced in debate.

This orientation has important implications for the development of Islam, Christianity, and atheism going forward. While this book has focused on the development of atheism as a response to Judeo-Christian, monotheistic understandings of God, which subsequently set the agendas of the movement, the same can be said of Islam in the context of Fontain's ministry. For him, the interaction of Islam and Christianity in the West is oriented toward Christian belief and the extent to which he can make Islam recognizable to his audience, even by arguing that the belief that Christians already hold is in fact an Islamic faith. While this appropriation of Christian faith for the purposes of dawah is useful for Fontain, the consequence is a persistent foregrounding of Christian theology and one that has the possibility of influencing how the faith of individuals develops.

Debates are, of course, neither intrinsically positive nor negative. The Internet and the connectivity of users simply foregrounds how faiths can no longer be isolated and must, in these contexts, respond to the dominant ideologies in the cultures in which they are developing. Debate among people of faith and of no faith is a natural response to this proximity and a potentially useful way of understanding one's own position in relation to another. In this sense, they can as useful ways of practicing critical skills and developing a nuanced understanding of one's own position. The interaction, however, need not always be constructive, as seen in the development of online religious radicalization, which encourages a rejection of the dominant ideological structures and an attempt to change them through violence. The results of the debate and how one is led to respond to them are then of important consequence in how users understand themselves and their faith or lack of faith in a larger social world.

Argument is embedded in how all three of the users respond and present themselves to others. theamazingatheist foregrounds his point-by-point refutations of Christians, John Fontain does dawah on the street, and Joshua Feuerstein "challenges" atheists and Muslims. Where there are attempts to find common ground, as seen repeatedly in Fontain's videos, they are oriented toward convincing someone to take on the position of the other. Fontain's attempt to reconcile Islam with Christianity is specifically an attempt to convince Christians to accept Islam. While the presentation is kinder and more empathetic than theamazingatheist, the end goal of both is the same – they are both attempting to present Christianity as illogical, and to offer implicitly or explicitly their own position as the correct one.

Argument, however, does not seem support the growth of tangible affiliation among users or communities, at least in the sense that we have conceived of them, either as practice-oriented (Lave and Wenger, 1991) or in terms of a sense of "belonging" (Lundby, 2011). Users affiliated with each other at times, but these alignments appeared to be hierarchical, with users primarily affiliating with the main user, whoever it may be. Where users on Feuerstein and Fontain's pages showed support for others, these appeared to be motivated by larger religious commitments, as evidenced in the particular registers they employed. Users affiliate with others they recognize as sharing their belief. Affiliated users could be conceived as part of larger community of practices (which might contribute to a sense of belonging both on and offline), but communities didn't appear to be created in the interaction investigated in this book. They are features of Christian life or the Muslim *ummah* (community) more generally.

With the personality-driven nature of the users in this book, where individuals play a central role on each of the channels or pages, the lack of community is perhaps unsurprising. However, on YouTube in particular, many users encourage and name their "fan communities," be they the follows popular users like Hank and John Green – the Nerdfighters – or Philip Defranco – the Nation. Communities can and do emerge around users, with varying degrees of commitment, practices, and affiliation, and with users reporting senses of belonging. In these cases, users leverage their (micro-) celebrity status to help the communities develop through explicitly naming the community, facilitating its growth through reference to it in videos, and supporting fan-led initiatives. In the examples of Fontain and Feuerstein, there seems to be little acknowledgment of viewership and the audience, beyond thanking people for watching and sharing their videos. Instead, Feuerstein focuses on producing videos that reach out to anyone that might share them. He very rarely returns to recurring themes that might require some background history to understand. Fontain also focuses on video content that can stand alone and is internally complete. There is no need for any user to have a broader understanding of him or his work to view and appreciate a specific video. In both cases, however, users interact with the content as a part of a larger faith community, be it through exhorting each other in Arabic or offering up their prayers for other users. There is an implicit community of faith and one that other members of the same faith can recognise through shared discourse.

No similar practices can be observed on theamazingatheist's video pages. While the keyword analysis showed registers in both the Christian and Muslim user comments, similar patterns could not be seen in the atheist dataset, beyond a common theme of talk about science and swear words. In cultivating an image as an antihero outside the mainstream, a fan community is not useful for his self-presentation or the development of the channel. Moreover, with theamazingatheist's stated lack of interest in the arguments "being about him" (see 2014.07.29 AA Video), it is perhaps unsurprising that a community does not appear to emerge around his videos. The extent to which this might be applied to other channels which focus on atheism could be a topic of further research and one that will be of interest to researchers in sociology investigating atheist experience, belief, and identity.

While it might be difficult to observe community practices in the comments sections of theamazingatheist's videos, it's clear that the presence of atheist voices online does serve to emboldened people to "come out" as atheists and provides them with a place of connection and discussion, something observed in Cimino and Smith's (2011) research. Users like theamazingatheist then, regardless of their own feelings about their centrality, might find themselves as *de facto* community leaders, even while resisting the label. While believers within Christian and Muslim communities draw on long histories of doctrine, theology, and community practice in their interaction in online spaces, atheism as it emerges in the twenty-first century has a less cohesive history. Although movements to organize atheist communities to come together around shared values in places like the "atheist churches" (Wheeler, 2013), their long-term success and development will be a necessary area of research going forward. What seems clear, however, is that users playing antagonistic roles like theamazingatheist, despite their prominence, are unlikely to put themselves forward as leaders. How then the movement develops, the political stances it takes, and whether a united voice continues to emerge will remain an important topic for discourse analysts and sociologists.

The same fundamental questions about the future of Christianity and Islam do not appear to exist. Social media and online interaction so far have developed within the larger communities of faith, with physical community gatherings and leaders throughout the world. While atheism and arguments against the existence of God might have gained prominence in online spaces, Christian and Muslim voices continue to emerge as well, with the support of long and established cultural histories. The world may be changing, but Muslim and Christian communities have long adapted to change. How they develop, and how the communities adapt to the online tools that believers use to share their belief will continue to tell us as much about belief and how it works, as it will about whatever new technology emerges in the immediate future.

Context collapse and the constant presence of opposing voices in religious communities will likely continue to impact religious practice, as smart phones and tablets allow for offline speech and interaction within physical religious communities to be shared immediately. Evangelists and religious influencers will need to be aware of diverse audiences wherever the setting, be they actively presenting themselves on Facebook or speaking to audiences in their own physical contexts. This presence of the other does certainly have disadvantages. However, the presence of an unknown audience who can speak back at any time is also a moderating force, requiring users to reach potential converts in a context where extremism is likely to be met with strong opposition. Although this can be dangerous, pushing extremists underground, the need to appeal to the mainstream has potentially positive outcomes. It means a presentation of faith must at least be aware of the voices of others.

With users going back and forth in arguments, navigating opposition to professions or rejections of faith will continue to be an issue. Those pushbacks can create a new environment for the discussion of faith in public settings, something that is again neither good nor bad in and of itself. It can give rise to a multitude of possible outcomes, both known and unknown. In all three personalities in this book, the focus was on pushing ideas out to audiences and responding to others when it could be seen as beneficial. This was not always successful – throughout the analysis we've seen how users can fail to connect to with one another. At the same time, the users observed here developed a unique and successful practice, speaking to their audience and achieving their desired effect, particularly as their social media presence and micro-celebrity developed.

Whatever future exists, the continued spread of technology in the short to medium term seems certain. Faith and religious belief will continue to be a part of social interaction, with the lines between what occurs online and offline blurring as mobile technologies improve. With the history of antagonism and the popularity of drama and argument, discourse involving religion is likely to continue to have some degree of animosity. At the same time, the access to a diversity of voices will continue to provide comfort and a sense of belonging and connection that has been observed among all the categories of users in this study: atheist, Christian, and Muslim users. How these interactions develop and what possibilities can be found for mutual understanding and engagement has yet to be fully discovered. In the end, all the proximity that technology provides is simply an affordance.

Appendix

Joshua Feuerstein Videos

Description	Date	URL
POT SMOKING ATHEIST turns CHRISTIAN and BAPTIZED in JESUS NAME! #60seconds #churchofchampions #boom #GODSNOTDEAD	10/05/2014	www.facebook.com/ video.php?v= 524401924329161
60 seconds on "The Power of a Problem"!!! Gotta see this . . .	10/02/2014	www.facebook.com/ video.php?v= 522933154476038
Trash or Treasure?? Which are YOU?? 90 seconds of pure inspiration!!!! #shareifyoucare	10/02/2014	www.facebook.com/ video.php?v= 522657767836910
FACING A PROBLEM? 60 seconds of powerful encouragement on turning your problem into a blessing!!! #shareifyoucare	09/30/2014	www.facebook.com/ video.php?v= 521719027930784
Wow!!! Some SCARY SCARY truth about why we as Americans are not really free and why the world could END for us TOMORROW!!!!	09/26/2014	www.facebook.com/ video.php?v= 520034264765927
If YOU see this . . . God wants you to know this 60 second PRAYER is for you!!! #shareifyoucare	09/25/2014	www.facebook.com/ video.php?v= 519573821478638
Heeeeeeey . . . YOU . . . shhhh . . . Listen to this secret. . . . #youarebeautiful	09/16/2014	www.facebook.com/ video.php?v= 516658811770139
The VALUE of a LADY! Every man MUST WATCH! #rayrice #mustshare #forREALMEN OUR NEW PROJECT –> http://www.gofundme.com/cjwrxk Help us spread the word!!!	09/10/2014	www.facebook.com/ video.php?v= 514320968670590
Developing in the Darkness!! A 90 second video the promises to change your life!!! #shareifyoucare	09/02/2014	www.facebook.com/ video.php?v= 509212385848115
No Strings Attached Sex: Condoms can't protect your heart! MUST WATCH!!!!! MUST SHARE!!!!	08/29/2014	www.facebook.com/ video.php?v= 505723482863672

(cont.)

Description	Date	URL
PREACHER GETS MAD AND TEARS PAGES OUT OF THE BIBLE . . . but makes a very powerful point!!!! You gotta listen and share this. . . .	08/28/2014	www.facebook.com/video.php?v=504575839645103
Do you feel like God doesn't hear you, Has abandoned you?	08/25/2014	www.facebook.com/joshua.feuerstein.5/posts/502428446526509
WOW! Powerful life changing one minute video . . . in WALMART! Lol. Are you troubled, down, discouraged? This video is for YOU!	08/19/2014	www.facebook.com/video.php?v=499221086847245
Help save CHILDREN from being BEHEADED with one click of a button!!! So sad . . . #thousandsDEADalready	08/11/2014	www.facebook.com/video.php?v=496171727152181
Do you feel like you are CONSTANTLY UNDER ATTACK? Thieves don't break into empty vaults! 90 seconds to change your life!	07/30/2014	www.facebook.com/video.php?v=490226101080077
Dear Mr Muslim Reuploaded	07/17/2014	https://youtu.be/V3K-tmcu7Y0
It's TIME for your COMEBACK! 3 minutes of Life Changing ENCOURAGEMENT and TRUTH! Share w/ anyone down, discouraged, hurting, depressed or beaten up by life!!!	07/06/2014	www.facebook.com/video.php?v=480606392042048
Dear Mr. Atheist reuploaded	06/08/2014	www.youtube.com/watch?v=pB2RMBzFg6A
It's not REJECTION! It's RE-DIRECTION! To those feeling rejected . . . #shareifyoucare	08/18/2014	www.facebook.com/video.php?v=459104107525610
90 seconds every MAN must watch !!! #shaaaaare	05/20/2014	www.facebook.com/video.php?v=455003107935710
90 Seconds Every Person Ever Hurt in a Relationship (or Friendship) MUST WATCH!	05/09/2014	www.facebook.com/video.php?v=454674741301880
MUST SHARE! Do you feel like you have a HOPELESS or IMPOSSIBLE situation????? This is FOR YOU!!	05/08/2014	www.facebook.com/video.php?v=453239138112107
Straight Rap Saturday: UP ALL NIGHT TO GET LUCKY? . . . for every young man or woman. #shareifyoucare	05/04/2014	www.facebook.com/video.php?v=452910884811599
To Those Surrounded by Negativy! #shareifyoucare	05/03/2014	www.facebook.com/video.php?v=452415724861115
National Sexting Day! "Get in Her Heart . . . Not Her Pants!" MUST WATCH! #respectWOMEN #respectYOURSELF	4/22/2014	www.facebook.com/video.php?v=449333938502627

(cont.)

Description	Date	URL
The Beauty in The Storm! MUST WATCH for anybody going through a dark season! #SHAREifyouCARE	4/22/2014	www.facebook.com/video.php?v=449019238534097
SHOCKING CONFESSION: I'm A Preacher . . . But I Love Prostitutes! #SHAREifyouCARE	04/15/2014	www.facebook.com/video.php?v=446087242160630

John Fontain Videos

Title	Date	URL
iERA Dawah USA	10/01/2014	www.youtube.com/watch?v=WLksXOADct8&list=UUzBBG_OZUVVtNVb9HGVcm4A
SNOOP DOGG MUSLIM? 3 Reverts Discuss Islam [MUST SEE]	08/30/2014	http://youtu.be/dIqKlhlWvlY?list=UUzBBG_OZUVVtNVb9HGVcm4A
Street Dawah Brazil – Jew believes but refuses to accept Islam – Final Day 25	07/20/2014	www.youtube.com/watch?v=82n8ZQayrII&feature=youtu.be&list=UUzBBG_OZUVVtNVb9HGVcm4A
Dawah - Invitation 2 Islam – John Fontain	07/16/2014	www.youtube.com/watch?v=5zDRnHpIfSY&feature=youtu.be&list=UUzBBG_OZUVVtNVb9HGVcm4A
Dawah to Christian in Brazil – Day 24	07/15/2014	http://youtu.be/lNdiRuGCkDw?list=UUzBBG_OZUVVtNVb9HGVcm4A
Praying on the Street, Brazil World Cup Day 23	07/14/2014	www.youtube.com/watch?v=CXMWDe2IMEw
A heart melting story from the Brazil I World Cup Day 6	06/27/2014	www.youtube.com/watch?v=FNLWvR7FpTo&list=UUzBBG_OZUVVtNVb9HGVcm4A
Dawah to Hare Krishnas in Brazil – Day 4	06/26/2014	www.youtube.com/watch?v=9u7d-tJC4iE&list=UUzBBG_OZUVVtNVb9HGVcm4A
Sister accepts Islam – Dawah Night Manchester Rusholme	06/13/2014	www.youtube.com/watch?v=GdEx7EB_W9U
Dear Joshua Feuerstein Muslim Response John Fontain	06/01/2014	www.youtube.com/watch?v=eLN9pRvt1VY
Christian Accepts Islam – Magic, Diamonds And Music [MUST WATCH]	05/26/2014	https://bwww.youtube.com/watch?v=PlALN2s3uM&list=UUzBBG_OZUVVtNVb9HGVcm4A

(cont.)

Title	Date	URL
BRITAIN FIRST Invade Manchester Mega Mosque! – ITS GONE TOO FAR! – John Fontain	05/16/2014	www.youtube.com/watch?v=jhQbOtcShJc&list=UUzBBG_OZUVVtNVb9HGVcm4A
Christian asks a Muslim for protection from two atheists – John Fontain	05/15/2014	http://youtu.be/EgYjYy11fF4?list=UUzBBG_OZUVVtNVb9HGVcm4A
Eddie accepts Islam in Chicago – John Fontain	04/09/2014	www.youtube.com/watch?v=R9LPsU2pSOc&list=UUzBBG_OZUVVtNVb9HGVcm4A
Judaism led me to Islam – Ustadh Ramiz Ibrhaim, John Fontain	04/08/2014	www.youtube.com/watch?v=ps21Y64ynCs&list=UUzBBG_OZUVVtNVb9HGVcm4A
SHAHADA!!! Sheikh Abu Hafsa Clare – John Fontain	04/08/2014	www.youtube.com/watch?v=JqGCoTFiH9w&list=UUzBBG_OZUVVtNVb9HGVcm4A
My Husband is Muslim! SHAHADA – John Fontain – The Deen Show – Street Dawah	12/20/2013	www.youtube.com/watch?v=E5ZJbzbQrg4&list=UUzBBG_OZUVVtNVb9HGVcm4A
Revealed John Fontain – Jesus & the Injeel	12/09/2013	https://youtu.be/fs5gtyFGtnk
Englishman accepts Islam (Cambodia) – John Fontain	11/12/2013	www.youtube.com/watch?v=rxtn3sZIPx4&list=UUzBBG_OZUVVtNVb9HGVcm4A
SUBHANALLAH!!! The Power of Dua in Dawah – Ali Da'Wow & John Fontain	11/11/2013	www.youtube.com/watch?v=LPn7SNLpeAc&list=UUzBBG_OZUVVtNVb9HGVcm4A
Jesus & The Injeel – John Fontain	10/24/2013	https://youtu.be/3rsX53VNF9E

theamazingatheist Videos

Title	Date	URL
Josh Feuerstein DESTROYS ATHEISM AGAIN!	10/22/2014	www.youtube.com/watch?v=-PFjvoJamRw
ISLAM AND THE ISLAMIC STATE	10/15/2014	www.youtube.com/watch?v=P3855_NUNmk
Kevin Sorbo Says More Dumb Stuff	09/19/2014	www.youtube.com/watch?v=V4S-a8r5AAg&list=UUjNxszyFPasDdRoD9J6X-sw
FEMINIST COMICS	09/18/2014	www.youtube.com/watch?v=qbGQuYvgENw&list=UUjNxszyFPasDdRoD9J6X-sw
Ray Rice & The NFL's Hypocrisy	09/08/2014	www.youtube.com/watch?v=iivkzO0xaMQ&list=UUjNxszyFPasDdRoD9J6X-sw

(cont.)

Title	Date	URL
Kevin Sorbo: SHUT UP, ATHEISTS!	08/27/2014	www.youtube.com/watch?v=LP5O9zgTuT8&list=UUjNxszyFPasDdRoD9J6X-sw
Religion: Does Anyone REALLY Believe It?	08/26/2014	www.youtube.com/watch?v=arJE7QoOdQ0&list=UUjNxszyFPasDdRoD9J6X-sw
Josh Moronstein's 100 Kajillion Dollar Aunicornist Challenge	08/25/2014	www.youtube.com/watch?v=qr8eMPjK7gg&list=UUjNxszyFPasDdRoD9J6X-sw
Not A Feminist, Not A Sexist	08/14/2014	www.youtube.com/watch?v=5_saS417Pe8&list=UUjNxszyFPasDdRoD9J6X-sw
Ebola Is God's Judgment?	08/09/2014	www.youtube.com/watch?v=fBxcpDAi-0w&list=UUjNxszyFPasDdRoD9J6X-sw
Rape, Feminism, and The Amazing Atheist	07/29/2014	www.youtube.com/watch?v=K6ys-OklTOA&list=UUjNxszyFPasDdRoD9J6X-sw
The Amazing Atheist vs. Josh Feuerstein	07/28/2014	www.youtube.com/watch?v=2wWNpbABYZ4&list=UUjNxszyFPasDdRoD9J6X-sw
Gravity Disproved In 2 Minutes	07/18/2014	www.youtube.com/watch?v=JisCl6-q2fA&list=UUjNxszyFPasDdRoD9J6X-sw
Whats Going On?	07/10/2014	www.youtube.com/watch?v=LFZdiJxeJXM&list=UUjNxszyFPasDdRoD9J6X-sw
COPS WANT TO PHOTOGRAPH KID'S ERECTION	07/09/2014	www.youtube.com/watch?v=b3RfS_Kj1I8&list=UUjNxszyFPasDdRoD9J6X-sw
UK SMOKING BAN	06/30/2014	www.youtube.com/watch?v=80mIcAatRqY&list=UUjNxszyFPasDdRoD9J6X-sw
EVOLUTION DISPROVED AGAIN! STUPID ATHEISTS!	06/16/2014	www.youtube.com/watch?v=2gtoSggP6oM&list=UUjNxszyFPasDdRoD9J6X-sw
Atheists Don't Exist?! What?!?!	06/05/2014	www.youtube.com/watch?v=j4Cyq3Nx208&list=UUjNxszyFPasDdRoD9J6X-sw
Christian "Disproves" Evolution?	06/02/2014	www.youtube.com/watch?v=ieIxQtKogl4

References

Abbott, H. Porter. (2008). *The Cambridge introduction to narrative*. Cambridge: Cambridge University Press.

Abboud, Peter F. (1988). Speech and religious affiliation in Egypt. In Mohammad Ali Jazayery & Walter Winter (Eds.), *Language and cultures: Studies in honor of Edgar C. Polome* (pp. 21–27). Berlin: Mouton de Gruyter.

Abrams, Dominic, & Hogg, Michael. (2010). Social identity and self-categorization. In J. Dovidio, M. Hewstone, P. Glick, and V. Esses (Eds.), *The Sage handbook of prejudice, stereotyping and discrimination* (pp. 179–193). London: Sage.

Adamic, Lada, & Glance, Natalie. (2005). The political blogosphere and the 2004 US election: Divided they blog. Paper presented at the Proceedings of the 3rd International Workshop on Link Discovery, New York, NY.

Al-Rawi, Ahmed. (2016). Facebook as a virtual mosque: The online protest against innocence of Muslims. *Culture and Religion*, *17*(1), 19–34. doi:10.1080/14755610.2016.1159591

Allington, Daniel. (2007). "How come most people don't see it?": Slashing the Lord of the Rings. *Social Semiotics*, *17*(1), 43–62.

Allington, Daniel, & Swann, Joan. (2009). Researching literary reading as social practice. *Language and Literature*, *18*(3), 219–230.

Anderson, Jon W. (2003). The Internet and Islam's new interpreters. In Dale F Eickelman & Jon W Anderson (Eds.), *New media in the Muslim world: The emerging public sphere* (pp. 45–60). Bloomington, IN: Indiana University Press.

Androutsopoulos, Jannis. (2008). Potentials and limitations of discourse-centred online ethnography. *Language@Internet, 5*. Retrieved from www.languageatinternet.org/articles/2008/1610

(2010). Localising the global on the participatory web. In N. Coupland (Ed.), *Handbook of language and globalization* (pp. 201–231). Oxford: Wiley-Blackwell.

(2014). Languaging when contexts collapse: Audience design in social networking. *Discourse, Context and Media*, 4–5, 62–73. http://dx.doi.org/10.1016/j.dcm.2014.08.006

Angouri, Jo, & Tseliga, Theodora. (2010). "You have no idea what you are talking about!": From e-disagreement to e-impoliteness in two online fora. *Journal of Politeness Research: Language, Behavior, Culture*, *6*(1), 57–82.

Arensberg, Conrad M. (1954). The community-study method. *American Journal of Sociology*, *60*(2), 109–124.

Aufderheide, Patricia, Milosevic, Tijana, & Bello, Brian. (2015). The impact of copyright permissions culture on the US visual arts community: The consequences of fear of fair use. *New Media and Society*, *18*(9), 2012–2027. doi:10.1177/1461444815575018

Ayoub, Mahmoud. (1995). Jesus the Son of God: A study of the terms Ibn and Walad in the Qu'ran and Tafsir tradition. In Ybonne Yazbeck Haddad & Wadi Haddad (Eds.), *Christian-Muslim encounters* (pp. 65–81). Gainsville, FL: University of Florida Press.

Baker, Paul. (2006). *Using corpora in discourse analysis*. London: Bloomsbury.

Baker, Paul, Gabrielatos, Costas, & McEnery, Tony. (2013). *Discourse analysis and media attitudes: The representation of Islam in the British press*. Cambridge: Cambridge University Press.

Bakhtin, Mikhail. (1981). *The Dialogic imagination*. Austin, TX: University of Austin Press.

Bamberg, Michael. (1997). Positioning between structure and performance. *Journal of Narrative and Life History*, *7*(1–4), 335–342.

(2004). Considering counter narratives. In Michael Bamberg & Molly Andrews (Eds.), *Considering counter narratives: Narrating, resisting, making sense* (pp. 351–371). Amsterdam: John Benjamins.

Bansal, Monisha. (2007). Blasphemy site "playing texas hold 'em with eternity." Retrieved from www.cnsnews.com/news/viewstory.asp?Page=/Culture/archive/200702/CUL20070205a.html

Barker, Valerie, Dozier, David M, Weiss, Amy Schmitz, & Borden, Diane L. (2015). Harnessing peer potency: Predicting positive outcomes from social capital affinity and online engagement with participatory websites. *New Media and Society*, *17*(10), 1603–1623. doi:10.1177/1461444814530291

Barnett, Emma. (January 11, 2010). Facebook's Mark Zuckerberg says privacy is no longer a "social norm." *The Telegraph*. Retrieved from www.telegraph.co.uk/technology/facebook/6966628/Facebooks-Mark-Zuckerberg-says-privacy-is-no-longer-a-social-norm.html

Baron, Naomi. (2008). *Always on: Language in an online and mobile world*. Oxford: Oxford University Press.

Barzilai-Nahon, Karine, & Barzilai, Gad. (2005). Cultured technology: The Internet and Religious Fundamentalism. *The Information Society*, *21*(1), 25–40.

Bebbington, David W. (1989). *Evangelicalism in modern Britain: A history from the 1730s to the 1980s*. London: Routledge.

Becker, Carmen. (2011). Muslims on the path of the Salaf al-Salih. *Information, Communication and Society*, *14*(8), 1181–1203. doi:10.1080/1369118X.2011.597414

Bermingham, Adam, Conway, Maura, McInerney, Lisa, O'Hare, Neil, & Smeaton, Alan. (July 20–22, 2009). Combining social network analysis and sentiment analysis to explore the potential for online radicalisation. Paper presented at ASONAM 2009 – Advances in Social Networks Analysis and Mining, July 20–22, 2009, Athens, Greece.

Biggs, John. (2007). YouTube launches revenue sharing partners program, but no pre-rolls. Retrieved from https://techcrunch.com/2007/05/04/youtube-launches-revenue-sharing-partners-program-but-no-pre-rolls/

Bijlefeld, Willem A. (1995). Christian-Muslim studies, Islamic studies, and the future of Christian-Muslim encounter. In Ybonne Yazbeck Haddad & Wadi Haddad (Eds.), *Christian-Muslim encounters* (pp. 13–40). Gainesville, FL: University of Florida Press.

Billig, Michael. (1996). *Arguing and thinking: A rhetorical approach to social psychology*. Cambridge: Cambridge University Press.

Bou-Franch, Patricia, & Garcés-Conejos Blitvich, Pilar. (2014). Conflict management in massive polylogues: A case study from YouTube. *Journal of Pragmatics*, *73*, 19–36. doi: http://dx.doi.org/10.1016/j.pragma.2014.05.001

boyd, danah. (2011). Social network sites as networked publics: Affordances, dynamics, and implications. In Z. Papacharissi (Ed.), *A networked self: Identity, community, and culture on social network sites* (pp. 39–58). London: Routledge.

(2014). *It's complicated: The social lives of networked teens*. New Haven, CT: Yale University Press.

boyd, danah, & Ellison, Nicole. (2007). Social network sites: Definition, history, and scholarship. *Journal of Computer-Mediated Communication, 13*(1), 210–230. doi:10.1111/j.1083-6101.2007.00393

Brandtzæg, Petter Bae, Lüders, Marika, & Skjetne, Jan Håvard. (2010). Too many facebook "friends"? content sharing and sociability versus the need for privacy in social network sites. *International Journal of Human-Computer Interaction, 26*(11–12), 1006–1030. doi:10.1080/10447318.2010.516719

Brown, Penelope, & Levinson, Steve. (1987). *Politeness: Some universals in language usage*. Cambridge: Cambridge University Press.

Broxton, Tom, Interian, Yannet, Vaver, Jon, & Wattenhofer, Mirjam. (2011). Catching a viral video. *Journal of Intelligent Information Systems, 40*(2), 241–259. doi:10.1007/s10844-011-0191-2

Bruckman, Amy. (2002). Ethical Guidelines for Research Online. Retrieved from www.cc.gatech.edu/~asb/ethics

Bunt, Gary R. (2009). *iMuslims: Rewiring the house of Islam*. Chapel Hill, NC: University of North Carolina Press.

Burgess, Jean, & Green, Joshua. (October 15–18, 2008). Agency and controversy in the YouTube community. Paper presented at the Internet Research 9.0: Rethinking Community, Rethinking Place, Copenhagen.

(2009). *YouTube: online video and participatory culture*. Cambridge: Polity Press.

Caers, Ralf, De Feyter, Tim, De Couck, Marijke, Stough, Talia, Vigna, Claudia, & Du Bois, Cind. (2013). Facebook: A literature review. *New Media and Society, 15*(6), 982–1002. doi:10.1177/1461444813488061

Cameron, Lynne. (2007). Patterns of metaphor use in reconciliation talk. *Discourse and Society, 18*(2), 197–222.

(2011). *Metaphor and reconciliation: The discourse dynamics of empathy in post-conflict conversations*. London: Routledge.

(2015). Embracing connectedness and change: A complex dynamic systems perspective for applied linguistic research. *AILA Review, 28*(1), 28–48.

Cameron, Lynne, & Maslen, Rob (Eds.). (2010). *Metaphor analysis: Research practice in applied linguistics, social sciences and the humanities*. London: Equinox.

Campbell, Heidi A. (2012). *Digital religion: Understanding religious practice in new media worlds*. London: Routledge.

(2005). *Exploring religious community online: We are one in the network*. New York: Peter Lang.

Campbell, Heidi A., & Lövheim, Mia. (2011). Introduction. *Information, Communication and Society, 14*(8), 1083–1096. doi:10.1080/1369118X.2011.597416

Chafe, Wallace. (1994). *Discourse, consciousness, and time*. Chicago, IL: University of Chicago Press.

Cheong, Pauline Hope, Huang, Shirlena, & Poon, Jessie P. H. (2011). Cultivating online and offline pathways to enlightenment. *Information, Communication and Society, 14*(8), 1160–1180. doi:10.1080/1369118X.2011.579139

Cimino, Richard, & Smith, Christopher. (2007). Secular humanism and atheism beyond progressive secularism. *Sociology of Religion*, *68*(4), 407–424.

(2011). The new atheism and the formation of the imagined secularist community. *Journal of Media and Religion*, *10*(1), 24–38. doi:10.1080/15348423.2011.549391

(2014). *Atheist awakening: Secular activism and community in America*. Oxford: Oxford University Press.

Clift, Rebecca, & Helani, Fadi. (2010). Inshallah: Religious invocations in Arabic topic transition. *Language in Society*, *39*(03), 357–382.

Cohen, Joshua. (2012). YouTube gives 24-karat gold "play button" to channels with 1m+ subs. *Tubefilter*. Retrieved from www.tubefilter.com/2012/06/29/youtube-gold-play-button-million-subscribers/

Cosentino, Victor J. (1994). Virtual legality. *Byte*, *19*(3), 278.

Craig, William Lane. (1993). *Theism, atheism, and big bang cosmology*. Oxford: Oxford University Press.

Creese, Angela. (2008). Linguistic ethnography. In Nancy Hornberger- (Ed.), *Encyclopedia of language and education*, vol. 2 (pp. 229–241). New York, NY: Springer.

Crystal, David. (2001). *Language and the Internet*. Cambridge: Cambridge University Press.

Cunningham, Stuart, Craig, David, & Silver, Jon. (2016). YouTube, multichannel networks and the accelerated evolution of the new screen ecology. *Convergence: The International Journal of Research into New Media Technologies*, 22(4), 376–391. doi:10.1177/1354856516641620

Dawkins, Richard. (1986). *The blind watchmaker: Why the evidence of evolution reveals a universe without design*. London: W. W. Norton and Company.

Dembski, William A. (2002). *Intelligent design: The bridge between science and theology*. Champaign-Urbana, IL: InterVarsity Press.

Dorst, Aletta, & Klop, Marry-Loïse. (2017). Not a Holy Father: Dutch Muslim teenagers' metaphors for Allah. *Metaphor and the Social World*, *7*(1), 67–87.

Edwards, Charlie, & Gribbon, Luke. (2013). Pathways to violent extremism in the digital era. *The RUSI Journal*, *158*(5), 40–47. doi:10.1080/03071847.2013.847714

Edwards, Lee, Klein, Bethany, Lee, David, Moss, Giles, & Philip, Fiona. (2013). Framing the consumer: Copyright regulation and the public. *Convergence: The International Journal of Research into New Media Technologies*, *19*(1), 9–24. doi:10.1177/1354856512456788

Ellison, Nicole B., Steinfield, Charles, & Lampe, Cliff. (2007). The benefits of Facebook "friends": Exploring the relationship between college students' use of online social networks and social capital. *Journal of Computer-Mediated Communication*, *12*(3), 1143–1168. doi:10.1111/j.1083–6101.2007.00367

Ernst, Carl. (2004). *Rethinking Islam in the contemporary world*. Edinburgh: Edinburgh University Press.

Eronen, Maria. (2014). Moral argumentation as a rhetorical practice in popular online discourse: Examples from online comment sections of celebrity gossip. *Discourse and Communication*, *8*(3), 278–298. doi:10.1177/1750481313510818

Esposito, John L. (Ed.). (2003). *The Oxford dictionary of Islam*. Oxford: Oxford University Press.

Ess, Charles. (1996). *Philosophical perspectives on computer-mediated communication*. Albany, NY: SUNY Press.

Estes, Douglas. (2009). *SimChurch: Being the church in the virtual world.* Grand Rapids, MI: Zondervan.

Etling, Bruce, Kelly, John, Faris, Robert, & Palfrey, John. (2014). *Mapping the Arabic blogosphere: Politics, culture, and dissent.* Retrieved from www.ikhwanweb.com/uploads/lib/HNFNAB99APYNXAK.pdf

Fairclough, Norman. (1995). *Critical discourse analysis: The critical study of language.* London: Pearson.

(2001). *Language and Power.* Essex: Pearson.

Feinberg, John S. (2013). *Can you believe it's true?: Christian apologetics in a modern and postmodern era.* Wheaton, IL: Crossway.

Fernback, Jan, & Thompson, Brad. (1995). Virtual communities: Abort, retry, failure? *International Communication Association.* Retrieved from www.rheingold.com/texts/techpolitix/VCcivil.html

Feuerstein, Joshua. (2016a). 7 more officers shot!! I have a solution . . . Retrieved from www.facebook.com/joshua.feuerstein.5/videos/804387082997309/

(2016b). Personal Facebook page. Retrieved from www.facebook.com/joshua.feuerstein.5/

Fossheim, Hallvard, & Ingierd, Helene (Eds.). (2015). *Internet research ethics.* Kristiansand, Norway: Cappelen Damm Akademisk.

Foucault, Michel. (1981). The orders of discourse. In Robert Young (Ed.), *Untying the Text: A post-structuralist reader.* London: Routledge.

Freund, Katharina. (2014). "Fair use is legal use": Copyright negotiations and strategies in the fan-vidding community. *New Media and Society.* doi:10.1177/1461444814555952

Fuchs, Christian. (2012). The Political Economy of Privacy on Facebook. *Television and New Media, 13*(2), 139–159. doi:10.1177/1527476411415699

Gal, Noam, Shifman, Limor, and Kampf, Zohar. (2015). "It Gets Better": Internet memes and the construction of collective identity. *New Media and Society,* 1698–1714. doi:10.1177/1461444814568784

Georgakopoulou, Alexandra. (2015). Sharing as rescripting: Place manipulations on YouTube between narrative and social media affordances. *Discourse, Context and Media,* 9, 64–72. doi: http://dx.doi.org/10.1016/j.dcm.2015.07.002

Georgalou, Mariza. (2016). 'I make the rules on my Wall': Privacy and identity management practices on Facebook. *Discourse and Communication, 10*(1), 40–64. doi:10.1177/1750481315600304

Gibbs, Raymond. (2011). The Allegorical Impulse. *Metaphor and Symbol, 26*(2), 121–130.

Gilesnan, Michael. (2000). *Recognizing islam: Religion and society in the modern arab world.* New York: Pantheon Books.

Gillespie, Marie, Herbert, David, and Greenhill, Anita (Eds.). (2013). *Social Media and Religious Change.* Berlin: De Gruyter.

Goddard, Hugh. (2000). *A history of Christian-Muslim relations.* Chicago: New Amsterdam Books.

Goggin, Gerard. (2014). Facebook's mobile career. *New Media and Society, 16*(7), 1068–1086. doi:10.1177/1461444814543996

Gordon, Eric, and e Silva, Adriana de Souza. (2011). *Net locality: Why location matters in a networked world.* Oxford: John Wiley and Sons.

Gottschalk, Peter, and Greenberg, Gabriel. (2008). *Islamophobia: Making Muslims the enemy*. Lanham, Maryland, USA: Rowman and Littlefield Pub Inc.

Grady, Joseph Edward. (1997). *Foundations of meaning: Primary metaphors and primary scenes*. Berkeley, CA: University of California Press.

Grady, Joseph, Oakley, Todd, and Coulson, Sean. (1999). Blending and metaphor. In Raymond W. Gibbs and Gerard Steen (Eds.), *Metaphor in cognitive linguistics* (pp. 101–124). Amsterdam: John Benjamins.

Graham, Sage Lambert. (2007). Disagreeing to agree: Conflict, (im)politeness and identity in a computer-mediated community. *Journal of Pragmatics*, *39*(4), 742–759. doi: http://dx.doi.org/10.1016/j.pragma.2006.11.017

Hanson, Hilary. (2015). Former Pastor Suggests Christians Should Fight Gay Rights with Guns. www.huffingtonpost.com/entry/christians-gay-rights-guns_55abeacee4b065dfe89e989a (Accessed on December 11, 2015).

Hardaker, Claire. (2010). Trolling in asynchronous computer-mediated communication: From user discussions to academic definitions. *Journal of Politeness Research. Language, Behaviour, Culture*, 6, 215).

Hardaker, Claire, and McGlashan, Mark. (2016). "Real men don't hate women": Twitter rape threats and group identity. *Journal of Pragmatics*, *91*, 80–93. doi: http://dx.doi.org/10.1016/j.pragma.2015.11.005

Hargittai, Eszter, Gallo, Jason, and Kane, Matthew. (2008). Cross-ideological discussions among conservative and liberal bloggers. *Public Choice*, *134*(1–2), 67–86.

Harré, Rom. (2000). The social construction of terrorism. In Fathali Moghaddam and Anthony Marsella (Eds.), *Understanding terrorism: Psychosocial roots, consequences, and interventions* (pp. 91–102). Washington, D.C.: APA Press.

Harré, Rom, Moghaddam, Fathali M., Cairnie, Tracey Pilkerton, Rothbart, Daniel, and Sabat, Steven R. (2009). Recent Advances in Positioning Theory. *Theory and Psychology*, *19*(1), 5–31. doi:10.1177/0959354308101417

Harré, Rom, and van Langenhove, Luk. (1998). *Positioning Theory: Moral contexts of intentional action*. London: Blackwell Publishers.

Haugh, Michael. (2010). When is an email really offensive?: Argumentativity and variability in evaluations of impoliteness. *Journal of Politeness Research: Language, Behavior, Culture*, *6*(1), 7–31.

Heatherly, Kyle A, Lu, Yanqin, and Lee, Jae Kook. (2016). Filtering out the other side? Cross-cutting and like-minded discussions on social networking sites. *New Media and Society*. doi:10.1177/1461444816634677

Heffelfinger, Chris. (2011). *Radical Islam in America: Salafism's journey from Arabia to the West*. Lincoln, Nebraska, USA: Potomac Books.

Herring, Susan. (2003). Computer-mediated discourse. In Deborah Schiffrin, Deborah Tannen, and Hiedi Hamilton (Eds.), *The handbook of discourse analysis* (pp. 612–634). Oxford: Blackwell.

(2004a). Computer-mediated discourse analysis: An approach to researching online behavior. In Sasha Barab, Rob Kling, and James Gray (Eds.), *Designing for virtual communities in the service of learning* (pp. 338–376). Cambridge: Cambridge University Press.

(2004b). Slouching toward the ordinary: Current trends in computer-mediated communication. *New Media and Society*, *6*(1), 26–36.

Hick, John. (1991). Jesus and Muhammad In Dan Cohn-Sherbok (Ed.), *Islam in a world of diverse faiths* (pp. 114–118). Basingstoke: MacMillan.

Hogg, Michael. (2004). Social Identity Theory. In A.H. Eagly, R.M. Baron, and V. Hamilton (Eds.), *The social psychology of group identity and social conflict: Theory, application, and practice* (pp. 111–136): American Psychological Association.

Hopkins, Mark. (1863). *Lectures on the evidences of Christianity: Before the Lowell Institute, January, 1844*. Boston: T.R. Martin.

Housley, William, and Fitzgerald, Richard. (2002). The reconsidered model of membership categorization analysis. *Qualitative Research*, *2*(1), 59–83.

(2009). Membership categorization, culture and norms in action. *Discourse and Society*, *20*(3), 345–362.

Howard, Robert Glenn. (2011). *Digital Jesus: The making of a new Christian fundamentalist community on the Internet*. New York: NYU Press.

Hutchings, Tim. (2007). Creating church online: A case-study approach to religious experience. *Studies in World Christianity*, *13*(3), 243–260.

(2011). Contemporary religious community and the online church. *Information, Communication and Society*, *14*(8), 1118–1135. doi:10.1080/1369118X.2011.591410

Janson, Torsten. (2003). *Your cradle is green: The Islamic foundation and the call to Islam in children's literature* (Vol. 18). Lund: Lund University.

Jones, Steven. (1995). Understanding community in the information age. In Steven Jones (Ed.), *Cybersociety: Computer-mediated Communication and Community* (pp. 10–35). Thousand Oaks, CA: Sage.

Justdawah.org. (n.d.). Just Dawah: Conveying the Message homepage. www.justdawah.org/ (Accessed on March 22, 2016).

Karagiannis, Emmanuel. (2012). European converts to Islam: Mechanisms of radicalization. *Politics, Religion and Ideology*, *13*(1), 99–113.

Kelly, Patricia. (1999). Integration and identity in Muslim schools: Britain, United States and Montreal. *Islam and Christian–Muslim Relations*, *10*(2), 197–217. doi:10.1080/09596419908721180

Kerr, David A. (1991). The Prophet Muhammad in Christian theological perspective. In Dan Cohn-Sherbok (Ed.), *Islam in a World of Diverse Faiths*. Basingstoke: MacMIllan.

Kiesler, Sara, Siegel, Jane, and McGuire, Timothy W. (1984). Social psychological aspects of computer-mediated communication. *American Psychologist*, *39*(10), 1123–1134. doi:10.1037/0003–066X.39.10.1123

Kim, Jin. (2012). The institutionalization of YouTube: From user-generated content to professionally generated content. *Media, Culture and Society*, *34*(1), 53–67. doi:10.1177/0163443711427199

Know Your Meme. (n.d.). The amazing atheist. http://knowyourmeme.com/memes/people/the-amazing-atheist (Accessed on March 29, 2017).

Kress, Gunter, and Van Leeuwen, Theo. (2006). *Reading images: The grammar of visual design*. London: Routledge.

Kwan, Grace Chi En, and Skoric, Marko M. (2013). Facebook bullying: An extension of battles in school. *Computers in Human Behavior*, *29*(1), 16–25.

Kwon, Ohbyung, and Wen, Yixing. (2010). An empirical study of the factors affecting social network service use. *Computers in Human Behavior*, *26*(2), 254–263. doi: http://dx.doi.org/10.1016/j.chb.2009.04.011

Labov, William. (1972a). *Language in the inner city*. Philadelphia: University of Pennsylvania Press.

(1972b). *Sociolinguistic patterns*. Philadelphia: University of Pennsylvania Press.

Lakoff, George. (1987). *Women, fire, and dangerous things: What categories reveal about the mind*. Chicago: University of Chicago Press.

Lakoff, George, and Johnson, Mark. (1980). *Metaphors We Live By*. Chicago: University of Chicago Press.

Lange, Patricia. (2006). What is your claim to flame? *First Monday, 11*(9). http://firstmonday.org/htbin/cgiwrap/bin/ojs/index.php/fm/article/view/1393/1311 (Accessed on March 21, 2010)

(2007a). *Commenting on comments: Investigating responses to antagonism on YouTube*. Paper presented at the Society for Applied Anthropology Conference, Tampa, FL.

(2007b). Publicly private and privately public: Social networking on YouTube. *Journal of Computer-Mediated Communication, 13*(1), 361–380.

(2007c). *Searching for the 'You' in 'YouTube': An analysis of online response ability*. Paper presented at the EPIC 2007, Keystone, CO.

Larsen-Freeman, Diane, and Cameron, Lynne. (2008). *Complex Systems and Applied Linguistics*. Oxford: Oxford University Press.

Lave, Jean, and Wenger, Etienne. (1991). *Situated learning: Legitimate peripheral participation*. Cambridge: Cambridge University Press.

LeDrew, Stephen. (2012). The evolution of atheism: Scientific and humanistic approaches. *History of the Human Sciences, 25*(3), 70–87. doi:10.1177/0952695112441301

(2013). Discovering atheism: Heterogeneity in trajectories to atheist identity and activism. *Sociology of Religion, 74*(4), 431–453. doi:10.1093/socrel/srt014

Leonard, Karen. (2003). American Muslim politics: Discourses and practices. *Ethnicities, 3*(2), 147–181. doi:10.1177/1468796803003002001

Lewis, Bernard. (1993). *Islam and the West*. Oxford: Oxford University Press.

Lewis, C.S. (1952). *Mere Christianity*. San Franciso: Harper Collins.

Lipka, Michael. (2015). *7 facts about atheists*. www.pewresearch.org/fact-tank/2015/11/05/7-facts-about-atheists/ (Accessed on March 22, 2016)

Litt, Eden. (2012). Knock, knock. Who's there? The imagined audience. *Journal of Broadcasting and Electronic Media, 56*(3), 330–345. doi:10.1080/08838151.2012.705195

Litt, Eden, and Hargittai, Eszter. (2016). The imagined audience on social network Sites. *Social Media + Society, 2*(1), 1–12. doi:10.1177/2056305116633482

Lorenzo-Dus, Nuria, Garcés-Conejos Blitvich, Pilar, and Bou-Franch, Patricia. (2011). On-line polylogues and impoliteness: The case of postings sent in response to the Obama Reggaeton YouTube video. *Journal of Pragmatics, 43*(10), 2578–2593. doi: http://dx.doi.org/10.1016/j.pragma.2011.03.005

Luchjenbroers, J., and Aldridge-Waddon, M. (2011). Paedophiles and politeness in email communications: Community of practice needs that define face-threat. *Journal of Politeness Research. Language, Behaviour, Culture, 7*(1), 21–42.

Lundby, Knut. (2011). Patterns of belonging in online/offline interfaces of religion. *Information, Communication and Society, 14*(8), 1219–1235. doi:10.1080/1369118X.2011.594077

Malley, Brian. (2004). *How the Bible works: An anthropological study of Evangelical Biblicism.* Walnut Creek, CA, USA: AltaMira Press.

Markham, Annette, and Buchanan, Elizabeth. (2012). Ethical decision-making and Internet research 2.0: Recommendations from the AoIR ethics working committee. http://aoir.org/ethics/ (Accessed on February 10, 2015).

Marwick, Alice, and boyd, danah. (2011). I tweet honestly, I tweet passionately: Twitter users, context collapse, and the imagined audience. *New Media and Society, 13*(1), 114–133.

McDonald, Aleecia, and Cranor, Lorrie. (2009). The Cost of reading privacy policies. *I/S: A Journal of Law and Policy for the Information Society, 4*(3), 543–568.

McLeod, Jack M, and Lee, Nam-Jin. (2012). Social networks, public discussion and civic engagement: A socialization perspective. In Holli A. Semetko and Margaret Scammell (Eds.), *The Sage handbook of political communication* (pp. 197–208).

Mission Dawah. (n.d.). Dawah Missions Overview. www.missiondawah.com/training/dawah-missions-overview/ (Accessed on March 21, 2016).

Moor, Peter J., Heuvelman, Ard, and Verleur, Ria. (2010). Flaming on YouTube. *Computers in Human Behavior, 26*(6), 1536–1546. doi: http://dx.doi.org/10.1016/j.chb.2010.05.023

Morrow, John A. (2006). *Arabic, Islām, and the Allāh lexicon: How language shapes our conception of God.* Lewiston: Edwin Mellen Press.

Moyer, Justin Wm. (2015). Starbucks 'removed Christmas from their cups because they hate Jesus,' Christian says in viral Facebook video. *The Washington Times.* www.washingtonpost.com/news/morning-mix/wp/2015/11/09/starbucks-removed-christmas-from-their-cups-because-they-hate-jesus-christian-says-in-viral-facebook-video/ (Accessed on March 22, 2016)

Neill, Stephen Charles. (1964). *A history of Christian missions.* London: Penguin books.

Nishimura, Yukiko. (2010). Impoliteness in Japanese BBS interactions: Observations from message exchanges in two online communities. *Journal of Politeness Research: Language, Behavior, Culture, 6*(1), 35–55.

Nitschke, Paula, Donges, Patrick, and Schade, Henriette. (2016). Political organizations' use of websites and Facebook. *New Media and Society, 18*(5), 744–764. doi:10.1177/1461444814546451

O'Halloran, Kieran. (2014). Deconstructing arguments via digital mining of online comments. *Literary and Linguistic Computing, 30*(4), 559–588. doi:10.1093/llc/fqu034

O'Sullivan, P. B., and Flanagin, A. J. (2003). Reconceptualizing "flaming" and other problematic messages. *New Media and Society, 5*(1), 69–94.

Osteen, Joel. (2004). *Your best life now: 7 steps to living at your full potential.* Brentwood, TN, USA: FaithWords.

Owen, William Foster. (1984). Interpretive themes in relational communication. *Quarterly Journal of Speech, 70*(3), 274–287.

Packer, James Innell. (1973). *Knowing God.* London: Hodder and Stoughton.

Page, Ruth. (2010). Re-examining narrativity: Small stories in status updates. Text and Talk, 30, 423–444).

(2012). The linguistics of self-branding and micro-celebrity in Twitter: The role of hashtags. *Discourse and Communication, 6*(2), 181–201. doi:10.1177/1750481312437441

(2013). *Stories and social media: Identities and interaction.* London: Routledge.

Pariser, Eli. (2011). *The filter bubble: What the Internet is hiding from you.* New York City: Penguin UK.

Parshall, Phil. (2003). *Muslim evangelism: Contemporary approaches to contextualization.* Grand Rapids, Michigan, USA: Biblica.

Partington, Alan. (2004). "Utterly content in each other's company": Semantic prosody and semantic preference. *International Journal of Corpus Linguistics*, *9*(1), 131–156. doi:10.1075/ijcl.9.1.07par

Partington, Alan, Duguid, Alison, and Taylor, Charlotte. (2013). *Patterns and meanings in discourse: Theory and practice in corpus-assisted discourse studies (CADS)* (Vol. 55). Amsterdam: John Benjamins Publishing.

Peek, Lori. (2005). Becoming Muslim: The development of a religious identity. *Sociology of Religion*, *66*(3), 215–242.

Peplow, David. (2011). "Oh, I've known a lot of Irish people": Reading groups and the negotiation of literary interpretation. *Language and Literature*, *20*(4), 295–315.

(2016). *Talk about books: A study of reading groups.* London: Bloomsbury.

Pfannenstiel, A. N. (2010). Digital literacies and academic integrity. *International Journal for Educational Integrity*, *6*(2), 41–49.

Phillips, Whitney. (2011). *LOLing at tragedy: Facebook trolls, memorial pages and resistance to grief online.*

Piamenta, Moshe. (1979). *Islam in everyday Arabic speech.* Leiden: E.J. Brill.

Pihlaja, Stephen. (2011). Cops, popes, kings, and garbage collectors: Metaphor and antagonism in an atheist/Christian YouTube video thread. *Language@Internet*, 8(1). www.languageatinternet.org/articles/2011/Pihlaja/ (Accessed on 6 June 2013)

(2013a). 'It's all red ink': The interpretation of biblical metaphor among Evangelical Christian YouTube users. *Language and Literature*, *22*(2), 103–117.

(2013b). Truck stops and fashion shows: A case study of the discursive construction of Evangelical Christian group identity on YouTube. In D. Herbert and M. Gillespie (Eds.), *Social Media, Religion and Spirituality* (pp. 165–184). Berlin: De Gruyter.

(2014a). *Antagonism on YouTube: Metaphor in Online Discourse.* London: Bloomsbury.

(2014b). 'Christians' and 'bad Christians': Categorization in atheist user talk on YouTube. *Text and Talk*, *34*(5), 623–639.

(2015). Antagonism in religious discourse on YouTube. In Sariya Cheruvallil-Contractor and Suha Shakkour (Eds.), *Digital Methodologies in the Sociology of Religion.* London: Bloomsbury. (pp. 49–58)

(2016a). Expressing pleasure and avoiding engagement in online adult video comment sections. *Journal of Language and Sexuality*, *5*(1), 94–112.

(2016b). 'What about the wolves?': The use of scripture in YouTube arguments. *Language and Literature*, *25*(3), 226–238.

(2017) More than 50 shades of grey: Creative content and copyright on social networking sites. *Applied Linguistics Review.* 8/2-3:213-228. DOI: 10.1515/applirev-2016-1036

Planchenault, Gaëlle. (2010). Virtual community and politeness: The use of female markers of identity and solidarity in a transvestites' website. *Journal of Politeness Research: Language, Behavior, Culture*, *6*(1), 83–103.

Poston, Larry. (1992). *Islamic da'wah in the West: Muslim missionary activity and the dynamics of conversion to Islam.* Oxford: Oxford University Press.

Prior, Markus. (2007). *Post-broadcast democracy: How media choice increases inequality in political involvement and polarizes elections*. Cambridge: Cambridge University Press.

Rampton, B., Tusting, K., Maybin, J., Barwell, R., Creese, A., and Lytra, V. (2004). UK Linguistic Ethnography: A Discussion Paper. Retrieved from www.ling-ethnog.org.uk. (Accessed on August 14, 2012)

Rational Response Squad. (2007). The Blasphemy Challenge. www.blasphemychallenge.com/ (Accessed on December 11, 2015).

Rayson, Paul. (2008). From key words to key semantic domains. *International Journal of Corpus Linguistics, 13*(4), 519–549.

Reilly, Paul. (2015). Every little helps? YouTube, sousveillance and the 'anti-Tesco' riot in Stokes Croft. *New Media and Society, 17*(5), 755–771. doi: 10.1177/1461444813512195

Renard, John. (2011). *Islam and Christianity: Theological themes in comparative perspective*. London: University of California Press.

Rheingold, H. (2000). *The virtual community: Homesteading on the electronic frontier*. Cambridge, MA: MIT Press.

Richardson, Peter. (2012). A closer walk: A study of the interaction between metaphors related to movement and proximity and presuppositions about the reality of belief in Christian and Muslim testimonials. *Metaphor and the Social World, 2*(2), 233–261.

Ritchie, L. David. (2010). "Everybody goes down": Metaphors, Stories, and Simulations in Conversations. *Metaphor and Symbol, 25*(3), 123–143. doi:10.1080/10926488.2010.489383

Roof, Wade Clark. (1999). *Spiritual marketplace: Baby boomers and the remaking of American religion*. Princeton: Princeton University Press.

Ruesch, Michelle Anna, and Märker, Oliver. (2012). *Real Name Policy in E-Participation*. Paper presented at the CeDEM 12 Conference for E-Democracy and Open Government, May 3–4, 2012. Danube-University Krems, Austria.

Rushfield, Richard, and Hoffman, Claire. (2006). Mystery fuels huge popularity of web's Lonelygirl15. *Los Angeles Times*. http://articles.latimes.com/2006/sep/08/entertainment/et-lonelygirl8 (Accessed on May 4, 2016)

Sabat, Steven R. (2001). *The experience of Alzheimer's*. Oxford: Blackwell.

(2003). Malignant positioning and the predicament of people with Alzheimer's disease. In Rom Harré and Fathali Moghaddam (Eds.), *The Self and Others Positioning Individuals and Groups in Personal, Political, and Cultural Contexts*. Westport, CT, USA: Praeger.

Sacks, Harvey. (1992). *Lectures on conversation*. Oxford: Blackwell.

Schrage, Michael. (1997). Mr. Bozo, meet Miss Courtesy Worm. *Computerworld*, 31(8), 37.

Schultze, Quentin J. (2003). *Televangelism and American culture: The business of popular religion*. Eugene, Oregon, USA: Wipf and Stock Publishers.

Scott, Mike. (1997). PC analysis of key words—and key key words. *System, 25*(2), 233–245.

Seargeant, Philip, and Tagg, Caroline. (2014). *The language of social media: Identity and community on the internet*. Basingstoke, UK: Palgrave Macmillan.

Sedghi, Ami. (2014). *Facebook: 10 years of social networking, in numbers. The Guardian*. www.theguardian.com/news/datablog/2014/feb/04/facebook-in-numbers-statistics (Accessed on March 22, 2016)

Shafaat, Ahmed. (1991). The Abrahamic Ummah. In Dan Cohn-Sherbok (Ed.), *Islam in a world of diverse faiths* (pp. 188–200). Basingstoke: MacMIllan.

Shifman, Limor. (2012). An anatomy of a YouTube meme. *New Media and Society*, *14*(2), 187–203. doi:10.1177/1461444811412160

Sider, Ronald J. (1975). Evangelism, salvation and social justice. *International Review of Mission*, *64*(255), 251–267.

Siegel, Jane, Dubrovsky, Vitaly, Kiesler, Sara, and McGuire, Timothy W. (1986). Group processes in computer-mediated communication. *Organizational Behavior and Human Decision Processes*, *37*(2), 157–187. doi: http://dx.doi.org/10.1016/0749–5978(86)90050-6

Simon, Stephanie. (2008). Atheists reach out – just don't call it proselytizing. *Wall StreetJournal.*

Simpson, Paul. (2004). *Stylistics: A resource book for students*. London: Routledge.

Sledgianowski, Deb, and Kulviwat, Songpol. (2009). Using Social Network Sites: The Effects of Playfulness, Critical Mass and Trust in a Hedonic Context. *Journal of Computer Information Systems*, *49*(4), 74–83. doi:10.1080/08874417.2009.11645342

Smith, Christian, and Emerson, Michael. (1998). *American evangelicalism: Embattled and thriving*. Chicago, Illinois, USA: University of Chicago Press.

Smith, Christopher, and Cimino, Richard. (2012). Atheisms unbound: The role of the new media in the formation of a secularist identity. *Secularism and Nonreligion*, *1*(0), 17–31. doi: http://doi.org/10.5334/snr.ab

Smith, Jesse M. (2011). Becoming an atheist in America: Constructing identity and meaning from the rejection of theism. *Sociology of Religion*, *72*(2), 215–237. doi: https://doi.org/10.1093/socrel/srq082

(2013). Creating a Godless community: The collective identity work of contemporary american atheists. *Journal for the Scientific Study of Religion*, *52*(1), 80–99. doi:10.1111/jssr.12009

Smithers, Rebecca (2011). Terms and conditions: Not reading the small print can mean big problems. www.theguardian.com/money/2011/may/11/terms-conditions-small-print-big-problems (Accessed on September 17, 2015).

Solomon, Norman. (1991). Stereotyping other theologies. In Dan Cohn-Sherbok (Ed.), *Islam in a world of diverse faiths* (pp. 104–113). Basingstoke: MacMillan.

Stelma, J. H., and Cameron, L. J. (2007). Intonation units in spoken interaction: Developing transcription skills. *Text and Talk*, *27*(3), 361–393.

Stempel, Jonathan. (2014). Google, Viacom settle landmark YouTube lawsuit. www.reuters.com/article/2014/03/18/us-google-viacom-lawsuit-idUSBREA2H11220140318 (Accessed on September 17, 2015).

Stewart, Anna Rose. (2011). Text and response in the relationship between online and offline religion. *Information, Communication and Society*, *14*(8), 1204–1218. doi:10.1080/1369118X.2011.592206

Stommel, Wyke. (2008). Conversation analysis and community of practice as approaches to studying online community. *Language@Internet*, 5, *article 5.*

Subrahmanyam, Kaveri, Reich, Stephanie M., Waechter, Natalia, and Espinoza, Guadalupe. (2008). Online and offline social networks: Use of social networking sites by emerging adults. *Journal of Applied Developmental Psychology*, *29*(6), 420–433. doi: http://dx.doi.org/10.1016/j.appdev.2008.07.003

Tabak, Alan. (2004). *Hundreds register for new Facebook website. The Harvard Crimson*. www.thecrimson.com/article/2004/2/9/hundreds-register-for-new-facebook-website/ (Accessed on May 4, 2016)

Tagg, Caroline. (2012). *Discourse of text messaging: Analysis of SMS communication*. London: Continuum/Bloomsbury.

Tajfel, Henri. (1981). *Human groups and social categories*. Cambridge: Cambridge University Press.

(1983). *Social identity and intergroup relations*. Cambridge: Cambridge University Press.

Tajfel, Henri, Billig, Michael, Bundy, R.P., and Flament, Claude. (1971). Social categorization and intergroup behaviour. *European Journal of Social Psychology*, *1*(2), 149–178.

Tajfel, Henri, and Turner, John. (1979). An integrative theory of intergroup conflict. In Henri Tajfel (Ed.), *Differentiation between social groups: Studies in the social psychology of intergroup relations* (pp. 33–47). London: European Association of Experimental Social Psychology by Academic Press.

Taylor, Keith. (2006, December/January). Atheists in cyberspace. *Free Inquiry*, *26*(6), 51–52.

Theocharis, Yannis, and Quintelier, Ellen. (2016). Stimulating citizenship or expanding entertainment? The effect of Facebook on adolescent participation. *New Media and Society*, *18*(5), 817–836. doi:10.1177/1461444814549006

Thiselton, Anthony C. (2009). *Hermeneutics: An introduction*: Wm. B. Eerdmans Publishing.

Thoburn, Nicholas. (2003). *Deleuze, Marx and politics*. London: Routledge.

Thunderf00t. (2008). Game over man, game over . . . https://youtu.be/TIVRIyBGkhU?list=PL4244972AB1AAE8C9 (Accessed on March 30, 2017).

Trammell, Jim. (2015). Jesus? There's an app for that! Tablet Media in the "New" Electronic Church. In Mark Ward (Ed.), *The electronic Church in the digital age: Cultural impacts of evangelical mass media*. Westport, Connecticut, USA: Praeger.

Turner, John. (1981). Towards a cognitive redefinition of the social group. In Henri Tajfel (Ed.), *Social identity and intergroup relations* (pp. 15–40). Cambridge: Cambridge University Press.

Turow, Joseph. (2012). *The daily you: How the new advertising industry is defining your identity and your worth*. New Haven, CT, USA: Yale University Press.

Van Leeuwen, Theo, and Jewitt, Carey. (2001). *The handbook of visual analysis*. London: Sage.

Van Til, Cornelius. (1955). *The defense of the faith*. Phillipsburg, New Jersey, USA: Presbyterian and Reformed Publishing Company.

van Zoonen, Liesbet, Vis, Farida, and Mihelj, Sabina. (2010). Performing citizenship on YouTube: Activism, satire and online debate around the anti-Islam video Fitna. *Critical Discourse Studies*, *7*(4), 249–262. doi:10.1080/17405904.2010.511831

(2011). YouTube interactions between agonism, antagonism and dialogue: Video responses to the anti-Islam film Fitna. *New Media and Society*, *13*(8), 1283–1300. doi:10.1177/1461444811405020

Vie, Stephanie. (2014). "You Are How You Play": Privacy policies and data mining in social networking games. In Jennifer deWinter and Ryan M. Moeller (Eds.), *Computer games and technical communication: Critical methods and applications at the intersection* (pp. 171–187).

Vis, Farida, van Zoonen, Liesbet, and Mihelj, Sabina. (2011). Women responding to the anti-Islam film Fitna: Voices and acts of citizenship on YouTube. *Feminist Review, 97*(1), 110–129.

Vogelstein, Fred. (2009). The Wired Interview: Facebook's Mark Zuckerberg. *Wired. com.* www.wired.com/2009/06/mark-zuckerberg-speaks/ (Accessed on January 21, 2016).

Vonderau, Patrick. (2016). The video bubble: Multichannel networks and the transformation of YouTube. *Convergence: The International Journal of Research into New Media Technologies.* doi:10.1177/1354856516641882

Vorvoreanu, Mihaela. (2009). Perceptions of corporations on Facebook: An analysis of Facebook social norms. *Journal of New Communications Research, 4*(1), 67–86.

Wagner, Rachel. (2012). You are what you install: Religious authenticity and identity in mobile apps. In Heidi A. Campbell (Ed.), *Digital religion: Understanding religious practices in new media worlds* (pp. 199–206). London: Routledge.

Walther, Joseph. (2002). Research ethics in Internet-enabled research: Human subjects issues and methodological myopia. *Ethics and Information Technology, 4*(3), 205–216.

Watt, William Montgomery. (2013). *Muslim-Christian encounters: Perceptions and misperceptions.* London: Routledge.

Weber, Max. (2002 [1905]). *The Protestant ethic and the spirit of capitalism and other writings.* New York: Penguin.

Wesch, Michael. (2009). Youtube and you: Experiences of self-awareness in the context collapse of the recording webcam. *Explorations in Media Ecology, 8*(2), 19–34.

West, Anne, Lewis, Jane, and Currie, Peter. (2009). Students' Facebook 'friends': public and private spheres. *Journal of Youth Studies, 12*(6), 615–627. doi:10.1080/13676260902960752

Wheeler, Brian. (2013). What happens at an atheist church? *BBC Magazine.* www.bbc.co.uk/news/magazine-21319945 (Accessed on March 22, 2016)

Wilken, Rowan. (2014). Places nearby: Facebook as a location-based social media platform. *New Media and Society, 16*(7), 1087–1103. doi:10.1177/1461444814543997

Wilkinson, David, and Thelwall, Mike. (2011). Researching Personal Information on the Public Web: Methods and Ethics. *Social Science Computer Review, 29*(4), 387–401. doi:10.1177/0894439310378979

Wilson, Andrew. (2007). *Deluded by Dawkins? A Christian response to the God delusion.* Colorado Springs, CO: Kingsway Books.

Wodak, Ruth, and Meyer, Michael. (2002). *Methods for critical discourse analysis.* London: Sage.

Yates, Timothy. (1996). *Christian mission in the twentieth century.* Cambridge: Cambridge University Press.

YouTube. (2016). Statistics. www.youtube.com/yt/press/en-GB/statistics.html (Accessed on March 21, 2016).

Yung-Tzu Joyce, Lin, Meng-Yen Tom, Lin, and Kuo-Chen, Li. (June 22–24, 2015). Consumer involvement model of fan page: Mining from Facebook data of a real celebrity fashion brand. Paper presented at the 2015 12th International Conference on Service Systems and Service Management (ICSSSM).

Zacharias, Ravi. (2008). *The end of reason: A response to the new atheists.* Grand Rapids, MI: Zondervan.

Index